A PEOPLE NUMEROUS AND ARMED

Reflections on the Military Struggle
for American Independence

Revised Edition

JOHN SHY

Ann Arbor Paperbacks
THE UNIVERSITY OF MICHIGAN PRESS

2010   2009   2008   2007   16   15   14   13

Library of Congress Cataloging-in-Publication Data

Shy, John W.
    A people numerous and armed : reflections on the military struggle
for American independence / John Shy. — Rev. ed.
      p.   cm.
    Includes bibliographical references and index.
    ISBN 0-472-09431-9 (alk. paper). — ISBN 0-472-06431-2 (pbk. :
alk. paper)
    1. United States—History—Revolution, 1775-1783—Campaigns.
    2. United States—History—Revolution, 1775-1783.   I. Title.
E230.S5 1990
973.3'3—dc20   89-40806
                                      CIP

The following essays are reprinted by the kind permission of their original publishers:
    Chapter 2 © 1963 by John Shy; first printed in *The William and Mary Quarterly*, 3rd
series, XX (1963); here slightly revised.
    Chapter 3 from *Anglo-American Political Relations, 1675-1775*, edited by Alison Gilbert
Olson and Richard Maxwell Brown. Copyright © 1970 by Rutgers, the State University. Reprinted by permission of the Rutgers University Press.
    Chapter 4 from *George Washington's Opponents*, edited by George A. Billias. Copyright
© 1969 by William Morrow & Co., Inc.
    Chapter 5 from *Reconsiderations on the Revolutionary War*, edited by Don Higginbotham
(Westport Conn., Greenwood Press, Inc., 1978). Copyright © 1978 by Don
Higginbotham.
    Chapter 6 from *George Washington's Generals*, edited by George A. Billias. Copyright
© 1964 by George A. Billias. Originally published by William Morrow & Co., Inc.,
1964.
    Chapter 8 originally published in *The Loyalist Americans: A Focus on Greater New York*,
edited by Robert A. East and Jacob Judd (Tarrytown, N.Y.: Sleepy Hollow Restora-
tions, 1975).
    Chapter 9 from *The Southern Experience in the American Revolution*, edited by Jeffrey J.
Crow and Larry E. Tise. Copyright © 1978 by the University of North Carolina Press.
Published by the University of North Carolina Press and sponsored by the North Carolina Bicentennial Committee, 1978.
    Chapter 10 from *Essays on the American Revolution*, edited by Stephen Kurtz and James
Hutson. Copyright © 1973 by the University of North Carolina Press. Published by
the University of North Carolina Press for the Institute of Early American History and
Culture, 1973.
    Chapter 11 from *Legacies of the American Revolution*, edited by Larry R. Gerlach, James
A. Dolph, and Michael L. Nicholls. Copyright © Utah State University, 1978.
    Chapter 12 from *The Journal of Interdisciplinary History*, I (1971), 205–228, by permission
of *The Journal of Interdisciplinary History* and the M.I.T. Press, Cambridge, Massachusetts.

ISBN 978-0-472-06431-1 (pbk. : alk. paper)

A People Numerous and Armed

For my family

Preface to the Revised Edition

More clearly than at the time of their collection and publication in 1976, these essays appear to me now as a product of the Vietnam era in American history. Historians usually dislike the labeling of their work by the name assigned to whatever "Great Crisis of the Contemporary World" may have been playing on their minds during the act of creation.[1] Labeling in this way seems to relegate the results of hard scholarly labor to the status of historiographical artifacts. Of course historians regularly do this to one another in teaching graduate students about other historians, especially about those who are safely dead, unable any longer to explain themselves.

I am not dead, yet, but neither does it seem useful or honest to pretend that a period of great upheaval, the 1960's and 1970's, did not exert an important influence on my reading of evidence for the American Revolution, particularly on a growing sense that the Revolutionary War—a long, violent struggle for national independence—was crucially important in shaping post-Revolutionary America. Previous historians of the Revolution may have been too repelled by the slaughterhouse quality of all warfare, or perhaps too aware that nothing in the American Revolutionay War much resembled the technological and or-

ganizational monstrosity of even the American Civil War, to
be able to find anything in that earlier war, except its outcome,
of great historical significance. But post-1945 wars of decoloni-
zation and "national liberation," often tentative, attritional
struggles between weak and divided resistance forces and inept, sometimes half-hearted regimes, have served to remind us
that the scale, ferocity, and efficiency of warfare are not automatic measures of the social and political significance of the
contest. During much of the American Revolutionary War
both sides seemed to lack either the skill or the will to achieve
a decisive military result.

Lethality in these modern "little wars" may seem limited in
comparison with the incredible body counts of the two world
wars, and at the same time more repulsive, because so often
the violence of the "little war" is perpetrated by or against
civilians, who are supposed to enjoy the protected status of
"noncombatants." The irregular violence of these post-1945
struggles has restored to warfare the visceral, ugly, face-to-face
quality somewhat diluted by the technologized, long-range killing of modern military methods. The bodies, British and
American, strewn along the Charlestown-Lexington roadside
in April 1775, or the hundred Loyalist corpses scattered through
the North Carolina woodland by "Light Horse Harry" Lee in
early 1781, or the dead rebel soldiers ruthlessly cut down after
they had failed to defend New London, Connecticut, later in
the same year—all testified that this American war, however
small when compared to contemporary European wars, could
be atrocious in its conduct, and traumatic in its likely effects.

Since the original edition of this work appeared in 1976, other
historians have published important work that has deepened
our understanding of the Revolutionary War and its effects.
John Dann has combed the thousands of military pension files
for the Revolution, preserved in the National Archives, to give
us a remarkable selection from those revealing, unpolished accounts of direct personal involvement.[2] Robert Gross, focusing

on a single community, has carefully traced the effects of the war in Concord, Massachusetts.[3] Charles Royster has explored the changing relationship between the American people and its Continental Army, 1775–83, in search for that elusive quality, "national character."[4] Richard Buel for the state of Connecticut and Wayne Carp for the war as a whole have studied the problems of voluntarily mobilizing and distributing the material resources demanded by armed resistance to Britain.[5] Even a recent, insightful biography of George Washington, by John Ferling, has improved our understanding of the military performance of that mysterious central figure.[6]

Compared to some of these new works of thorough scholarship, the essays that follow are for the most part suggestive and impressionistic. If they retain value, it is in their sense of pattern and process, that at some level the eight-year struggle, full of waste and futility as well as death and destruction, can be made to make the kind of sense that historians who do not normally study war and warfare but concentrate on more edifying forms of human activity will recognize as relevant to their own concerns.

I have taken advantage of the chance to reprint the book to make minor revisions and in a few cases respond to criticism. From the original 1976 edition I have removed the historiographical essay on Lawrence Henry Gipson, whose great work, although heavily military in subject matter, may also be said to avert its gaze from what the author regarded as the terrible debacle that began in 1775; and I have added three essays published during the later years of the American Revolution Bicentennial, essays in which I attempted to explore points touched lightly in the original chapters. These added essays are chapters 5, 9, and 11. Finally, the concluding brief "Further Reflections" has been completely revised.

I must thank The University of Michigan Press for making this new edition possible, and Mary Erwin, who patiently oversaw its production. Other scholarly debts incurred since

1976 are to Richard Buel, Robert Calhoon, David Chesnutt, Tom Condon, Jeffrey Crow, John Dann, Jim Dolph, Larry Gerlach, Stephen Grossbart, Don Higginbotham, Linda Kerber, Jessica Kross, Debbie Mahoney, Mike Nicholls, Mark Odintz, Jacob Price, George Rogers, Charles Royster, Larry Tise, Darold Wax, Esmond Wright, and as ever, to my wife, Arlene.

Ann Arbor, 1989

Contents

Introduction to the Original Edition

This book might have been subtitled "Accidental Essays on the American Revolution," because each was written at the unexpected invitation of another party, to lecture, to read a paper, or to contribute to a symposium. For some of the essays, research and ideas were simply waiting to be put into final written form; for others, responding to the invitation meant seizing an opportunity to conduct my own education. The essays on colonial militia, Ellis and Pownall, Thomas Gage, and "Long Bill" Scott fall in the former category, while those on Charles Lee and Loyalism are examples of starting from scratch. But in every case, the timing and to some extent the form were not part of a master plan of work, but accidental—the result of an outside force intervening in my scholarly life.

Reading them again, together, I do not find them as disparate as I feared they might be. There is more consistency of viewpoint, which is good, and less change in my thinking over more than fifteen years, which may be not so good. In any event, certain concerns and themes appear and reappear, and a few introductory words about them are in order, at the risk of telling readers more than they may want to know about the author.

For twenty years, since entering graduate school, my chief academic interests have been two, one very fashionable, the other very unfashionable. The fashionable interest has been in revolution, especially the American Revolution and its long-term background in British and colonial American history, but also the English and French Revolutions. The other interest has been in war, armies and navies, and military history generally—a subject never quite respectable in the twentieth-century university. It is strange that two phenomena so similar in their use of collective violence, and in their cataclysmic nature and effects on society, as revolution and war, should be so differently regarded by scholars. But that is the case, and it has been so for a long time; here is not the place to explain it. Perhaps it is enough to say that most written military history, however fascinating in itself, does not "connect" very well with other areas of history, and non-military historians have felt justified in disregarding books from which they learn so little about the non-military past. Some of the problem may be intrinsic to the subject matter of war and military institutions, but most of it stems from the way in which military historians have chosen to treat their subject. This "disconnection" of military history from history in general has always seemed wrong and sad, and in a sense I have tried to be an evangelist for a "new" military history which would make students of history pay attention to a subject they were ignoring at their peril.

This book, then, may be read as an evangelical tract, preaching a new perspective on war, using the history of one war to carry the message. The message is that war changes society, that strategy and military policy are aspects of politics, that the incidence of military service reflects and affects social structure, that the events and patterns of armed struggle help to shape the way people think about themselves and others, and so on through a catalogue of specific ways in which the impact of armed force may be felt. No great knowledge or special insight is required to see truth in this message, but like many other obvious ideas it has failed at the level of execution; scholars have not taken the trouble to show what it means concretely. Enormous effort has been spent on studying the causes of the American Revolution, and an almost equally enormous effort has been invested in the events leading up to the drafting, ratification, and implementation of the Constitution. But, with some exceptions, more than seven years of armed struggle have been left to the military historians, who have generally been preoccupied with recounting military operations and assessing generalship. That situation is changing, and would continue to change in a healthier direction even without my own efforts; but the essays in this book are intended to contribute to a better understanding of how the Revolutionary War links what caused it to what it produced.

My other chief interest, in the history of revolution generally and the American Revolution in particular, is meant to appear in these essays as something more than a mere carrier for an evangelical concern with a "new" military history. The American Revolution, possibly like all revolutions, seems fated to be encumbered with an endless debate, about what kind of revolution it was, and whether it was a "real" revolution at all. Protagonists in this debate, at their worst, seem to have a vision, one part *Communist Manifesto,* one part *Tale of Two Cities,* against which the reality of revolution is to be measured. How much class conflict? how many bloodied heads? how much upward social mobility? are the key questions supposed to test American revolutionariness. Bernard Bailyn has pointed out that revolution may, in the ultimate sense, be a mentality; do people see themselves as being in or having been through a revolution? My own contribution to this debate is to assert that a protracted war, especially one so reliant on popular, more or less voluntary military service, is itself a kind of revolution, whether one takes the crude body-count approach or Bailyn's psycholo-

gical approach to the definition of revolution. Beyond this assertion of the revolutionary nature of war itself, I am convinced that the military factor permeates both the origins and
the outcome of the Revolution, that one sees it in the marked
shift in British colonial policy after 1760 and in Alexander
Hamilton's nightmare of a spastic confederation failing to survive in the international jungle of the 1780's and 1790's, and
that this aspect of the Revolutionary epoch has been badly neglected by historians.

Several other, more limited themes run through the essays.
One, reflected in the title of the book, is the widely ramifying
effects of a legally armed population. The National Rifle Association may find aid and comfort in this volume, though I hope
not, because every question of power and policy in the Revolutionary period was skewed by the fact that almost all white men
had guns, and by the unusual importance given to this fact by
the state of eighteenth-century military technology. Government—imperial, provincial, state, or Federal—could rarely
choose to rule even a small area by force alone; primitive
weapons limited the capacity to do so, and even that capacity
could be quickly eroded by a failure to persuade or motivate
people. Far more than in our own time of rubber bullets and
data banks and news management and armored personnel car-
riers, eighteenth-century American politics was a politics of
consent, and the distribution of weaponry had done more than
anything else to produce that political situation. Faced with
rebellion a century before Lexington and Concord, Governor
William Berkeley of Virginia had bewailed the lot of the man
who must rule a people "Poore Endebted Discontented and
Armed." Though poverty among Americans diminished in the
next hundred years, indebtedness and discontent did not; they
kept their guns, and their numbers grew twentyfold.

Governor Berkeley's lament points to a second theme running through most of the essays: the importance of perception
to decision and action. The way people saw their situation is

one of the most accessible aspects of history; diaries and letters are full of exactly dated pictures of what their writers *thought* was going on; it has even been said that written history is nothing except a history of ideas, because all that documents can convey are ideas—contemporary perceptions. But no aspect of history has proved more fragile, perhaps because the temptation to read our own knowledge of outcomes back into the words and sentences of people who did *not* know the outcome of their situation seems almost irresistible; once we spot the glimpse of the future in the historical document, we are very likely to twist the meaning present in the writer's mind at the time he wrote. So I have tried, especially in the essays on Ellis and Pownall, Gage, Lee, and Loyalism, to rescue the contemporary perception of decision-makers from anachronistic distortion.

Finally, I have sought patterns. Politics and strategy usually provide a story, with beginning, middle, and end. But the politics and strategy of the Revolution are what we know most about, and where there is least left for the historian to discover and say, and other sectors of life do not have the neat narrative form provided by politics and strategy. Without a story to tell, what does the historian do? Normally he asks questions and tries to answer them. What caused the Revolution? Why did it succeed? Etc. But for the military history of the Revolution the debated questions are not very good ones, and truly good questions are yet to be debated seriously. I have tried to raise a few questions about the military aspect of the Revolution in these essays. More valuable, however, than my question-asking may be a less ambitious approach, which begins with a simple belief that the war must have been important, and goes on to sift through as much of the historical record of the war, its background and its aftermath, as I could with the aim of making some sense of countless vignettes, and of giving some system and precision to my hunch that the war was important. The stories, such as they are, in these essays are biographical and illustrative; they are there admittedly to entertain, but mainly to make clear whatever pattern has slowly filtered through from documents to brain. There is a pattern to British strategy, a pattern to American military response, patterns in the mind of Thomas Pownall and Charles Lee, a crazy-quilt pattern of colonial militia structure, and an awesomely continuous pattern in American military experience before, through, and many years beyond the Revolution. At least I think I see such patterns; and therein lies the historian's problem, with the intricate way his mind works on an infinitude of facts which most assuredly do not speak for themselves. Having flayed a few predecessors in the notes to these essays for their blindness to patterns that are plain to me, I will say no more, and prepare to meet my critics.

Those critics should spare the people named below who have contributed to my education, and to the development of one or more of these essays, but who must not be held responsible for anything I say. Above all, David Bien has helped with criticism, inspired by example, and sustained with friendship through the years represented in this book. Frank Craven will always have his own niche in any list of my intellectual obligations. Peter Paret more than anyone else has shaped my conception of what military history ought to be. It would be invidious and probably inaccurate to list others in any but alphabetical order: Jim and Harriet Agnew, William Baldwin, James Banner, Randy Beers, George Billias, John Bowditch, Richard Maxwell Brown, Richard Challener, Thomas Collier, Marcus Cunliffe, Jack Greene, Jonathan House, John Howe, Al Hurley, Kermit and Lynn Johnson, Michael Kammen, Laura Daniel, Charles Lesser, Gerald Linderman, Kenneth Lockridge, Paul Lucas, Patricia McCommon, Piers Mackesy, Louis Morton, Elizabeth Muenger, John Murrin, Alison Gilbert Olson, Robert Palmer, Howard Peckham, Bradford Perkins, Lionel Rothkrug, Jerrold Seigel, Marianne Sheldon, DeWitt Smith, Lawrence Stone, William Stryker, John Tottenham, Sam Bass Warner,

William Wilcox, Vann Woodward, and Henry Young. The friendly and efficient staff of the U.S. Army Military History Research Collection at Carlisle Barracks, where I was a visiting professor when the book was being finished, helped in more ways than they know.

Faculty research funds fron Princeton University and the University of Michigan, and support from the National Endowment for the Humanities and the American Council of Learned Societies, provided much of the time and research travel needed to write the essays in this book. Other debts, more readily acknowledged than described, are to my wife, Arlene Phillips Shy, to my parents, and to my children.

London, 1976

CHAPTER ONE

The American Revolution Today

This first essay was delivered originally as the Harmon Memorial Lecture at the U.S. Air Force Academy in 1974 and again, slightly revised, at the U.S. Army War College in 1975. Although it addresses an audience of military professionals, its main arguments, about historical relevance and the nature of armed force, recur and are more fully explored in the subsequent essays, and so it has not undergone any major revision here.

"The American Revolution Today," as a title, must sound vaguely familiar. Surely we have read or heard this one before, somewhere, in the Sunday magazine section or on television. If the title seems banal, that was the intention, because it seemed more appropriate here not to strive for profundity or esoteric reinterpretation of the American Revolution as an armed struggle, but to deal directly with certain aspects of the Revolutionary War so obvious and so elementary that they are easily overlooked. The first, perhaps most important, aspect has to do with the connection, if any, between a war fought two hundred years ago and now.

"Relevance" was never a strong word. Vague, and a little soft at the center, it simply could not carry the load placed upon it during the 1960's, when a silent, accepting generation gave way to one that was vocal and full of doubt. And now the word is exhausted. Sophisticated people visibly react, wincing or smirking, when others use the word, as if the speaker were wearing an odd piece of clothing gone out of style. We (at least we in history departments, who have suffered during the last decade a hemorrhage of students to more obviously relevant disciplines like psychology and sociology) relish signs of a counterattack that will administer the coup de grace to "relevance," as in a sign recently tacked on a history office door: "The surest way not to find relevance," it said, "is to go looking for it." With a sigh of relief, teachers of history watch enrollment figures bottom out, then begin to climb again, and they go back to teaching history, not trying to explain why history is worth studying.

And yet, that weak word, muttered and shouted by a generation of students now moving toward middle age, a generation that may never have thought carefully about what it was demanding when it demanded "relevance," that word makes a vital point. There ought to be a better, stronger, clearer word, but there isn't, so "relevance" has had to do what it could to make that vital point. The point is: historians inhabit two worlds, the world of the present, and the world of the past.[1] And it is not just any "past" world, but some particular location in time and space which each historian probably knows as well or better than he knows the world of the present. Most historians read the documents of the past more systematically and carefully than they read today's newspaper. They reconstruct the physical environment of the past with painstaking care, while usually taking their own almost for granted, often hardly noticing their immediate surroundings. The vital point, so feebly made by the cry for "relevance," is that these past and present worlds not only *ought* to connect, but they absolutely *do* connect, whether we like it, or are aware of it, or not. There is simply no escaping the subjective quality of historical study; "history" is memory, and the human mind is the inevitable filter through which every gritty historical fact either does, or does not, pass. We may smile wisely at those who still demand relevance; but then we go back to work, our present world subtly dictating the past time and place we choose for intensive study, dictating our priorities for research, dictating our preliminary hypotheses and our angle of attack, dictating when we can meet to talk about history, who our audience will be, and even suggesting what that audience would like to hear.

Consider, briefly, how the historical "present" has affected study and understanding of the Revolutionary past. Historians who lived through the great Civil War focused on the Constitution, that miraculous and delicate achievement which had bound together disparate, scattered groups of people; for these historians of the nineteenth century, the Revolution was primarily the story of the long road to the Philadelphia Convention of 1787, and the question lurking in the backs of their minds was how the Constitution could contain the forces of disruption which threatened the Republic in the 1860's and 1870's. For a later generation of historians, those who lived and worked through an era of great reform and great depression, of Woodrow Wilson and the two Roosevelts, the concerns were

different. In both the causes and the consequences of the Revolution, they looked for the effects of class conflict and economic
interest, and of course they found them. For a still later generation, profoundly affected by the Second World War and
working under the influence of the Cold War, the chief concern seems again very different: it was with the essential unity
and goodness of eighteenth-century American society, not con-
trived at Philadelphia in 1787 so much as sprung from the
basic equality and security of life, and from the basic soundness
of belief, in colonial and Revolutionary America, giving the nation the strength and purpose—then and now—needed both to
defend itself and to lead the world by example. Needless to say,
the most recent generation of historians has begun to raise
questions about this view, less by direct refutation than by exploration of some of the disturbing sides of life in eighteenth-century America—slavery, poverty, violence, Indian relations, and
the place of women, to mention a few.[2]

But our focus is not the Revolution as a whole, but the role
played by armed force in the Revolution. More than a decade
ago there was noted a revival of interest in the military side of
the Revolution.[3] Between the Civil War and the Second World
War historians had moved away from the study of military history. Many, reacting to the horrors of the First World War,
simply found war a repulsive subject (which of course it is), and
others thought (not unreasonably) that for too long excessive
attention to military history had caused other important aspects
of the past to be neglected. But with the Second World War
and the Cold War came another shift.[4] War again seemed interesting, and its study respectable. By looking at a few examples of the forms taken by this revived interest in military
history, we can see again how the mid-twentieth-century
"present" and the Revolutionary "past" have interacted.

Piers Mackesy of Oxford gave us a radically new perspective
on the Revolutionary War by putting it into a global context,
and by making us see it from London; King George III and his

cabinet could not match the British performance of 1939–45, but it is hard to imagine Mackesy's book without the Second World War to serve as a concealed analytical framework.[5] My own study of the British army in America before the Revolution, and what some reviewers thought excessive preoccupation with the confusion and contradictions in British military policy for America before 1775, was at least partly a product of what seemed the appalling confusion of American military policy under Eisenhower, the dreary interservice wrangling and contemporary failure to think through basic assumptions about the use of force.[6] Ira Gruber of Rice, in his study of the unfortunate Howe brothers, focused on the actual use of force; and if I do not misunderstand him, he has been fascinated by the effort to make war an extension of politics in the formulation of Clausewitz, whose reputation as a military thinker rose in the course of the great strategic debate of the later 1950's and early 1960's (when Professor Gruber was doing his work) over how, after Korea, the United States could best make war an effective political instrument.[7] Whether his study of the Howes contains any lesson for our own times, or whether the author ever thought about Clausewitz, Flexible Response, and all that, only Professor Gruber can say.

Don Higginbotham of North Carolina is a last example. Daniel Morgan, the subject of his first book, was not exactly a guerrilla, but he certainly was irregular in many respects, and he was the kind of effective and charismatic soldier who turns up in the revolutionary wars of our own time.[8] Vietnam, especially, created an interest in seeing the American Revolution as a truly revolutionary war, with guerrilla tactics, popular attitudes, and even counterinsurgent methods getting new attention. Higginbotham's next book, a general history of the war, gave full scope to these "revolutionary" elements in the military conflict, but he also pointed a still more recent trend—toward interest in the deeper effects of the war on American society. More than any previous military historian, Higginbotham

began to ask particularly about what mobilization of manpower
and ruinous inflation did to people, how the Revolutionary
War as a protracted, strenuous public event affected thousands
and thousands of private lives. Somehow, as I compare the air
fare to Colorado Springs this year with what it was in 1969,
when I last attended the symposium, or watch my own personal
response to the televised ordeal of Watergate, I find those few
pages in which Higginbotham discusses wartime psychology
and the effects of runaway inflation highly relevant.[9] It seems
strange that military historians have waited so long to study
war, not merely as a series of maneuvers and battles, but as a
kind of revolution in its own right.

   Now it is important to be as clear as possible about how the
historian's own present world impinges on his understanding
of the past. The present has a powerful effect on what seems
most relevant, but it does not dictate conclusions, although it
may nudge those conclusions in a certain direction. Mackesy
thought that Britain might have won the war had it persevered
a year or so longer. Gruber thought the Howes virtually lost
the war because they let their political role fatally compromise
their military performance. Other historians, equally fascinated
by the global nature of the conflict and by the interplay of politics and strategy, would strenuously disagree. The danger that
historians will tell lies about the past in order to serve present
political or ideological ends is less than the risk that, by responding to the lure of relevance, we will distort the past by
being one-sided. To have many students of British strategy and
military policy, but too few students of the grass-roots American response to wartime pressures, will produce a lopsided understanding of the Revolutionary War. But that kind of risk is
not peculiar to the study of history and the perils posed by a
quest for historical relevance; it goes with simply being alive
and trying to understand anything.

   What then is the right approach to the American Revolutionary War today? My audience is mainly military, brought

together primarily by a felt need to do something about the two-hundredth anniversary of the Revolution. Military professionals hope, like militant students, to learn something relevant. Over us all looms the Bicentennial, so far an embarrassing mess, in part because so far too few have had the heart or displayed the imagination required to celebrate it properly. Our lack of heart, and our paucity of imagination, are themselves symptoms of a "present" that seems all the more disheartening when we look at the evidence of energy and brilliance two hundred years ago. And so, speaking directly to soldiers, who seek guidance, and impelled but disconcerted by the Bicentennial occasion and its doomed desire for profundity, what is there to say about the Revolutionary War? Or is there anything to say?

We can begin to find an answer if we let ourselves be guided by the pressures of relevance. The military, like all other professions outside of the academic world, seeks knowledge not for its own sake, but for its professional uses. Humbly consulting experts, soldiers try to pick out the professionally useful in whatever the experts convey. Are there lessons, or other useful knowledge, for the American military professional in the story of the Revolution? It is a fair question, better brought into the open than suppressed by academic impatience with utilitarian concerns.

The other side of "today"—the Bicentennial—does not point so clearly. But let me try to define the problem: it is mainly in the sense of remoteness that we feel from the Revolution. It is not only a problem of distance in time. For many people today, the Civil War has an immediacy, a palpability, that the Revolution lacks, however much we may admire George Washington, Monticello, or early American furniture. Lincoln lives, but Washington is a monument. The heart of the matter is in the very success of the Revolution. The Civil War, like every other major event in American history including (we now begin to see) the Second World War, has a tragic, human, two-sided quality that the Revolution seems to lack. Whatever was done or decided in 1775 or 1777 or 1781, the outcome justified it, and the whole complex of events takes on a smooth, self-contained character that makes it very difficult to get an emotional grip on the subject. The American nation was a success story from the beginning; the nation began with the Revolution; *quod erat demonstrandum.* In short, finding something useful to the military profession, and breaking down the barrier posed by time and success, are the tasks imposed on me by "today." Let us start with the most basic facts, and try to work our way toward some useful and satisfying result.

The first fact about the Revolutionary War is that the British lost it. And the inevitable question follows, for soldier as well as historian, why? It is easy to assemble a whole catalogue of answers: military failure to adjust to American conditions; blunders by the field commanders; incompetence and corruption in London; stubborn and obtuse misunderstanding of American grievances by both Crown and Parliament; and collapse of British public support for the war after Yorktown. But a second look at each of these answers raises a new set of questions.

From early on, the British and their German and American allies seem as adept at irregular warfare, at the tactics of hit and run, as do the rebels. For every British tactical blunder like Bennington there is a comparable rebel blunder. British tactics might have been better, sooner, but it is hard to put much weight on the tactical factor.[10] The quality of high command in America is another matter. From the faulty planning of the march to Concord in 1775, through the Yorktown fiasco in 1781, British field commanders made serious mistakes. More than anything, they repeatedly misjudged the American military and popular response. In retrospect, it is easy to say what they should or might have done. But as I look at the men and their decisions, several things occur to me: one is that none of these men—Gage, Howe, Clinton, Carleton, Cornwallis, even

Burgoyne—was notably incompetent.[11] Their military ac-
complishments justified giving each of them high military command. Second, a few mistakes—like the failure to seal off the
southeastern exit from Trenton on January 2, 1777—are the
kinds of lapses that inevitably occur in every war, that every
commander in history has been guilty of committing or permitting. Third, the other mistakes—like not destroying Washington's army in the autumn of 1776, like expecting to reach
Albany from Canada without too much trouble in the summer
of 1777, like expecting to re-establish a sea line of communication from the Virginia tidewater in 1781—seem reasonably calculated risks, which of course in the event were *mis*-
calculated. That historians can still argue vigorously about
these decisions suggests that the commanders themselves, however hapless they may have been, were at least not stupid or
grossly incompetent. For example: Professor Gruber thinks
Howe should have pursued Washington to destruction after
the battle of Long Island in 1776.[12] Hindsight strongly suggests
that Gruber is right. But the length of the British casualty list at
Bunker Hill, plus Howe's belief that the beaten American army
would probably fall apart and his fear that pointless killing of
the king's American subjects might have a boomerang effect,
led him to play a cat-and-mouse game during those months
after Long Island. A mistake, probably, but not a foolish or irresponsible one. We may hold high military commanders to an
unrealistic, Napoleonic standard; when they fail to meet the
standard, we may judge them too quickly as incompetents. British commanders, as a group, were not unusually bad, and I
think it is a mistake to tie the can of British defeat to their
tails.[13]

As for the situation in Britain itself, Lord George Germain
and the Earl of Sandwich may have been unattractive people,
but the sheer size of the unprecedented British financial, administrative, and logistical effort which Germain and Sandwich,
as the responsible cabinet ministers for army and navy, mobi-

lized and directed suggests that corruption and confusion in
London were at most a marginal part of our explanation for
failure.[14] Likewise, the crucial collapse of British public opinion
after Yorktown needs to be seen against fairly solid popular
support for the war at the outset, even among many who had
been critical of British policy in America before 1775, and a miraculous revival of that solidarity when it was threatened in the
aftermath of Burgoyne's defeat by French entry into the war,
by the danger of a cross-Channel attack, and by an almost revolutionary economic and political crisis in the home islands
themselves.[15] Finally, whether greater political flexibility in the
cabinet and House of Commons, more generous and timely
concessions to American demands, might have split and dissi-
pated the Revolutionary movement, is a fascinating but impossible question to answer. Certainly American leaders were
afraid of just such an event. The timing of the Declaration of
Independence was, in part, a Congressional coup intended to
foreclose serious negotiations which the British seemed ready
to undertake.[16] But the basic British line on negotiation was
that previous flexibility had been repeatedly misread by Americans as weakness and irresolution, and that only major concessions, extracted by the pressure of armed force from the Americans themselves, could mean the start of a negotiated peace. A
wrong-headed position, perhaps, but one which we, of all people, ought to be able to recognize as not completely unreasonable.

Should we conclude then that the root cause of British defeat
was not so much in the failure of British leaders or British people, but in the circumstances of the war? That Britain's objective was simply not attainable without great good luck or divine
intervention? That there was a disjunction between British
ends and British means? That they were trapped in a set of
basic assumptions about their problem that made the American
Revolutionary War a British Tragedy?

"Tragedy" is a word with a seductive ring to it, especially

when the tragedy happened to someone else, long ago. But if we stay close to the facts, we find some knowledgeable, relatively detached observers on the spot who did not see the British problem in tragic terms. They thought the British had a good chance to win, and they believed the margin between winning and losing lay well within the available range of military power and strategic perception. To take only one example: Colonel Louis Duportail was one of the ablest French officers to serve the American cause. He became chief engineer, and rose to the rank of major general in the Continental army. He was also a spy for the French minister of war. In a long, brutally candid letter written after Burgoyne's surrender and on the eve of Valley Forge, a letter that never reached its destination because the British intercepted it, Duportail stated that the British could win if they replaced General Howe, which they did, and if they could maintain an army in America of 30,000 men, a figure actually surpassed in 1776 and not maintained subsequently because forces were dispersed.[17] Duportail based his estimate on weaknesses in the American situation, which I will turn to in a moment. Deciding whether Duportail and some others who agreed with him were exactly right is less important than seeing that such opinions existed. Major American defeats in Canada in 1775, around New York City in 1776, on the Brandywine in 1777, at Charleston and Camden in South Carolina in 1780, as well as the collapse of the American position in New Jersey in 1776, later in large areas of the South, and still later in the transappalachian West, suggest that we must take Duportail seriously. The British lost, but they were fighting within that zone of contingencies where both winning and losing are not unlikely outcomes.

And what of the American revolutionaries? The second most obvious fact about the Revolutionary War seems to be that the rebels won. But a safer, more accurate statement is that they did not lose. If we look closely at the American side of the war, we see a very mixed picture—impressive in some ways, but very unedifying in others. From the outburst of enthusiasm in the spring of 1775, genuine support for the war appears to have declined through the next six years. The service and pension files in the National Archives indicate that a large proportion of the white male population, and a significant part of the black male population as well, performed active military service, but only a tiny part of the population performed truly extended military service.[18] People seemed to get tired. They got tired of serving, and they got tired of contributing. Of course, they got angry when British or Hessian or Tory troops misbehaved, but they also grew weary of being bullied by local committees of safety, by corrupt deputy assistant commissaries of supply, and by bands of ragged strangers with guns in their hands calling themselves soldiers of the Revolution. They got very tired of worthless and counterfeit money. Duportail, for one, also thought Americans were soft. He said that supply shortages were wrecking the Revolution, not shortages of munitions, but of things like linen, sugar, tea, and liquor. They were not, he said, a warlike people, but were used to living comfortably without working too hard. Of course the European peasant was his standard of comparison, but those peasants—the poorest, most miserable and desperate, toughest ones—comprised the backbone of every European army. Duportail, himself committed fully to the American side, told the French government, "There is a hundred times more enthusiasm for this Revolution in any Paris café than in all the colonies together." Surely he exaggerated, but too much other evidence supports the line of his argument to reject it out of hand.[19]

This realm of simple and obvious facts in which we have been operating is slippery. American revolutionaries did not *win* the war, but they did not lose it. What do these words mean, and what is the point of the distinction? Clearly, that they mustered enough strength from internal and foreign sources of support not to be defeated decisively, and that they hung on long enough to discourage the British government and people. Though not beaten as the Confederacy in 1865 and Germany in 1945 were beaten, neither did they win mili-

tarily as the Union won and the Allies won. The point of the
distinction has to do with the character of the struggle, which
went on for more than seven years. In characterizing the war
from the Revolutionary viewpoint, what stands out is weakness,
part of which Duportail noted, the rest of which was not yet apparent to him.

In discussing American revolutionary weakness, we must be
careful. There is danger of distortion and exaggeration. Obviously, the rebels could have been much weaker than they
were. Moreover, military historians are too apt to look for
someone to blame. As we asked about the British, so we ask
about American revolutionaries: were the generals incompetent, Congress irresponsible, the States selfish, and the people
apathetic? These may be the wrong questions, leading us to irrelevant answers. If politicians squabbled endlessly, if commanders repeatedly committed elementary military mistakes, if
States ignored Congress while the Army damned it, if ordinary
people quit and went home or hid their cows or even packed
up and went to Vermont or across the mountains to get away
from the war and its ceaseless demands—and all these things
did in fact happen frequently in the later years of the war—
then it is beside the point to blame the politicians, the soldiers,
or the people. One wonders why the whole affair did not simply collapse, what kept it going so long.

Some good American patriots at the time wondered the same
thing. Did war take on a life of its own, like the Thirty Years'
War as portrayed in Bertolt Brecht's *Mother Courage,* with people virtually forgetting what it was about, and trying to do no
more than survive, even if survival meant collaborating with
the impersonal machinery of mobilization? That is not the way
we like to think about the origins of the American nation, but
there is evidence to support such a view (though the Revolution
never attained the far-flung ferocity of that most brutal and
protracted of the religious wars). The years from 1776 to 1782
might indeed be recounted as horror stories of terrorism,

rapacity, mendacity, and cowardice, not to blame our ancestors for these things, but to remind us what a war fought by the weak must look like. The bedrock facts of the American Revolutionary struggle, especially after the euphoric first year, are not pretty.

But everything turned out all right. The British went home, even the French went home; thousands of German prisoners of war blended into the Pennsylvania landscape, and only the Spanish, the Indians, and black slaves were left to deal as best they could with the victorious revolutionaries. How a national polity so successful, and a society so relatively peaceful, could emerge from a war so full of bad behavior, including perhaps a fifth of the population actively treasonous (that is, loyal to Crown), must be a puzzle.[20]

Duportail, like many other observers on all sides, thought that the United States would split into fragments once the war was over. The Hessian Colonel Dincklage was even more pessimistic as he looked into the future:

> They may have peace but not happiness when the war is over. It matters little whether the Americans win or lose. Presently this country is the scene of the most cruel events. Neighbors are on opposite sides, children are against their fathers. Anyone who differs with the opinions of Congress in thought or in speech is regarded as an enemy and turned over to the hangman, or else he must flee.
>
> We give these refugees food, and support most of them with arms. They go on patrol for us in small groups and . . . into their home districts to take revenge by pillaging, murdering, and burning. . . .
>
> If peace comes after an English victory, discord between the two parties will flare up underneath the ashes and nobody will be able to resolve it. If the rebels should win, they will break their necks, one by one. What misery the people have plunged themselves into.[21]

Dincklage, like Duportail, was too pessimistic and his prediction was wrong. Yet even the most prominent leaders of the Revolution had similar fears.

A brilliant young staff officer, Alexander Hamilton, after several years of watching the course of the war from Washington's headquarters, confided to his closest friend:

> . . . our countrymen have all the folly of the ass and all the passiveness of the sheep in their compositions. They are determined not to be free and they can neither be frightened, discouraged nor persuaded to change their resolution. If we are saved, France and Spain must save us. I have the most pigmy-feelings at the idea, and I almost wish to hide my disgrace in universal ruin.[22]

Thomas Jefferson, who saw most of the war from Philadelphia and Virginia, and whose optimism allegedly contrasts with Hamilton's cold-eyed conservatism, occasionally revealed similar fears, especially once the unifying British threat had passed:

> I know no danger so dreadful and so probable as that of internal contests. . . . The states will go to war with each other in defiance of Congress; one will call in France to her assistance; another Gr. Britain, and so we shall have all the wars of Europe brought to our own doors.

Jefferson predicted that "From the conclusion of this war we shall be going down hill." [23] Having faced apathy, riot, and even secessionism as governor of Virginia when he had tried to mobilize the state against British invasion in 1781, Jefferson had reason to worry about the postwar prospects of the United States.[24] Jefferson, at his gloomiest, sounded not unlike Dincklage and Duportail.

Why were they all wrong? When Shays' Rebellion broke out in 1786, and again when the Whiskey Rebellion erupted in 1794, many thought that the beginning of the end had come. As predicted, the unwieldy, centrifugal Republic, like Poland, was collapsing into anarchy. Even Hamilton and Jefferson, as emergent party leaders in the 1790's, were acting out the scenario both had written: sectional conflict and violent rhetoric followed by apparent appeals for foreign intervention and cries of treason. But it did not happen. Affluence—what Duportail dis-

paraged as the soft life—is part of the explanation; no matter
how aggrieved or deprived, no one was likely to starve in
America, so insurrection seemed to lack the desperate edge
that it could have in England, Ireland, or France.[25] But more
than mere affluence explains post-Revolutionary success.

Part, perhaps the most important part, of the explanation
lies in the character of the war itself, and in contemporary perceptions of the armed struggle. Bitter experience of fighting
from weakness had all but obliterated the naïve optimism of
1775, and had sensitized Americans to their own political peril.
Fearful prophecies, based on dismal fact, functioned to defeat
those prophecies by channeling political energies into the
struggle against anarchy. Leaders thought, talked, and even
compromised, shrinking from the last act of the scenario that
they knew so well; people listened, talked back, occasionally
resisted, but ultimately acquiesced, at least for the crucial season when the future of the Republic hung in the balance.

Nothing was feared more by leaders in the postwar era than
disunion, and most people felt the same way. Disunion meant
failure and disgrace, so widely predicted and expected, and the
fear itself generated extraordinary efforts to prevent it. All had
learned the lessons of a dirty revolutionary war that had ended,
not with Napoleonic victories or massive defections from the
enemy armies, but with ragged unpaid American soldiers drift-
ing down the Hudson valley to sign on as sailors in the ships
which were evacuating British forces, while American officers
back at Newburgh half-heartedly planned a coup d'état to get
the money owed them by Congress.[26] The Revolution, as an
armed struggle, ended with a whimper.

Where in all this are the lessons for the soldier, and the Bicentennial message? For the Bicentennial there is only a
greater sense of reality, of immediacy, of (I hope) honesty in
looking at the Revolutionary War as it actually was. In a way,
the Bicentennial itself, and our anxiety about it, is a continuation of the national myth which began in the 1780's, when the

elation of ultimate victory combined with the sour memories of widespread human weakness and depravity as revealed in the seven-year struggle, to produce a wonderfully creative period in American politics. The ink was barely dry on the Treaty of Paris before myth and reality about the Revolutionary War were becoming entwined. The Bicentennial is indeed a birthday, and we all know the strange emotional effects induced by birthday parties. Being born the way we were was glorious? We think. Or was it? Or is it? Much about the event called the Revolutionary War had been very painful and was unpleasant to remember; only the outcome was unqualifiedly pleasant; so memory, as ever, began to play tricks with the event, which is not always a bad thing, though it makes the historian's task difficult.

And the lessons for soldiers? The most important lesson may be more philosophical than practical. Soldiers, like other professionals, learn to see themselves as the center of the activity that defines their professionalism. But the use of force is a weird activity. What most impresses me about the War of the Revolution is the sort of thing that professional military education does not dwell on, because it does not seem very practical and even sounds vaguely defeatist. It moves the commander from stage center into the chorus, if not, like Tolstoy's Kutuzov, into the orchestra or the audience. It reminds all of us, civilians as well as soldiers, of the deeply relativistic and contingent nature of violent encounters. Killing is a terribly easy thing to measure, and the results of killing called "victory" and "defeat" seem almost equally unequivocal. The British lost, so the Americans won. But when we stop fixating on military failure and success, and start scrutinizing that dynamic, unstable process of collectively trying to kill and not get killed which George Patton labeled war, then the commanders and their intentions and decisions become no more than one factor in a set of complexly interacting elements.[27] Because it may be an extreme case, the Revolution drives home the lesson that in war reality always seems to escape perception, results outrun intentions, and the final outcome is much more than the sum total of decisions made at headquarters. It may be a bleak sort of lesson for the professional soldier, but realism is better than illusion, and the lesson, if properly regarded, carries a certain cold comfort.

CHAPTER TWO

A New Look at the Colonial Militia

Produced under pressure while I was trying to turn a doctoral dissertation into a book, and delivered as a paper at a convention in Miami Beach at the end of a wild week in which Kennedy had made Khrushchev blink and Nixon had told the press that they wouldn't have him to kick around any more, this essay now strikes me as a little stiff and naïve. It is the first, chronologically, in the series. Escalation in Vietnam lay ahead, and a new streamlining Secretary of Defense was thinking about dropping the draft because it was so inefficient. My own best thought was that neither conscript nor volunteer armies were the early American tradition, and that the complexity and variety of the tradition defied those who would turn history into a comic strip for their own immediate purposes; not a very satisfying argument, perhaps, but, if pressed, I would stand by it. Although I find nothing to change in the historical presentation, the ambience of 1962 in which it was written now seems as remote as the eighteenth century itself. The essay originally appeared in The William and Mary Quarterly, *3rd series, XX (1963), 175–185; it is here slightly revised.*

The subject of the militia has produced some passionate writing by American publicists, soldiers, and historians. Defenders of the militia—those who believe that a universal military obligation is the proper way to defend a society—are fond of stressing that only when free men must themselves fight to protect their liberty are they likely to remain free. The colonial militia, in particular, represents the happy uniqueness of America, where Englishmen in the seventeenth century revived this relic of the middle ages just as, in Europe, it was sinking beneath the military superiority of the politically dangerous mercenary army. Critics of the militia—many of them professional soldiers—point a different moral, one that rests on the apparent inefficiency of militia in combat, and on the way that the myth of defense by "citizen soldiers" led again and again to tragic unpreparedness for war.

There is one point, however, where critics and defenders appear to agree: it is on the assumption that the militia, especially the colonial militia, was a fairly static institution; once its simple theory of organization has been described, there seems little need to watch it as closely for signs of deviation and change as one would watch, say, political institutions. Historians have tended to go along with this assumption, as they have generally accepted the major tenets of both defenders and critics; in short, the militia is usually regarded as both politically healthy and militarily inefficient, but in any case relatively uncomplicated.[1]

My aim is simply to raise a question about this conventional view, and to suggest that the early American militia was a more complicated—and more interesting—institution, that it varied from province to province, that it changed through time as the military demands placed upon it changed, and that these variations and changes are of some historical importance.[2] My motive is not to bolster the Pentagon, the House Armed Services Committee, or the *New York Times* in their latest disagreement over the draft or the volunteer army, not even to provide a new

key to the reinterpretation of the American Revolution, but
only to offer ways of thinking about our early military history,
and of more satisfactorily relating that history to the general
history of colonial America.

It is not difficult to understand why the militia has been
treated in terms of an unvarying sameness; one has only to
read the laws to know the answer. In 1632 the Virginia Assembly told every man fit to carry a gun to bring it to church, that
he might exercise with it after the service.[3] One hundred forty-
four years later, the legislature of Revolutionary Massachusetts
ordered men between the ages of sixteen and fifty to be
enrolled in the militia, to provide their own weapons and
equipment, and to be mustered and trained periodically by
their duly commissioned officers; that is, the same thing
Virginia had said in less sophisticated language.[4] In other ways,
the laws are much alike. Certain minor groups of men are exempted from duty. In time of emergency, individuals may be
impressed or levied or drafted—the word varies—from their
militia companies for active service. In most cases, the law provides that anyone so drafted can be excused by paying a fine,
sometimes also by finding an able-bodied substitute. The one
case of a clear legal difference—that company officers are
elected by their men in New England while they are appointed
by governors elsewhere—turns out on inspection to have made
little difference in practice. As in the case of colonial politics,
men of the "better sort" usually appear in office whatever the
process of selection; military organization and social structure
seem as yet undifferentiated.

In the beginning, of course, this is true quite literally: social
and military organization were the same thing. When John
Smith wrote of "soldiers," he meant only those inhabitants who
at that moment had guns in their hands and who had been ordered to help Smith look out for danger. But military change
in Virginia began very early. To make everyone a soldier when
men were still concerned about starving was to ensure that no

one would be much of a soldier, as Virginia learned several times. First, a few forts and garrisons were established, either by appropriated funds or, more often, by land grants. Then Negroes, and later most indentured servants, were excused from militia duty.[5] Indian policy had a direct bearing on military organization. For a time, Virginia attempted to treat all Indians as hostile, *ipso facto*.[6] But the military requirements of such a policy were too great, demanding large forces to make almost continuous raids into Indian country.[7] The policy was changed, and the system of defense changed with it; henceforth, Virginia relied on a buffer of friendly Indians, on several forts along the frontier, and—after Bacon's Rebellion of 1675-76—on a few dozen paid, mounted soldiers who "ranged" between the forts—the first rangers of American history.[8]

The year of Bacon's Rebellion, when both Chesapeake and New England colonies waged wars against the Indian, affords a convenient opportunity for comparison. Though there are many similarities in the way Virginia and Massachusetts responded to this danger, differences are equally evident and may be more important. Virginia had fewer enemies to contend with, and yet suffered political breakdown in the process of fighting its war, while Massachusetts did not. Governor William Berkeley's strategy of defense, which called for five hundred soldiers in the pay of the colony, required a level of taxation that most Virginia planters believed they could not bear. When Nathaniel Bacon and his followers later reshaped strategy, they called for a thousand soldiers, but planned to use them in raiding and plundering the Indian settlements; thus, Virginians would get not only the satisfaction of hitting back at their tormentors, but also the chance to make a burdensome war profitable.[9] The change from Berkeley to Bacon is more than a little reminiscent of European mercenary armies of the sixteenth and the early seventeenth century, when a government often lost control of a war while trying to wage it more ef-

fectively. Massachusetts and Plymouth lost many more lives
than did Virginia in 1675–76, but their governments never lost
control of the war. Crucial to New England success was its ability to draft large numbers of men when and where they were
needed. Of course there were grumbling and evasion as war-
weariness set in, but the point is that Boston could do it and apparently Jamestown could not.[10]

The reasons for this difference are not altogether clear.
There is always danger of neglecting the effect of the particular economic and political situation in each colony while making a military comparison. There is also the possibility that if
the danger to Virginia had been greater, it might have unified
and invigorated that colony. But it would seem that the principal factor is the different pattern of settlement. New England
towns were more scattered than Chesapeake farms, but each
town had a capacity for armed resistance that was lacking in an
individual plantation. A town could bear the burden of a military draft and still hope to maintain itself against attack, while
the loss of a man or two from a single, remote household often
meant choosing between abandonment and destruction. Despite shortages and complaints, a New England town could
usually house and feed a company of soldiers besides its own,
thus acting as an advanced military base. The meetinghouse,
large and centrally located, often doubled as the "garrison
house," strong point and refuge in case of attack. New England
promised its soldiers plunder in the form of scalp bounties,
profits from the sale of Indian slaves, and postwar land grants,
but such promises were merely contributory, and not essential
as they were in Virginia, to the procurement of troops. The
contrast between New England and the Chesapeake can be exaggerated, for many New England towns were destroyed or
abandoned during King Philip's War. But there remains an important difference: the clustering of manpower and the cohe-
sive atmosphere in the town community gave New England
greater military strength.

This point about the importance of atmosphere can be sharpened by adding the case of New York to the comparison. The Dutch West India Company made the initial error of promising protection to the settlers of New Netherland, and never thereafter could correct its mistake, although it tried.[11] Organized solely as a commercial enterprise, the colony acquired a social heterogeneity and an attitude toward war that subverted militia organization. The English conquest in 1664 brought the stereotype militia law, but it also brought a small garrison of regulars that tended to perpetuate the Dutch atmosphere of military dependency. Moreover, an accident of geography gave New York not the two-hundred-mile frontier of Massachusetts or Virginia, but a single center of danger—the Anglo-Dutch city of Albany, a city constantly torn by internal disputes. More straggling in its pattern of settlement than Virginia, and with much less of the sense of community that makes men fight for one another, New York depended for protection on its diplomatic and commercial connection with the Iroquois Confederation rather than on an effective militia; in time of trouble, it had to call for help.[12]

By the end of the seventeenth century, the principal threat to the British colonies was changing. Europeans—French and Spanish—became the main danger. Virginia found itself so little troubled by the new threat, and her Indian enemies so weak, that militia virtually ceased to exist there for about a half-century, a time when a handful of semi-professional rangers could watch the frontier. When the Tuscarora momentarily menaced Virginia in 1713, Governor Alexander Spotswood had little success in ordering out the militia. He then tried to recruit two hundred volunteers from the counties along the frontier ("for those that are far enough from it are little inclined to adventure themselves"), but soon learned that frontiersmen were understandably reluctant to leave their homes in time of danger. Spotswood, finally convinced that he could not make war, made peace.[13]

During the same period, the frontier of Massachusetts was under sporadic attack by French-supported Indians. After the loss of Deerfield in 1704, the colony developed a net of what have been called, in another time and place, "strategic villages," from Hadley to Wells in Maine, each protected by its own militia, and augmented by provincial troops who used horses in the summer, snowshoes in the winter, to connect the towns by patrols and to conduct raids into Indian country.[14] Clearly the New England militia was retaining much of its vitality.

But it was not simply the prevalence or absence of an external threat that determined military change. As New England bore the brunt of war with France, South Carolina occupied the post of danger against Spain. The Carolina militia came in from the country to repulse a Spanish attack on Charleston in 1706, and it rallied—with some help from North Carolina and Virginia—to save the colony during the Yamassee War in 1715, though not before most of the outlying settlements had been abandoned. But South Carolina came to have a more scattered population than either Virginia or New York. In 1720 the Council and Assembly complained to the British Board of Trade that it was difficult to react to any sudden danger because the colony's 2000 militiamen were spread over 150 miles.[15] In 1738 Lieutenant Governor William Bull reported to the Board that, brave as the Carolinians might be, an effective defense was, as he phrased it, "Inconsistent with a Domestick or Country Life." [16]

Bull neglected to mention South Carolina's other major difficulty in defending itself—slavery. Under the earliest militia law, officers were to "muster and train all sorts of men, of what condition or wheresoever born." In the Yamassee War, four hundred Negroes helped six hundred white men defeat the Indians.[17] But as the ratio of slaves to whites rapidly increased, and especially after a serious slave insurrection in 1739, Carolinians no longer dared arm Negroes; in fact, they hardly dared leave their plantations in time of emergency. The British government tried to fill the gap, first by organizing Georgia as an all-white military buffer, then by sending a regiment of regulars with Oglethorpe in 1740. But increasingly the South Carolina militia became an agency to control slaves, and less an effective means of defense.[18]

Elsewhere the new, European threat of the eighteenth century called forth responses that went far beyond the original conception of militia. War against France and Spain required larger forces serving for a longer time and traveling greater distances. These were volunteer forces, paid and supplied, often armed and clothed, by the government. The power of the governor to raise and command the militia accordingly came to mean less and less, while the military role of the legislature grew larger. The shift in power from royal governor to colonial assembly had many causes, but the change in the character of warfare was not the least of them.

Less important perhaps, but also less obvious, was the changing character of recruitment in the eighteenth century. So long as military service was nearly universal, one might imagine that volunteers for active duty necessarily must have been militiamen who received a reminder of their military obligation along with a little tactical drill at the militia muster, three or four times a year. This, it would appear, is not wholly true. There were several classes of men, whose total number was growing after 1700, who fell outside the militia structure. These classes were: friendly and domesticated Indians, free Negroes and mulattoes, white servants and apprentices, and free white men on the move. These were precisely the men who, if given the chance, were most willing to go to war. As the militia companies tended in the eighteenth century to become more social than military organizations, they became the hallmarks of respectability or at least of full citizenship in the community. Evidence gathered so far is not full nor does it admit of any quantitative conclusions, but it does indicate that a growing number of those who did the actual fighting were not the men who bore a military obligation as part of their freedom.[19]

It is difficult to believe that the colonial volunteers of the eighteenth century had more in common with the pitiable recruits of the contemporary European armies than with the militia levies of an earlier period; nevertheless, changes in the social composition of American forces between about 1650 and 1750 were in that direction. By impressing vagabonds in 1740, the Virginia Assembly filled its quota of men for the expedition against Cartagena. Six years later, when Governor William Gooch sought to recruit volunteers for another expedition, he found few men willing to enlist, the usual sources apparently depleted by the previous draft. For the expedition against Fort Duquesne in 1755, Virginia was drafting "such able bodied men, as do not follow or exercise any lawful calling or employment, or have not some other lawful and sufficient maintenance," and carefully exempting from the draft all "who hath any vote in the election of a Burgess or Burgesses to serve in the General Assembly of this colony." Two years later, having recognized that voters ought not to be troubled by active military service, the House of Burgesses spelled out who ought to be the first to fight: Those who

> shall be found, loitering and neglecting to labor for reasonable wages; all who run from their habitations, leaving wives or children without suitable means for their subsistance, and all other idle, vagrant, or dissolute persons, wandering abroad without betaking themselves to some lawful employment.[20]

Perhaps the vital change was in the tone of active service: with more social pariahs filling the ranks, and military objectives less clearly connected to parochial interests, respectable men felt not so impelled by a sense of duty or guilt to take up arms. Only when a war approached totality (as in the Puritan crusade to Louisbourg in 1745, when an impressive percentage of Massachusetts manpower served in the land and sea forces) might the older attitude appear. Otherwise fighting had ceased to be a function of the community as such. It seems never to have crossed the introspective mind of young John Adams that he was exactly the right age to serve in the Seven Years' War, and he was shocked when a friend expressed envy in 1759 of the heroic warriors who had begun to win victories in North America.[21]

In fact, volunteer units so constituted could perform well under certain circumstances, but generally suffered from low morale and slack discipline. At least one British general in the Seven Years' War understood that there were two kinds of provincial troops: those levied from among the militia on the basis of a legal military obligation, and those who were recruited for all the wrong reasons—money, escape, and the assurance of easy discipline.[22] It is instructive to note that before Pitt's promise of reimbursement permitted the colonial governments to pre-empt the recruiting market with high pay and enlistment bounties, British regiments, despite their notoriously low pay and harsh discipline, enlisted about 7500 Americans after Braddock's arrival.[23] Again in 1762, when the colonies themselves used supplementary bounties to recruit regulars for General Jeffery Amherst, almost 800 enlisted.[24] There are hints that some of these recruits—for the provincial as well as the regular regiments—were Indians and Negroes, and better evidence that many of the white men were second-class citizens of one sort or another.[25]

The generally low opinion acquired by most British officers of the American fighting man, an opinion that later would have disastrous consequences for them, originated with the kind of provincial units they saw during the Seven Years' War. When Massachusetts resorted to the draft to fill a quota, it now—like Virginia—provided first for the impressment of "strollers." [26] Once the British had seen the American encampment at the head of Lake George in 1756—"nastier than anything I could conceive," reported one officer—most provincial regiments were relegated by the British command to an auxiliary function, becoming toward the end of the war "hewers of wood and drawers of water," as James Otis put it.[27] This was ignoble and backbreaking work, often on short rations, so that low morale and poor discipline declined still further. Add to this the frequency of epidemics among the Americans, whose officers probably had never heard of the elementary rules of field sanitation set down by Dr. John Pringle in 1752 and could not have enforced them even if they had. Contributory to certain kinds of disease was the absence—not the presence—of women among the provincial troops. These poor creatures—ridiculed in the drawings of Hogarth and maligned by the Puritan clergy—at least kept some semblance of cleanliness about the camp, hospitals, and person of the British regular.

Because the Seven Years' War in America was primarily an attack on Canada with New England supplying most of the provincial troops, it was the Yankee in particular who came to be regarded as a poor species of fighting man. This helps explain the notion of the British government in 1774 that Massachusetts might be coerced without too much trouble. The government and most British officers failed to understand that those provincials who had mutinied, deserted, and died like flies during the Seven Years' War were not militia units; those who did understand the difference apparently failed to see that the New England militia had not decayed to the extent that it had elsewhere. Even after Bunker Hill, General Thomas Gage seems still to have been somewhat confused: "In all their Wars against the French," he wrote to the Secretary of State, "they never Shewed so much Conduct Attention and Perseverance as they do now." [28]

In a society whose history, from the beginning, is so heavily marked by sectional and regional diversity, and by constant, rapid change, it would be strange to find the military sector of life untouched by these characteristics. In fact, it was not. Tidy colonial laws, imposing a military obligation on almost every free adult white male, became less and less an accurate mirror of military reality, particularly in times of danger. Similarly, basic social differences, between clustered population centers and more scattered settlements, between developed seaboard areas and economically marginal frontier, between slave and non-slave societies, to name only three of the most obvious forms of difference, were reflected in military response and performance. Contrary to the implication of much traditional writing on the subject, military history does not occur in a vacuum. When its study is set in its social, political, economic, and even intellectual context, non-military historians will begin to pay attention to what it can teach them. The colonial period is no exception.

CHAPTER THREE

The Spectrum of Imperial Possibilities: Henry Ellis and Thomas Pownall, 1763–1775

A last afternoon, at the end of several weeks of research in the Henry E. Huntington Library and Art Gallery, produced this essay. Planned work in the manuscript collections completed, those final few hours might well have been spent in the California sunshine or looking at the Gallery's magnificent paintings. Instead, some whim sent me digging in the printed books, where I stumbled over the anecdote with which the essay begins. Recalling that Ellis and Pownall had both been able colonial governors, with a special concern for the military problems of the colonies, and that Pownall had written a book on colonial policy, I took the next step, after which the essay virtually wrote itself. It was first published in Anglo-American Political Relations, 1675–1775, *edited by Alison Gilbert Olson and Richard M. Brown (New Brunswick, 1970).*

Little more than a year after Great Britain had given up the fight to hold her North American colonies, a remarkable meeting took place at Marseilles, where ancient ruins, the winter's sun, and fate brought Thomas Pownall and Henry Ellis southward to the same supper table. A generation earlier, during the critical years of what Lawrence Gipson labeled the Great War for the Empire (1754–1763), each man had governed one of the American provinces: Ellis in Georgia, Pownall in Massachusetts. After their coincidental return to England in 1760, their careers had diverged. Ellis had soon withdrawn from politics altogether; Pownall only lately had taken the same course. They were wealthy, cultivated men—both were Fellows of the Royal Society—and they would appear to have been finding solace for the recent wreck of Empire in the study of classical Greece and Rome. But there is no evidence that they ever spent an evening together before, or after, their meeting in Marseilles.

The meeting was remarkable, if more ironic than historic in its significance, because Ellis and Pownall are a matched pair for those who would relate British politics to the American Revolution. Their careers are full of parallels. Both were born just as Robert Walpole was climbing to the top of British government; both lived on into their eighties and saw Napoleon at his zenith; they died almost at the same time, in the years of Trafalgar, Austerlitz, and the death of the younger Pitt. Brilliant and leisured dilettantes, yet serious enough about antiquity, natural science, and political theory to write and publish, they are almost caricatures of the Enlightenment. Patronized as young men by the Earl of Halifax, reform-minded president of the Board of Trade, they were two of the ablest governors ever to serve in the Old Empire, although neither was willing to bury himself for more than a few years in the remote and primitive cities of North America.

The differences between the two are equally striking, how-

ever. Even their host was moved to record the contrast between
them: [1]

> Governor Pownall was splendid and magnificent in his dress;
> Governor Ellis was covered with a Scotch plaid cloak, and the cut
> of his coat beneath, had not been changed for the last thirty
> years; and though abundantly rich, he would not visit in a car-
> riage, but left his wooden clogs at the door.

Differences went deeper than mere appearance: Ellis was a
great wit, an idiosyncratic bachelor who had run off to sea as a
boy, begot numerous natural progeny, regularly visited Vol-
taire, gave parties that were legends, and followed the seasons
through Europe "like certain birds." In his twenties he had
spent a winter camped on Hudson Bay looking for the
Northwest Passage and then had written a book about it; in his
forties he was content simply to enjoy life as far as money, uncertain health, and the eighteenth century would allow.[2] Pownall, on the other hand, had matriculated at Trinity College,
Cambridge, and then followed his elder brother John to a
clerkship at the Board of Trade. He became known for his
pursuit of rich women—marrying two of them—and otherwise
spent much of his health, and their wealth, "making a figure"
in the House of Commons, the bookstalls of the City, and the
drawing rooms of Mayfair.[3] No one ever accused Pownall of
being a great wit, but some thought he was a great pedant; one
especially unkind contemporary used Shakespeare to describe
the onetime governor of Massachusetts: [4]

> . . . and in his brain,
> Which is as dry as the remainder biscuit
> After a voyage, he hath strange place cramm'd
> With observation, the which he vents
> In mangled forms.

Their host at Marseilles was more sympathetic: "Pownall and
Ellis, both men of deep erudition, kept the uninitiated at an
awful distance; they were both excellent when separate, but as

they rarely agreed on any learned topic, I never wished them to meet . . ." [5]

The evening when they did meet was a protracted and contentious dialogue between the "two great dictators," as they were branded for their behavior. Evidently the question in dispute concerned the ancient ruins at Arles, but beneath the surface of an antiquarian argument lay a less remote, more painful question. That question: Who lost America?

Pownall and Ellis are sufficiently important figures in the coming of the American Revolution to deserve study, but they are also interesting because they typified certain attitudes and opinions. Both men were consulted by government on major points of colonial policy; both exerted influence in other, less direct ways; each came to stand for what appeared to be opposed approaches to the problem of America. Ellis was associated with those who took a hard line: he was the most influential adviser to the Grenville ministry 1762–63; he was asked in vain by the notoriously "firm" Earl of Hillsborough to serve as Undersecretary of State for the Colonies in late 1767; and in 1774, on the eve of war, he urged the government to take coercive measures.[6] In short, Henry Ellis would seem to be the kind of "Tory" who filled the fantasies of John and Samuel Adams. In contrast to Ellis, Pownall was one of the most outspoken advocates of a conciliatory approach to America. For a decade, in his writings on the colonies and in his speeches to a rudely inattentive House of Commons, he hammered on the urgent need to listen sympathetically to colonial grievances and demands. His gloomiest predictions were soon realized with the onset of Anglo-American conflict, but his mind also played with the possibilities of a radically different basis for Empire, one similar to that which developed in the nineteenth century and would be called Commonwealth. If any British politician saw the way to prevent an imperial revolution, it would seem to have been Thomas Pownall.

Considered together, then, Ellis and Pownall offer a new way

of looking at an old subject—the limits of historical possibility
from 1763 to 1775, and in particular the range of policies for
America actually perceived by informed, influential, and typical
men in London before war brought an end to negotiation. It is
hardly surprising that the evening at Marseilles was an unpleasant memory to their host, for each of his "great dictators" must
have loathed not merely the sight of the other but even more
the reminder of what the other's kind of thinking had produced. Each surely knew the answer to the question, Who lost
America? Ellis knew that it had been lost by ill-advised ap-
peasement and the seditious promise of further concessions.
Pownall knew that it had been lost by foolish rigidity and the
tyrannical propensity to use force. The lucky record of their
meeting invites us to consider how neatly these two men stood
at the poles of possibility, and to look once again, closely, at the
distance between those poles.

Henry Ellis does not require extensive analysis. His position
was fairly clear, consistently maintained, and the one usually assumed by successive British governments in the period between
the end of the Great War for the Empire and the outbreak of
the American Revolution. Compared with Pownall, he wrote
and said little about America. He was concerned, but not obsessed, with the colonies—a sense of proportion characteristic
of all except a few of his contemporaries in the British political
community. Equally characteristic was his belief in the military
weakness of the colonists and the absurdity of their grievances.
That Ellis helped William Knox, perhaps as anti-American as
any British minister in history, to become Undersecretary of
State for the Colonies in 1770 is also worth remembering.

Ellis may have been variously bored and irritated by American affairs, but his whole attitude toward them was more complex. He had been an exceptionally able and successful governor of Georgia at a time of crisis, and the political skill with
which he got what he wanted from an elective assembly argues

for something better than mere dislike of obstreperous colonials.[7]

There may be a clue to his earliest thinking in his book on the Northwest Passage, published in 1748. His hostility toward some of the policies of the Hudson's Bay Company led him to contrast "public utility" with "private interest," to call for a truly "national" approach to the subject under consideration, and (after rehearsing the mercantilist arguments for further exploration of Hudson Bay) to write of the need to "awaken us from that slothful and drowsy State into which, through Indolence and too great Fondness for Pleasure, we are visibly fallen." [8] Eight years later, as wartime governor of Georgia, he was most impressed by the terrible defenselessness of unsupported colonies, and by the urgent need to find some way of adequately securing the Empire. And then for two years, from mid-1761 to mid-1763, he was in a position to make his views on imperial policy felt. As principal but unofficial adviser to the Earl of Egremont, Secretary of State for the Southern Department, his specialized talents, as well as Egremont's acute need for such assistance, gave Ellis more weight than anyone else in the transaction of American business.

The single most prominent theme running through his correspondence and memoranda for Egremont is the need for imperial security. Attack either Havana or St. Augustine, he argued in early 1762, despite all the objections being raised, in order to acquire permanent control of the Florida Strait, thus pulling the teeth of the Spanish threat in any future war. Placate and win over the Indians by concessions and the military enforcement of fair dealing, he argued on the eve of peace, because they are too strong and elusive to be held down by force, and they must never again become the tools of Britain's enemies. The peace treaty itself he defended as providing the territorial contiguity, the buffer areas, the strategic positions, and the clear and defensible boundaries which had long been needed to secure the North American continent. His opinions found their most authoritative expression in the Proclamation of 1763, which he was later accused of having written, and in the deployment and direction of the peacetime military establishment in the colonies.[9]

Throughout his career as governor and adviser Ellis had grown ever more certain that the traditional makeshift arrangements for defending the colonies were wasteful and dangerous. Vulnerable frontiers, mismanaged Indians, unregulated trade and settlement, and a hopelessly inefficient militia had cost an enormous amount of Anglo-American blood and money. The Great War in its early years had been all but lost, and it would be madness by any standard to return to the old system, so cheap and comfortable in peacetime, so disastrous in war. A little more military effort now, and a little more attention and expense in the postwar years, would literally secure the imperial future. One may disagree with Ellis, but it is difficult not to see and sympathize with the realism and rationality of his argument.

Though appointed governor of Nova Scotia and to several minor but lucrative sinecures at the end of the war, indolence and illness soon drew Ellis out of colonial administration and away from England itself. He could not stand London: "The Smoak, the foggs, and the cold humid air of that City, never agreed with me, even when I was a young man," he wrote to Knox.[10] But correspondence with Knox, whose star rose through the years of the developing imperial crisis, was an influential channel through which he occasionally expressed himself on American affairs, and his letters leave little doubt about his views. It may be safely inferred that Ellis had no sympathy with American complaints. Never, in his opinion, had British government so carefully and responsibly dealt with the vexed and bloody problem of colonial security as had government during and after the Great War; how then could Americans expect to be taken seriously when they refused even a small share of the burden which the solution to the problem required? Letters from Knox, who vehemently felt the same way, surely reinforced this opinion, as did occasional contact with Hillsborough and his friend Lord Barrington, Secretary at War.[11] Such, after all, was the opinion of the king himself. A year before the battle of Lexington, Ellis stated his position to Knox with clarity and vigor: [12]

> We know the real inability of the Americans to make any effectual resistance to any coercive method which might be employed to compel their obedience. They are conscious of it themselves, but may well give a scope to their insolent licentiousness when they have so long been suffered to practice it with impunity. What is decided upon [i.e., to crack down on Boston] appears judicious. . . .

Perhaps it is sufficient to note that Henry Ellis was entitled to his opinion; it had its roots neither in ignorance nor in lack of feeling. On the contrary, he seems to have known almost as much as anyone about America, and his own writing indicates that from his youth he had seen the Empire as something more noble and demanding than mere commercial venture. His success as a colonial governor was surely related to his evident concern for the need to protect colonists as well as colonies. He neither offered nor supported any sweeping program of imperial reform, but merely believed that certain undeniably acute problems demanded limited, reasonable changes. His later position—on the "hard line"—grew naturally from earlier experience and belief.

The symmetry suggested by the meeting at Marseilles must at last be sacrificed when we consider Thomas Pownall, for not only do his ideas require extensive analysis, but his position is in one sense not comparable to that of Ellis, because Pownall seems to stand for all those decisions not taken, and thus for events which did not occur. Ellis should be regarded as no more than a convenient foil, representing typicality and histori-

cal reality, against which to test Pownall's perception of what
might have happened.

Caroline Robbins, in her original and influential book on
British radical thought in the eighteenth century, has inducted
Pownall into the company of "Commonwealthmen." "His
ideas," she tells us, basing her judgment largely on a study of
his more general political and historical writings, "show more
originality than those of almost any of his contemporaries." [13]
Others, who have examined primarily his ideas on colonial policy, agree. His biographer thinks that "it is probable that no
one understood the total situation more completely" than Pownall, and Leonard Labaree, whose extensive investigation of
imperial government gives his conclusion unusual weight, calls
Pownall's *Administration of the Colonies*

> . . . The ablest and most discerning treatise on the major colo-
> nial problems written by an Englishman in the years of conflict
> before the Revolution. Though speaking as Englishman, Pow-
> nall showed a broader understanding of the colonial point of
> view than almost any other British public man could display.[14]

John Adams, at eighty-one, may be given the last word: "Pownall was a whig, a friend of liberty . . . the most constitutional
Governor, in my opinion, who ever represented the crown in
this province." [15]

This essay is concerned with his mind, and only incidentally
with his personality, but it is impossible to ignore Pownall's
enormous energy. From 1752, when he published his first
book, *The Principles of Polity,* until his retirement from the
House of Commons in 1780, he wrote extensively on archeol-
ogy, linguistics, the East India Company, Adam Smith's *Wealth
of Nations,* American geography, as well as colonial policy. One
finds Governor Pownall, at a time when British fortunes in the
Great War were ebbing, badgering Cadwallader Colden of New
York about obscure points of Iroquois etymology. His en-
graved sketches of American scenes were sold in London. His
lengthy proposals to the government for the conduct of mili-

tary operations in America are remarkably similar to what Pitt actually decided to do in carrying on the war. In the House after 1767, he spoke often, at length, and then polished his speeches for publication by his friend John Almon. Though his views on colonial policy went largely unheeded, he was able to draft and see enacted an important reform of the Corn Laws. After his retirement, the political tracts, archeological treatises, and other miscellaneous writings continued to appear. In 1782, he offered a prospectus for the scientific study of history; at the turn of the century he was drawing up plans for a revolution in Spanish America; and, shortly before his death, he produced a curious book—half psychology, half theology—called *Intellectual Physics,* which aimed to treat the human mind scientifically, and to prove the immortality of the human soul. At times in his life such energy and omnicompetence had struck unfriendly observers as pomposity or naked ambition. But whatever drove him to these intellectual efforts, they are nonetheless impressive.[16]

The concern here is with his ideas on colonial policy. These are most fully developed in *The Administration of the Colonies,* to which his speeches and few extant letters provide a gloss. Aside from its intrinsic interest, this book is peculiarly valuable because of its literally dynamic quality: there are five editions, distributed over the course of a decade of mounting crisis; Pownall tried to keep the book abreast of a changing situation. He wrote the first edition soon after the end of the Great War, before any tangible signs of crisis had appeared; the second when trouble over the Stamp Act was evident; the third after the repeal of that Act; the fourth as resistance to the Townshend Acts was growing; and the fifth just before the outbreak of the Revolutionary War. Through these successive editions it becomes possible to trace the relation between events in America and avowedly liberal ideas in Britain.

The opening words of the first, anonymous edition of *Administration of the Colonies* bear quotation, because they convey,

however turgidly, the almost mystical sense of great change
and new possibilities which was an important part of the postwar mood in England, and in all Europe. The prospect was
thrilling, a little frightening, and more readily felt than easily
defined: [17]

> The several changes in interests and territories, which have
> taken place in the colonies of the European world on the Event
> of Peace, have created a general impression of some new state of
> things arising . . . some general idea of some revolution of
> events, beyond the ordinary course of things; some general ap-
> prehension, of something new arising in the world; of some new
> channel of business, applicable to new powers;—something that
> is to be guarded against on the one hand, or that is to be carried
> to advantage on the other.
> . . . yet one does not find any where . . . any one precise com-
> prehensive idea of this great crisis. . . .
> I have seen and mark'd . . . this nascent crisis at the beginning
> of this war. . . .

Of course Pownall himself had worked out the "precise comprehensive idea of this great crisis": it was the need to formulate imperial policy measures that were systematically related to
"the interest of all as a One Whole" (p. 2).

Pownall's belief in the "wholeness" of imperial society, by
which he meant the natural harmony of interests created primarily by economic interdependence, had been set forth at
length in his *Principles of Polity* (1752), a book cast in the form
of a classical dialogue, and heavily dependent on the political
thought of James Harrington. The distribution and exchange
of property, the "scite" and circumstances of individual lives,
were for Pownall real, natural, and the origin of society and
government, whereas the administration of government was
epiphenomenal, becoming more artificial and "impractical" as
it diverged from basic social and economic reality. European
history had now entered its third phase, leaving the ages when
first naked violence, then religious superstition, had controlled
the affairs of men. In this third phase,

> . . . the spirit of *commerce* will become that predominant power,
> which will form the general policy, and rule the powers of
> Europe; and hence a grand commercial interest, under the
> present scite and circumstances of the world, will be formed and
> arise. The rise and forming of the commercial dominion is what
> precisely constitutes the present crisis. [p. 4]

Within the Empire, commerce was immutably real, and British
government could do no better than perceive and conform to
commercial reality. "It is not men that form great events, but
the crisis of events duly possessed and actuated that form great
men" (p. 5).

The outcome of the Great War had clearly put the chance to
lead in the hands of Englishmen. They must, however, cease
regarding their kingdom as a mere island with many provinces,
but see it "as a grand marine dominion, consisting of our pos-
sessions in the Atlantic and America." This idea, repeated
throughout the book, has since been treated as if it prescribed a
decentralized Empire, and even accepted a shift of power westward across the Atlantic. In 1764, at least, the idea was nothing
of the sort: "Forming all these Atlantic and American posses-
sions into a one dominion, of which Great Britain should be the
commercial center, to which it should be the spring of power, is
the *precise* duty of government at this crisis" (p. 6).

Mercantilist principles were, to Pownall, not artificial, but
basic. All profits of colonial agriculture and manufacturing
ought to center in the mother country, and the colonies were
her "sole and special" customers. Some of the present navigation laws in fact misapplied these principles, and therefore
ought to be amended. But there was nothing wrong, illiberal,
or unrealistic in the principles themselves: they were "mutually
coeval and coincident with the interests, rights and welfare of
the colonies." Interests, properly understood, naturally har-
monized (p. 25; also pp. 7–9, 22–24).

The most important reason for the occasional perversion of
mercantilist principles (as in the Molasses Act of 1733), as well

as the main source of trouble in colonial administration generally, was faulty organization. The first step in meeting the
present crisis, then, was to create a single center of colonial
government in England, an agency with the powers of a Secretary of State, the expertise of the Board of Trade, and all the
various strings of patronage and direction (which currently led
to the Treasury, Admiralty, War Office, Board of Ordnance,
and so on) firmly in its grasp. This was an old idea, finally
implemented half-heartedly and with disappointing results in
1768; the novelty lay in the emphasis, indeed precedence,
given to it by Pownall. Nothing was wanted more in colonial administration, he said, than greater efficiency (pp. 10, 15, and
especially 21).

The harmony of interests, the primacy of commerce, the
need for efficiency—these were the premises from which Pownall moved to a discussion of specific administrative problems.
There were current, he admitted, two views of the imperial
constitution: the one prevalent in America emphasized the
equal rights of all Englishmen, whereas the other, held widely
in Britain, stressed the necessary subordination of colonies.
Pownall saw these as conflicting claims, but not as contradictory
beliefs. The conflict could, and should, be resolved, not by a
tarnished royal prerogative, but by Parliament. By the enact-
ment of "a general bill of rights, and establishment of government on a great plan of union" for the colonies, Parliament
could "regulate and define their privileges; . . . establish and
order their administration; and . . . direct the channels of
their commerce." Until constitutional uncertainty was removed
once and for all, "there can be no government, properly so
called, but merely the predominance of one faction or the
other, acting under the mask of government" (pp. 28–32).[18]
The cardinal point was to clarify and strengthen the tie between each colony and Whitehall, but to do nothing that would
unify the colonies among themselves. Using one of the New-
tonian metaphors he found so compelling, Pownall saw danger
in united colonies acquiring an "equal force, which might recoil

back on the first mover," Great Britain. But the danger itself was remote, because the colonies were so inherently disunited that "nothing but a tampering activity of wrongheaded inexperience misled to be meddling, can ever do mischief here" (p. 34). This strong language may have been directed at his successor in Massachusetts, Francis Bernard, who was just then urging on government a thorough alteration of the whole imperial system. Only in Rhode Island, where flagrant abuses had occurred, might an exception be made, Pownall believed, to the rule of not carrying out drastic constitutional changes.

He was certain that the acute problems could be solved within the existing legal framework of Empire. The colonial claim to possess "the right of representation and legislation" was valid and ought to be respected; only some of its abuses and encroachments should be prevented. This would mean, above all, guaranteeing to the executive and judicial officers of provincial government an income free from legislative manipulation. Perhaps it would also be well to separate the provincial council into quite distinct bodies for the performance of executive and judicial functions, respectively, and to create several regional supreme courts of appeal which would further the cause of justice and produce greater legal "conformity." The legal and judicial systems were critical, for Pownall emphasized "how little the crown, or the rights of government, when opposed to the spirit of democracy, or even to the passion of the populace," could expect from colonial courts in the way of protection (pp. 56–57; also 61 and 63). These minor improvements would create an administration "that shall firmly, uniformly, and constitutionally govern the colonies" (p. 65).

The payment by the Crown of its colonial appointees raised the question of revenue. On this important question, Pownall's words deserve a most careful reading. Because the government already had

> the colony revenue under its consideration, I must, for the present, think myself precluded from entering into a discussion of those points. . . . However, I will just venture to suggest,

—that the best and surest funds of such revenue, will be, first,
the customs arising from the trade *regulated as hereafter to be mentioned:* secondly a stamp-duty . . . . [p. 65]

which he thought would raise a third more per capita than it
did in England; and, finally, "the quit rents, if duly laid and
collected" (p. 66).[19] To be sure, he expressed some doubts
about taxation, and these also require scrutiny. With respect to
any form of tax on real property, he said

> it is a point that ought very deliberately and dispassionately to be
> weighed, how far even the supreme government of the mother
> country can, consistently with general liberty, proceed in laying
> taxes on its colonists, where the consent of the people cannot be,
> in any constitutional way taken. [p. 67]

A different doubt, however, would arise in connection with
customs, excise, and stamp duties; and that doubt was

> how far these colonies, who, for the necessities of government,
> and the emergencies of service, have already, by their proper
> powers, laid these duties on the people, and granted the revenue
> arising therefrom to the crown, by acts which have received the
> consent of the crown. [p. 67]

In short, a land tax would raise the question of right, whereas
customs, excise, and stamp duties would raise only a question
of equity: taxes on real property might be unconstitutional, but
taxes on legal and commercial transactions, in which there was
inherent an element of consent, must only be kept commensu-
rate with the legitimate needs of government. Subsequent editions make clear that this distinction is neither a slip of Pownall's pen nor a perverse interpretation of his words.

The rest of the first edition is taken up with discussion of the
new military establishment, the colonial money supply, and the
reform of the navigation system. Pownall seems to take a liberal
position: he is critical of the military, and favorable to paper
currency and to relaxation of trade restrictions. But there are
limits to his liberalism: his brief attack on the military is confined to the office of Commander in Chief, which encroaches

on the power of royal governors and threatens to create that ever-dangerous union of the colonies. He supports paper currency, but not as legal tender. He favors extension of trade, but mainly through resident British "factories" and with precautions against foreign re-export of British goods. In Pownall's view, the desideratum of imperial economic policy is to discourage the growth of manufacturing in the colonies (pp. 129–131).

If prolixity, and reiterated calls to greatness and expressions of good will, is not allowed to obscure the author's more specific ideas, then the first edition of *The Administration of the Colonies* is seen to adumbrate much of what the government actually did or tried to do during the decade after the Great War. No sweeping changes are proposed, only what might be called "economical reform." Raise a modest revenue, being careful to be both legal and equitable in doing it. Use the money raised primarily to give Crown officials the independence no reasonable man would deny them, and what is left will help to pay for the new military establishment, essential to colonial security. Do not suppress paper money altogether, but curb the abuse of it passing as legal tender. Rationalize the laws of trade, putting national interest above vested interests. Centralize administration, but only in London. Perhaps reorganize provincial councils, but certainly ensure that colonial courts do justice. All of this to be effected by Act of Parliament.

The Sugar Act, the Currency Act, the Stamp Act, the Townshend Acts, the extension of vice-admiralty jursidiction, the creation of West Indian free ports and a Secretary of State for the Colonies, even threats to the Rhode Island charter, the alteration of the Massachusetts Council, and adamant opposition to intercolonial congresses—every one was at least suggested, none was clearly warned against, by Thomas Pownall in 1764. Of course this is not a fair indictment; his analysis is often perceptive and always knowledgeable though it is seldom lucid. His proposals for some form of regulated paper currency, greater freedom of trade, and perhaps even a colonial bill of rights, if enacted in time and with an informed benevolence, would have reduced American discontent to a significant degree. Nevertheless, the strongest impression created by the book is of an innocent, well-meaning articulation of the very attitudes that would soon lead to serious trouble; of a nearly total failure to anticipate that trouble; and of a dearth of other ideas sufficiently concrete to guide policy makers.

Judged in the harsh light of the coming Revolution, this first edition can be made to seem ridiculous, but it must also be regarded in another way. Pownall began his book with a passion for the imperial future that only his leaden prose had kept from soaring; yet he consistently rejected any program of reform that would have matched the grandeur of his emotion. Instead, he had tried to analyze the existing situation, problem by problem, and he had produced a set of truly modest solutions. In each case, his appeal had been to fact and reason; every argument had been anchored to the assumption that more explicit and rational practices and institutions would lead not only to greater efficiency but to a heightened awareness of mutual self-interest, the basic premise of all politics.

The second edition, which appeared as rioters against the Stamp Act roamed the streets of Boston and New York, reinforces the impression. Although he wrote to William Pitt for permission to publish a wartime document in an appendix, he dedicated the new version of the book to George Grenville.[20] This may seem a strange thing for a liberal on colonial policy to do, unless he did not yet perceive the polarization of opinion which is the subject of this essay. Grenville, according to the dedication, would "lead the people of the colonies, by the spirit of laws and equity to that true and constitutional obedience, which is their real liberty." Pownall's only expressed fear was that "false and mistaken patriots" in the colonies might create "undue impressions to their disadvantage."

There are many minor revisions of the text, which indicate that he had carefully reconsidered every sentence, and some of these little changes are interesting. The early section asserting the interdependence of the parts of the Empire is expanded by factual evidence, as if to refute any hint that economic tension or competition was inherent or natural (1765 ed., pp. 5–9; cf. 1764 ed., pp. 4–6). American and British interests, however, though they remain "coincident," have ceased in the second edition to be "coeval" (p. 27). Friction between royal officials in the colonies emerges as a new argument for a centralized administration in London, but the need to keep the colonies themselves disunited is now italicized (pp. 21–22, 36). The suggestion of 1764 that administrative reform would itself create the conditions for a new American spirit of obedience and cooperation disappears in 1765 (p. 87; cf. 1764 ed., p. 65).

Major additions concern taxation, Indian affairs, and military policy. On taxation, Pownall argues from logic, and his tone is huffy:

> I do suppose it will not bear a doubt, but that the supreme legislature of Great Britain is the true and perfect representative of Great Britain, and all its dependencies: and as it is not in the power of the House of Lords or Commons to exempt any community from the jurisdiction of the King, as supreme magistrate, so that it is not, nor ever was, or could be in the power of the crown, to exempt any persons or communities within the dominions of Great Britain, from being subject and liable to be taxed by parliament. [p. 89]

He cannot seriously entertain the idea that the King-in-Parliament is anything less than sovereign. There are, however, different "objects" of taxation; some are properly British, others provincial. Polls and estates are "the special internal private property" of the colonies, and ought to be left to them. "Duties," on the other hand, may be freely levied by Parliament so long as the principle of equalization of real obligations within the Empire is maintained. On this last point, he adds, the stamp duties may have been set too high through faulty information (pp. 90–96). But by conservative calculation, which he makes for the reader, a revenue of about £100,000 can easily be raised in America (pp. 97ff.).

A new, long section on Indian affairs is especially interesting because it clarifies part of the conclusion to the first edition (pp. 154–181; cf. 1764 ed., pp. 127–131). In the latter, he had said that the danger of colonial manufacturing would not become serious as long as colonial settlement was not restricted, whether by policy or by Indian pressure. Without the second edition, this passage might be interpreted as oblique criticism of the Proclamation of 1763, of the so-called Plan of 1764 to regulate trade with the Indians, and of the kind of thinking, which we have previously ascribed to Henry Ellis, that lay behind both measures. On the contrary: Given space in which to deploy his ideas on this question, Pownall expresses sympathy for the Indians and hostility toward the traders and frontiersmen who goad them to violence; he recognizes the practical impossibility of controlling the Indians by force or even of building effective military defenses against them; security lies, he believes, only in dealing fairly with them on matters of land and trade—"honesty" toward the Indians is "the best policy." He says nothing explicit about westward migration, but implies that it—like the Indian trade—will require some kind of imperial regulation. In short, this section might have been written by Henry Ellis himself.

His attack on the office of Commander in Chief is now longer and more vehement (pp. 54–70). The source of his animus was undoubtedly his own humiliating controversy when governor of Massachusetts with Lord Loudoun, the commander in chief for America 1756–57, but his arguments against having a supreme military commander with no civil counterpart are not frivolous or unreasonable, and they would later provide the text for more than one speech in the House of Commons. He does, however, recognize that a regular military establishment as such is "in the same manner and degree necessary in North America as in Britain or Ireland"; he simply wants to put that establishment under the control of the royal governors, who by their commissions are "Captains-General" of their provinces. In fact, a decade earlier he had argued for a more efficient and presumably more centralized system of colonial military administration (p. 69).[21] The appendix added to the 1765 edition deals exclusively with defense policy and its wartime background, which suggests the importance Pownall attached to that aspect of American policy in general. His long attack on the commander in chief concludes with the hope that the office will be weakened by the newly instituted brigadier-generals, regional commanders in Canada and Florida first proposed, it seems, in 1763 by Henry Ellis.[22]

The third edition, which appeared in 1766 after the repeal of the Stamp Act, was struck from the old plates, but contains a new appendix: "Considerations on the Points Lately Brought Into Question as to The Parliament's Right of Taxing the Colonies and of the Measures necessary to be taken at this Crisis." There is simply no question about the sovereignty of Parliament, Pownall asserts, nor is there any way to distinguish between taxation and legislation (Appendix, pp. 3–5). But he now shows a grudging willingness to move from legal and logical arguments toward one that is historical:

> I do not believe that there ever was an instance when this principle of the supreme Legislature's power to raise monies by taxes throughout the realm of Great Britain, was ever called in question. . . .

The whole controversy, as he sees it, has been stirred up by ignorant demagogues in America; nevertheless, expediency and history require that the claim of right should not be forced by the British government, but rather taught. But it is also obvious that the present situation, if permitted to drift, will eventually produce astronomical change:

> The center of power, instead of remaining fixed as it is now in Great Britain, will, as the magnitude of power and interest of the Colonies encreases, be drawn out from the island, by the

> same laws of nature analogous in all cases, by which the centre
> of gravity of the solar system, now near the surface of the sun,
> would, by an encrease of the quantity of matter in the planets,
> be drawn out beyond that surface.

What, then, is to be done?

> Form one general system of dominion by an union of Great
> Britain and her Colonies, fixing, while it may be so fixed, the
> common center in Great Britain. [Appendix, pp. 17–18]

The way to fix the center in Britain is to grant the colonies representation in Parliament, which measure is to be prepared by the dispatch to America of some *"very considerable person"* with full powers and an advisory council. Pownall refuses to elaborate on this proposal because, he says, even at that moment the government is considering it (Appendix, p. 33; also pp. 18, 48ff.).[23]

At this point, we may usefully consider the political atmosphere within which Pownall was thinking, writing, and publishing. Except for James Otis and Benjamin Franklin, the most important American spokesmen had already made it clear that colonial representation in Parliament was not an acceptable solution to the current crisis. Pownall hints as much in the 1766 edition, but somewhat lamely opines that the measure would still be effective if British government can act with great prudence, good temper, and "spirited council." As for his other proposals, the Rockingham government, allegedly receptive to all liberal ideas, was indeed considering them. William Dowdeswell, whose judgment was highly respected within and outside his party, discussed Pownall's plan in a letter to Rockingham. His tone was one of barely concealed contempt for the idea of sending the Duke of York (Pownall's *"very considerable person"*) as a viceroy to patch things up in America, and Rockingham's endorsement on the letter dismissed the idea of parliamentary representation as "Shirley's scheme." [24] Obviously, the political atmosphere was not congenial, and it is hardly surprising that these proposals did not flourish.

Pownall had bought himself a seat in the House of Commons by the time the fourth edition appeared in 1768. The book is now more than twice the length of the first edition, and its ideas have become far more qualified and convoluted. From the original sense of restrained excitement and programmatic zeal, the mood has shifted in four years to an unhappy mixture of alarm and resignation, with an occasional note of utter despair. Some bits of the newly composed preface are pathetic. He tries to weasel out of having dedicated the second and third editions to Grenville. He says he wants to end his days in America as an humble citizen (in one of his private letters he says that only his wife is holding him back).[25] Perhaps saddest of all is to hear him say: "It is a great pity that questions of this nature were ever raised. . . ."

But it is also in this edition that he is at his best, and the book as a whole is a richer, if less confident, analysis of Empire and its problems than earlier versions. The treatment of the nature of parliamentary power and colonial liberty becomes seriously and extensively historical; no longer satisfied with the easy answers he had been giving himself, Pownall obviously had done some research. Through a hundred pages of new material worked into the text, he wrestles with simple but baffling questions: Can a man separate himself from his political community? Can sovereign power be reconciled with restrictions on that power? After canvassing the law of emigration and the history of colonial charters, he finds an ingenious answer to the first question:

> . . . how much so ever the colonies, at their first migration, may be supposed to have been, or were in fact, without the Realm, and separated from it: Yet, from the very nature of that union of the community, by which all civil society must subsist, they could not have migrated, and been absolved of their communion and connection to the Realm, without leave or license; they had such leave [as his study of the charters has previously demonstrated], according to the then forms of the constitution, and the terms [on which permission to emigrate was granted] were, that

the society, community, or government which they should form, should neither act nor become anything repugnant or contrary to the laws of the Mother Country. [pp. 119–120]

"Here then," as he moves toward an answer to the second question, "is an express subordination to a certain degree." But he falters, because his research had taught him that the seventeenth-century constitution could not have incorporated colonies of the kind that had actually developed, and his mind is still caught on the hook of sovereignty:

There is no doubt, but that in the nature, reason, justice and necessity of the thing, there must be somewhere, *within* the body politic of every government, an absolute power. [p. 130]

But in the end it is necessary to choose. Either America is within the Realm, or it is outside. As matters now stand, Pownall admits, he cannot be certain of the correct answer, in which case one must act as if one or the other were correct. If America is outside the Realm, then the relationship is contractual—an alliance; and only request and requisition by the Crown to an American union are possible. History, however, points to the long-term consequences of such an arrangement:

If we keep the basis of this realm confined to this island, while we extend the superstructure, by extending our dominions: we shall invert the pyramid (as Sir William Temple expresses it) and must in time subvert government itself. If we chuse to follow the example of the Romans, we must expect to follow their fate. [pp. 162–163]

This would be an "artificial" system, and he clearly prefers the alternative: to consider the Americans as within the Realm. In that case, there is only one course: to grant them—force upon them if necessary—Parliamentary representation. "There is no other practicable or rational measure" (p. 152).

The problem, which Pownall now sees as a problem, is that representative government, "the very spirit of this country," trades recognition of equal rights for the acceptance of equal obligations. The precedents argue well enough that the extension of representation is right and can work—the annexation of the counties palatine of Chester and Durham, and the union with Scotland. But Americans must accept their obligations; the British debt is theirs as well, for the last two wars had been fought "solely in defence, and for the protection of the trade and actual existence of the colonies" (p. 167). Yet Pownall as much as admits that he knows they will not accept representation, even if government has the nerve to offer it. "One has only to hope, that the ruin is not inevitable, and that heaven may avert it" (p. 177).

Otherwise most of the original ideas are still there, tucked somewhere into the book. A few are trimmed or refurbished. The plan to pay the salaries of royal officials, which was just then being tried under the Townshend Acts, is dropped for reasons not made explicit, and a pension fund for ex-governors is suggested to perform roughly the same function. Pownall gives up his objections to legal-tender currency, and now presents a detailed plan to create a colonial money supply by Act of Parliament. The proposal to send a viceroy remains, but he knows that it will not be adopted. At this and a few other points in the fourth edition, one begins to feel that Pownall is writing for the record.

Not until war was only months away, late in 1774, did the fifth edition appear. Pownall was able to retain most of his original analysis of colonial problems by the device of changing verb tenses from present to past, but he finally felt compelled to recast the introductory paragraphs. The original sense of mystery, ambivalence, and high challenge disappears; in their place is put a flat assertion that the Great War created a new pattern of interests and a consequent shift of power, and that the government should have made the corresponding adjustments in policy. Pownall's feeling, more than his meaning, has changed in the course of a decade. Aside from these opening words, perhaps the most interesting revision is a note in which the author explains why his proposal for a unified Colonial Department, when adopted in 1768, had not produced the results he had predicted:

> It was sown in jealousy; so, in proportion as it arose in power, the resistance of cabinet faction obstructed it at home, and nursed up opposition to it abroad. To this an impracticable line of conduct, mistaken for system, and an unhappy tone of government misunderstood for firmness, gave ample scope; so that the last state of this unfortunate department became worse than the first. [p. 16n.]

The main cause of failure is obviously "faction."

Appearing first in 1764, growing sharply in 1768, echoing through his Parliamentary speeches and private letters to friends in Massachusetts, and rising to become a major theme in 1774, is this concern with the damage done by party politics and the spirit of faction. In 1768, he had gloomily predicted that

> the colonies will for some time *belong to some faction* here, and be the tool of it, until they become powerful enough to hold a party for themselves, and make *some faction their tool.* The latter stage of this miserable connection will be one continued struggle . . . until some event shall happen that will totally break all union between us. [1768 ed., pp. 29–30]

He had hoped for a reform of Empire in 1763, "but from the moment that American affairs became an object of politics, they became the tools and instruments of faction" (p. 45). In speeches and lectures afterward, he had proudly advertised his own independence of any party or group, and had repeatedly advised his friends in America to keep themselves and their problems free of British factions, by which of course he meant the Opposition splinters led by Chatham and Rockingham. In 1774 he still believed that the *"consensus obedientium* which is alone the bond and tie of practical and efficient government" was, by definition, incompatible with the existence of political parties, but he also had reluctantly come to modify his view that political conflict is wholly unnatural: "Nature knows no such distraction and separation of interests as the practices and powers of men have introduced"; yet "the very attraction which naturally draws them together—creates in their spirit, when they are thus drawn together, a principle of repulsion, that is too hard for nature, truth, and right" (1774 ed., II, pp. 8–9). Conflict may be ineradicable, but Pownall could not imagine that it was anything but a destructive force, a perversion of reason.

The illegitimacy of party politics in the eighteenth century is familiar, and it is not surprising to find an author resorting to this contemporary cliché as an explanation for political failure. In this particular context, however, one expects to find the argument being used exclusively by "conservatives"—the Henry Ellises, friends of the king and supporters of government—in order to blunt and confuse the Opposition "party" attack. Edmund Burke read the fourth edition of *The Administration of the Colonies,* or at least part of it, and Pownall's strictures on "party" drove Burke to make furious marginal comments, and perhaps even to adopt a hostile attitude toward the book as a whole. Burke's *Thoughts on the Causes of the Present Discontents* (1770), especially the latter pages where he makes his celebrated defense of political parties, when read in conjunction with some of Pownall's speeches and the 1768 edition of the book, seems almost a dialogue with Thomas Pownall. We will return to Burke's position with respect to Pownall later; here it is sufficient to note that Pownall's attack on "party" comes, like Thomas Jefferson's, not from the putative Right, but from the Left. Moreover, the attack is not merely the use of a handy weapon, for Pownall's earliest writing, *The Principles of Polity,* is largely taken up with the rejection of conflict as an acceptable premise for political theory. J. G. A. Pocock has recently written that the work of James Harrington, twisted into several shapes by his interpreters, did much to create the "mood" of eighteenth-century British politics; nowhere can Harrington's

influence, with its attendant confusion of "Right" with "Left,"
be seen more plainly than in the views of Thomas Pownall on
"party." [26] And, finally, it may be noted that Pownall rather
than Burke reflected the feelings of almost all their contemporaries on this matter.

On the current American crisis Pownall added another long
essay, as he had in 1766, "Wherein a Line of Government Between the Supreme Jurisdiction of Great Britain, and the
Rights of the Colonies is Drawn, and a Plan of Pacification is
Suggested." He had no illusions about the likelihood of its acceptance, but he hoped that his "line" would provide a basis for
negotiations whenever they once again became feasible. Although he still thinks that the best solution for all concerned is
colonial representation in Parliament, he at last admits that this
is not possible "since America as well as Great Britain will have
it so." He accepts the possibility of an American Union "incapa-
ble of being admitted to a perfect participation in the legislature, the soul of the British dominions," but instead *"subject to
the King as to their own head"* (II, pp. 11–12; italics mine). Here,
it seems, is recognition of James Wilson's argument for colonial
autonomy within a royal empire. But is it?

Pownall no sooner makes the concession than he begins to
analyze, qualify, and finally come near to withdrawing it. Using
the very words of James Harrington, he distinguishes between
"internal" or "national" government and "external" or "provincial" government.[27] Internal government relies on free will and
is essentially active; external government relies on coercion and
is essentially passive. A mixed form of government, appropriate to the present case, is "Colonial Government." It is "national" when operating on its own body, but the *"supreme sovereign power"* may act as "provincial government" whenever any
British subject or his property moves outside the jurisdiction of
the "national" government of his colony. In particular, any attempt to resist or reject colonial government, or to redefine its
composition, will have to be met with force, which is the essen-

tial characteristic of provincial, or external, government. This, says Pownall, is all that was meant by the Declaratory Act of 1766. At four different places in the essay he argues that the analogy of an omnipotent God giving man complete freedom of will is applicable—indeed is the solution—to the problem of Empire. The supreme power of Parliament, by which he means the King-in-Parliament, may be used only when the very existence of Empire is threatened.

Precisely what Pownall had in mind becomes steadily less clear in the course of the essay. But when he implies, after eighty pages, that the impossibility of an imperial relationship on the model of the union with Scotland means that the relationship must be modeled on the existing connection with Ireland, the reader may feel that he has drifted a long way from any vision of a modern Commonwealth. This feeling is strengthened by a "Postscript," in which the author rejects, one after another, the demands made by the Pennsylvania provincial congress that Britain give up her powers to punish treason in the colonies, to interfere with internal legislation, to lay taxes, and to regulate trade except by consent, as well as demands for repeal of the Quartering Act and other laws supporting the regular military establishment, for the abolition of vice-admiralty courts, and for the relinquishment of any right to alter colonial charters and constitutions. "The Colonies," Pownall had written truly in the introduction of his latest essay, "have so often shifted and advanced the ground of their claim of rights, that the best reasoning of their truest friends, even the most active zeal of their warmest partisans, have fallen short in the course" (1774 ed., II, p. 3). Pownall is in fact prepared to concede almost nothing, and his movement into Lord North's camp in the election of 1774 bears out this interpretation of the fifth edition of his book.[28]

How, it may be reasonably asked, could Thomas Pownall ever have been seen as a liberal on the American question, as "a true friend of the colonies"? The answer is simple: because he thought he was, and spoke and wrote in a way that persuaded himself and others that he was. Through ten years of mounting controversy, he had increasingly defended specific American actions and attacked specific British policies. His demolition of the government's case against Boston in 1769 was perhaps the high point of his Parliamentary career, and his explanation of the Boston Massacre as the inevitable result of irresponsible military power may have reduced the desire of the government to take any new, vigorous steps against Massachusetts in 1770. His speeches, like the later editions of the book, were suffused with sympathy for the Americans, and with dismay at those who held power in London. It is only when his ideas are disentangled from his feelings that Pownall's real position becomes evident.

To return briefly to Edmund Burke permits us to reconsider our premise in studying Pownall. It may be that the premise is wrong, that Pownall did not stand at the Left end of the political spectrum on the American question, and that he was somewhere to the Right of those other critics of the government, Burke and Shelburne. The results of the scholarly attention given to Shelburne's conduct in office would make it very difficult to sustain any such claim for him and for the Chathamites as a whole,[29] but what about Burke? Fortunately, Burke's marginalia in the 1768 edition of *Administration of the Colonies* make it possible to locate him, and presumably the whole Rockingham group, with some exactness on our spectrum.

When Pownall proposes a general inquiry into American grievances on the spot, Burke says it can be done as well in England, and besides "it is against the sound principles of government, to go about on officious and voluntary collection of grievances" (pp. 32–33).[30] When Pownall contrasts the unnecessary restrictions of the navigation system as it actually existed with the two basic principles of a commercial empire, and argues for investigation and liberalization, Burke simply—and ignorantly—notes "that all our plantation Laws have these two points certainly in their view, and that nothing is less necessary than *general* information on that subject" (p. 40). When Pownall refers to the dependence of American merchants on British credit, Burke dissents, again through ignorance: "Not the case of the Northern colonies, if I am rightly informed" (p. 41). And when Pownall tries to find some historical basis for the American claim to inalienable legislative rights, Burke will not even listen:

> These charters differed in no respect from those then and since given to all Trading corporations. They were forfeitable in Westminster Hall by process in *Quo Warrento*—might by the same process be carried into the *House of Lords in Error,* were ever subject to the Privy Council as a *Tribunal*—and it seems extremely absurd, that the Colonies should be *subject* to the *Judicial,* but free from the *Legislative* authority of their mother Country. [pp. 52–53]

In the end there may have been little substantive difference between the two men on the American question, but in the spectrum of attitudes Burke stands plainly to Pownall's Right.[31]

Finally we may come back to Caroline Robbins to test our premise in another way, by asking if her own praise of Pownall's originality and radicalism is mistaken. Could she have been deceived by rhetorical flourishes and political opportunism? The answer is certainly No. When his ideas on American policy are set in the context of his political career and his thought in general, two things stand out: one is that his ideas on the American question fit with everything else known about him, and the other is that he consistently and—as far as it is possible to judge—disinterestedly took what must be recognized for mid-eighteenth-century Britain as a fairly radical political position. His support of the government in 1774 ought not to count too heavily against him, because it followed from premises stated much earlier, and he was one of the first in the House of Commons to say flatly during the Revolutionary War that Britain had better recognize American independence. His ideas on reform of the navigation system were liberal, comprehensive, and—for his time—extreme. He publicly praised *Wealth of Nations* when it appeared, but politely argued in *A Letter to Adam Smith* (1776) that the farmer and wage-earner must be protected even though the cause of their suffering is the salutary and ineluctable operation of the "unseen hand." Otherwise, he said, developing a critique of classical economic theory that would be repeated and elaborated by the Left through the next two centuries, "we shall, in the triumph of our general prosperity, be the constant oppressors of those who have the best title to share in this prosperity" (pp. 6–7). His support for revolution in the Spanish Empire has already been mentioned, and his sympathy for the United States after the Revolutionary War could hardly have been stronger. His refusal, following Harrington, to find the guarantee of political liberty in a balanced mixture of monarchy, aristocracy, and commons, freed his mind from the kind of conservative paranoia that pervaded both British and American politics at the time, and his emphasis instead on *communitas* as the proper basis of all just and effective government is reminiscent of Rousseau (who, as far as I have been able to tell, was not directly influential in Pownall's political thought). A second look, then, shows that his credentials as a "Commonwealthman" are in good order; by any test, he stood near the Left edge of the British political community.

The main argument of this essay must now be clear: if Thomas Pownall and Henry Ellis are taken to represent the limits of what was conceivable in American policy between 1763 and 1775, then the range of historical possibilities was very narrow indeed. The argument is not new, but its opposite is more frequently encountered. A great deal of historical writing on the American Revolution contains at least the suggestion that there were available alternatives for British policy, and that what actually happened may be seen as a sad story of accident, ignorance, misunderstanding, and perhaps a little malevolence.[32] George Grenville is narrow-minded, Charles Town-

shend is brilliant but silly, Hillsborough is stupid and tyrannical, Chatham is tragically ill, Dartmouth is unusually weak, and
the king himself is very stubborn and not very bright. But if
politics had not been in quite such a chaotic phase, perhaps the
Old Whigs or an effective Chathamite ministry would have
held power, been able to shape and sustain a truly liberal policy
toward the colonies, and avoided the disruption of the Empire.
So the story seems to run.

Closely related to this view of might-have-been is the common assertion that the need for imperial reform in 1763 was
real and urgent, but that British leaders—Grenville especially—
had no master plans which threatened American liberty; on the
contrary, they were merely practical politicians, trying to solve
immediate problems with limited measures.[33] A little more
knowledge, a little more tact, a little more political sensitivity,
and it all might have turned out differently. As this bogey of a
master plan for Empire is exorcised, historical possibility seems
to widen out before us.

Though historians tend to dismiss speculation about what
might have happened as a futile exercise, their understanding
of any event is bound to be affected by what they think *could,*
and could *not,* have happened. Today the focus of attention in
the historiography of the Revolution seems to have shifted
away from the British side toward a preoccupation with events
in America. But before we leave what one historian has recently called "the dustbowl of English history," we ought to ask
the unfashionable question—what could have happened in
London?—if only to get some better measure of the American
side of the dispute. Of course such a question can only be answered in terms of probabilities; nothing can be proved, or
even demonstrated beyond reasonable doubt. And certainly the
study of one or two men cannot be conclusive for a question involving the politics of a whole society. Yet if one accepts the
proposition that men seldom do what they cannot imagine
doing, then the mind of Thomas Pownall provides a prima

facie case that British colonial policy in this period was neither fortuitous nor susceptible of change.

On this issue, as on so many others in early American history, Edmund Morgan has expressed some stimulating and influential thoughts. In his seminal essay on the historiography of the American Revolution, he finds a basic incompatibility between the so-called imperial and Namierist contributions to our understanding, and he therefore suggests the inadequacy, perhaps the unreliability, of both.[34] The imperial school, associated most readily with the name and work of Charles M. Andrews, seems to sympathize with those men who administered the Empire, to appreciate their difficulties, and especially to find in their efforts a body of ideas and principles that command respect. Andrews agreed with George Louis Beer that there was a basic shift by 1763 in their concept of the colonial relationship—from "mercantile" to "imperial"—and that this shift was a major factor in the coming of the American Revolution. The Namier school, on the other hand, appears to have taken "mind out of politics," to have reduced the historical importance of consciously held ideas and principles to nearly zero, at least for the explanation of British politics in the age of the American Revolution. Consequently, British politicians appear as petty, selfish, narrow men, with even the most able and serious of them absorbed in the complexities of a purely domestic game. Professor Morgan has asked how both schools— or either—can possibly be right.

This essay is meant to suggest an answer. Not only can everything of interest about Thomas Pownall and Henry Ellis be reconciled with the insights of Andrews and Namier, but a comparison of these two eighteenth-century lives sharpens our perception of what these two twentieth-century historians were trying to tell us about the British background of the American Revolution.

Pownall and Ellis, especially when considered together, offer support for the view that basic assumptions about empire, and the imperatives which followed from them, were undergoing a major change which was at first retarded, then accelerated and sustained by the Great War, 1754–1763.[35] The center of change appears to have been the obscure Earl of Halifax, though the roots of change can be traced back for decades; but the main point is its growing importance after mid-century. Whatever the explanation for it may be, the fact is that the colonies were coming to be regarded, even by the less informed and interested British politician, in a new way and with a new concern by about 1750. Perhaps Charles Townshend was brilliant and silly, but even his behavior is best explained in terms of an attitude—more highly developed and strongly held than one would expect in such a man—toward the Empire.[36] This new attitude can hardly be characterized as either "liberal" or "conservative"; it may more aptly be described as "enlightened." It was, or purported to be, factually better informed than previously held opinions about the colonies, and it took a broader view of relationships, a deeper view of value, and a longer view of time. Above all, it sought rationality.

"Rationality" is of course a treacherous abstraction, and a reader may hardly be blamed if he has not so far found either Thomas Pownall or Henry Ellis, or their British contemporaries, to be notably rational in attitude and argument. But surely Pownall and Ellis, like Shelburne and Burke, like Grenville and George III, saw themselves separated from earlier generations by their own readiness to subject government, in its political as well as its administrative dimensions, to rational analysis. As never before, chronic problems of government were to be first clearly formulated and then vigorously solved. Men might disagree about particular solutions, as differences of intellect and information might cause them to analyze particular problems in various ways, but the problem-solving approach to government was becoming universal, and it was new. There had always been those who sought to change colonial policies and procedures, and they had always tried to make reasonable arguments for change; but by 1763 there was something altogether different: a general dread of arrangements and practices that defied logical explanation, and a growing desire to rationalize them. Both the dread and the desire were themselves beyond reason: one simply knew that mysteries were dangerous, and that future happiness in some way required the elimination, or at least clarification, of the many mysteries of the colonial relationship.

Pownall, like Ellis, was moved to attack absurd and slovenly aspects of imperial government wherever he encountered them, and to call for policies that could pass the test of reason. They might stress different aspects of reform: to Ellis a more rational defense policy was the basic need, while Pownall argued that only a more rational administrative organization at the top could produce more rational policy. But they were very alike in believing that the time had come to rid the Empire of contradiction. When Ellis and Pownall attacked the Hudson's Bay and East India companies, respectively, they both subordinated private interest, and even property rights, to public interest and the common weal. When they examined the related problems of American security and Indian affairs, they both saw the long-run public interest, not to mention national honor, in a humane and fairly expensive plan of defense and Indian pacification. The essence of their thought on Empire— the same essence which had begun to percolate into the mind of the most blasé courtier or sleepiest country gentleman by 1763—was that equity and efficiency were the keys to a policy based on reason, and that a more reasonable policy was the key to a British greatness exceeding that of the empires of Rome and Alexander. The difficulty of course would come in deciding just what "equity" and "efficiency" should mean in practice, but the desire, often the passion, for the attainment of these ideals is clearly visible. It is what Andrews meant by a new view of Empire.

As important as the newness of the view is its remarkable

unity, and it is this latter quality that is more relevant to the influence on historical understanding of Sir Lewis Namier.[37] Namier shattered old, instinctive, and anachronistic notions about the popularity of British politics in the mid-eighteenth century. By analyzing away Whigs and Tories, he is often said to have atomized our picture of what was happening. But he also, though less explicitly, enabled us to see the deep consensus which gave politics its peculiar quality, and which provided his own frame of reference. Political disagreement and controversy, by getting all the publicity then and later, have obscured the unconscious agreement on standards of behavior, on the objectives of politics, and on the goals of life itself. Pownall and Ellis offer a footnote to Namier's insight. Their mutual dislike in 1784 mattered very much to them, apparently, but it should matter less to us than the remarkable, and not accidental, agreement of their views of Empire in and after 1763. If Pownall's mind was the broader and more flexible of the two, it was no less bound by the same canons of unthinkability. That "equity" could absolve the Americans from any share in the burden of Empire, that "efficiency" did not require in some way the recognition of Parliamentary sovereignty—both ideas were unthinkable, to Pownall as to Ellis. No trauma had yet shattered the controlling consensus in British political life, and this consensus channeled imperial policy as surely as it did other forms of thought and action.

There is nothing essentially wrong with the insights of Andrews and Namier on British politics in the American Revolution. Each looked at the evidence from a different perspective, but what they saw was mutually illuminating, not contradictory. If Namier stressed the complicated scurrying of politicians for places and prestige, Andrews saw that all were more or less afflicted by mounting anxiety for the future of the stage on which they scurried. America made enemies of Pownall and Ellis, but their antagonism seems to have had more to do with chance and perhaps temperament than with opposed principles. We must not be deceived by the rhetoric of the debate on America; disagreement follows, and does not precede, the event. The conventional categories of historical analysis, "liberal," and "conservative," are even more misleading than the largely discredited "Whig" and "Tory" for politics generally. The impulse that swept the British Empire toward civil war was powerful, and did not admit of any real choice.

CHAPTER FOUR

The Empire Militant:
Thomas Gage and the Coming of War

After writing a book on the British army in America before the Revolution, I was obviously prepared to write an essay on the man who had commanded that army. For months I had worked in his papers, which record in detail his twelve years as Commander in Chief. He had shipped them home in large wooden boxes, a box for each year, and eventually they were bought by the agents of William L. Clements, a Michigan tycoon, and brought to Ann Arbor, where they were carefully unpacked and beautifully mounted in great leather volumes. They fill one corner of the manuscript room of the Clements Library, and are among the most illuminating sources we have on the coming of revolution as seen through British eyes. But they are also puzzling and a little frustrating, because they contain almost nothing of a personal nature, and after all my research I felt that I knew Gage the military bureaucrat but not Gage the man. So the invitation to write the essay was welcome, because it forced me to think, one last time, about the fragments of information that I had accumulated about the man, and to make some sense of his life and his performance in the crisis of 1774–75. The essay first appeared in George Washington's Opponents, *edited by George A. Billias (New York, 1969).*

Thomas Gage, as commander in chief of the British army in North America in 1775, was trapped by historical forces he could neither control nor avoid. But his frantic efforts to elude the trap, if unsuccessful, were not inconsequential. He could not have prevented the American Revolution, but he could, and did, give its beginning a particular shape. The Revolutionary War began on land, under ambiguous circumstances, at the heart of rebel strength, in an area that could only be a dead end for British strategy, and with a series of humiliating setbacks for His Majesty's arms. In the years that followed, British policy could never quite shake free of this bad beginning—never again was the range of strategic and political choice as wide as it had been in 1775. There were others who must share the blame with Gage, but he more than anyone else might have made a different beginning. His personality and previous military experience suggest why he did not.

Thomas Gage was the second son of a noble family known primarily for its lack of distinction and its reluctance to give up Catholicism. His father, the first Viscount Gage, pursued an erratic course in British politics. Thomas's mother had a reputation for sexual promiscuity, while his brother's outstanding trait seems to have been absent-mindedness. His sister married into a Catholic family, and both of his parents, after living as nominal Anglicans, appear to have returned to the Catholic Church at the end of their lives. Great wealth entered the family only when Thomas's brother, who was the eldest, married a Jewish heiress. But long before that event, Thomas had to find his own way.

The church, the law, the army—these were the usual paths open to younger sons of nobility in eighteenth-century England, and so, after eight years at Westminster School, young Thomas set out on a military career. In getting a commission, he naturally had the help of his brother William, the future Lord Gage, who just as naturally would soon enter the House of Commons from the borough of Seaford, Sussex, one of whose seats was in the Gage family pocket. For fifteen years, Gage's military career was not unusual in any way: service in Flanders against the French, in North Britain against the Jacobites; a captain at twenty-three, a lieutenant colonel at just past thirty, both ranks acquired of course by the purchase of a vacant commission. As an officer with good "connexions," however, he was expected to serve some time at headquarters: "For a man who intends to be military nothing so pretty as an aide de camp in service with an intelligent general," was the advice of Jeffery Amherst, later conqueror of Canada, to his younger brother.[1] Accordingly Gage served on the staff—in "the family" was the phrase—of the Earl of Albemarle, father of his school friends at Westminster, the Keppels.

In 1755, he told an historian many years later, some American land speculators, among them George Washington, interrupted the typical pattern of Gage's military career, and incidentally started a world war.[2] But the British government at the time decided that the troubles of the governor of Virginia and his land-hungry cronies were caused by French aggression in the Ohio valley. Neither version was more than half true. The cabinet nevertheless took drastic action: it ordered British regulars to defend American territory and colonists, something rarely done in the past. The 44th, Gage's regiment, and the 48th, both stationed in Ireland, received orders to embark for Alexandria, Virginia, under the command of Major General Edward Braddock, who carried a commission as commander in chief for North America.

"My honest friend Gage is to be of the Ohio party," wrote James Wolfe when he heard the news of Braddock's expedition. It is interesting to learn that Wolfe, already known in the army as an exceptionally zealous and able officer, thought well of Gage.[3] But the Braddock campaign against the French at the forks of the Ohio turned into a disaster. Crippled at the start by problems of supply, Braddock lost the advantage that either a rapid march or a methodical approach might have offered.

When, after more than two hundred miles of marching, his column ran into ambush almost within sight of its objective, the French had had ample time to bring up reinforcements. The British force, on the other hand, was hungry and its march formation cluttered with wagons, cattle, and pack horses. Only a 300-man advance party was in position to prevent surprise and to protect the main body while it deployed, but the advance party failed. It collapsed at first contact, transmitted its panic to the entire force, and the advance-party commander, Lieutenant Colonel Thomas Gage, could do nothing to stop the ensuing rout.

Modern historians have criticized Gage on several grounds—failing to occupy the high ground near the line of march, leaving behind a pair of light cannon that might have turned the tide, even fleeing the battlefield—but all such criticism is captious, and some is merely uninformed, for no one criticized him at the time.[4] The French force, though outnumbered by the whole British column, simply overwhelmed the advance party. Surprise, fear, inexperience in forest warfare, and a faulty tactical arrangement of the main body did the rest. It was not a battle but a massacre.

Gage "distinguish'd himself by Encouraging the men as much as he Could," according to an anonymous eye-witness, and had "several narrow escapes."[5] But if he had minor wounds to prove his bravery, and in justice deserved little blame for the debacle, Gage had shown no special talent for leadership in combat. His own account of the battle puts all blame on the rank and file, which he certainly knew was an exaggeration. He had hardly reported the death of his colonel before he was asking for promotion to the vacancy. His assertion that he was the senior lieutenant colonel on the field, and that Braddock, "had he lived a few days longer," would have given him the regiment, hit a sour note even for the eighteenth century.[6] He did not get the colonelcy.

With Braddock's defeat, the British government found that

the small expedition was becoming a full-scale war, and Thomas Gage found that his military education in America was going to last more than a season. New commanders with new regiments came over with new plans; Gage and the 44th moved north toward Canada in keeping with those plans. British North America spent all of 1756 trying to reorganize its military effort, and Gage soon learned how low regular troops could sink under the primitive conditions of the frontier: he had seen a mutinous detachment of the 51st "in a filthy condition covered with vermin, . . . legs mortified thro dirt cold and want of change." [7] His own regiment was not much better: "The [44th] Regt is in Rags," wrote Lord Loudoun, the new commander in chief, but added that "they look like Soldiers" because "Lt Col Gage is a good Officer and keeps up Discipline Strictly." [8] In 1757, he was a member of the amphibious expedition that never quite reached its objective—the fortress of Louisbourg on Cape Breton Island. He did, however, manage to avoid the epidemic of back-biting and recriminations that infected the officer corps after the abortive campaign that summer which saw the fall of Fort William Henry and the slaughter of some of its garrison by Indians.

During the following winter Gage moved toward the colonelcy that had eluded him in 1755. All British officers with experience in America recognized the value of provincial rangers, armed woodsmen who were somewhat more dependable than Indians and more skillful than either British regulars or American militia in the techniques of forest warfare. Rangers were vital elements in gathering intelligence and in screening the army when it was in camp or on the move. But rangers were expensive because of their high rate of pay, they were unmilitary in dress and deportment, and, during the illness of their leader Robert Rogers, they had become unruly, even mutinous. Gage apparently saw his chance, and offered to raise a regiment of light infantry that could, in time, obviate the need for rangers.

It was a good idea, and often has been noted as a landmark in the history of the British army. There is little to suggest, however, that Gage was leading his British comrades toward a full acceptance of the lessons of Braddock's defeat. Gage raised his light infantry regiment, the 80th, and it served in 1758 alongside rangers and Indians in the unsuccessful campaign against Ticonderoga. But Gage himself, for some reason, hardly appears in the record. The 80th was parceled out among the three brigades of regulars, while Gage was an acting brigadier general and became second in command after the death of Lord Howe. But Gage seems to have done nothing to help the unfortunate General Abercromby avoid or retrieve his errors of judgment, which included a frontal attack without artillery support on a strongly fortified position. It is difficult to resist an impression that Gage had finally got his regiment, and was content. He improved his situation still more when at the end of the summer he hurried away from the sick and defeated army to marry Margaret Kemble, daughter of a wealthy New Jersey family.

His position as brigadier general became permanent in 1759, and that year he got his first independent command. Amherst, Abercromby's successor, sent Gage to take over the siege of Fort Niagara. Once the fort had fallen, Gage was to move against the French post of La Galette at the head of the St. Lawrence. While Wolfe attacked Quebec, and Amherst led his army down Lake Champlain toward Montreal, Gage was expected to exert pressure on Canada from the West. As in 1755, Gage, if he did not fail, at best failed to succeed.

He had excuses: the failure of the quartermaster at Albany to support him properly, the unexpected size of the French garrison at La Galette, and the attrition of his own force. But Amherst and especially Wolfe badly needed a diversionary attack, even if it were repulsed, and the commander in chief refused to accept the excuses. Gage had not carried out his orders, and "may not have such an opportunity [again] as long as he lives," was Amherst's judgment. "They have found out difficulties where there are none."[9] In the final campaign of the war on the continent in 1760, when Amherst accepted the surrender of Canada, he had Brigadier General Gage bringing up the rear.

Perhaps the rear was the right place for a general officer whose record indicated that running a regiment—making men look like soldiers and keeping strict discipline, as Loudoun had put it—was about the ceiling of his military abilities. In the rear he could keep the supplies moving forward, and the reserve forces in good order, ready for the commander's call. In the rear he could avoid the need to make quick decisions under pressure. There were some, though, who thought that Gage was not inept as a commander, only unlucky. Dr. Richard Huck, a highly intelligent surgeon on the headquarters staff, believed that Gage had received impossible orders and then been blamed when he could not execute them. "Gage is certainly none of the Sons of Fortune," Huck wrote to his old chief, Loudoun, and his epigram seems an apt description of Gage's entire wartime record, from Braddock's field to Bunker Hill. But even Huck reported that, according to French prisoners, the situation in Canada had been so desperate that two or three more days of pressure on La Galette would have brought collapse, and the doctor conceded that Gage perhaps had too much "Nonchalance" for his own good.[10]

In reviewing Gage's early military career in America, the record that he would carry into the opening battles of the Revolution, one is struck by how little combat experience he had had in six years. Twice he had been involved in an approach march through broken, unfriendly country: once with Braddock in 1755, and again near Ticonderoga in 1758. On both occasions he had seen a British army surprised. The result in 1755 had been panic and slaughter; in 1758, confusion, disorganization, and moderately heavy casualities. He had also taken part in an unsuccessful infantry assault on an entrenched position, at Ticonderoga in 1758, at a cost to the attackers of one-quarter of their force. The following year at Niagara, just a few weeks before he arrived to take command of the siege, a relief column of French regulars had smashed itself against an entrenched position in a small-scale repetition of the Ticonderoga attack; Gage must have seen the ground and heard the action described in detail.[11] Two surprise marches, two bloody infantry assaults—these made up his personal fund of tactical experience in American warfare before 1775.

The war ended for Gage in 1760. He did not go campaigning in the West Indies during 1761–62; instead, he served as military governor of Montreal, where combat experience was less important than some other qualities like intelligence, patience, honesty, and tact. Gage was a good governor, and became popular among people who had recently been his enemies. The "nonchalance" of which Dr. Huck had complained was an asset under peacetime conditions; a relaxed, understanding approach was what postwar Canada required.

But Montreal was cold and primitive, and, when peace came early in 1763, there was little to keep him there, or anywhere else for that matter, on active service. He held the rank of major general, and had become colonel of a senior regiment that would not be disbanded, as was the 80th, in the peacetime reduction of the army. Further promotion seemed unlikely. Few colonels actually served with their regiments, but merely enjoyed the honor and the emoluments. Gage could have done likewise, pleading perhaps that the climate of Canada was ruining his health, and have retired to Sussex or even New Jersey.

The Indian uprising of 1763 changed all such thoughts, which clearly Gage had been entertaining. The commander in chief, Sir Jeffery Amherst, had grossly underestimated the Indian problem after the war. For years the Indians had complained of traders who cheated them with rum and short weights, but now, with countervailing French power eliminated, they increasingly feared Anglo-American migration onto their hunting grounds. The war had taught Amherst to have utter contempt for Indians; he refused to listen to the pleas of Sir William Johnson, the Indian superintendent, and instead cut off their supply of ammunition and relied on small garrisons of regulars scattered through the West to hold them down by force. It was a stupid policy. The Indian uprising had been brewing for several years and may have been unavoidable, but when it broke out Amherst seemed the obvious culprit and was recalled. Thomas Gage took his place.

As the new commander in chief moved into his headquarters at New York, he faced two related problems: pacifying the northern Indian tribes, and managing a peacetime army scattered over a half-continent. For the first task he had the plans already developed by Amherst, the reinforcement by provincial troops which had been requested, and two able and experienced subordinates—John Bradstreet and Henry Bouquet. Bradstreet and Bouquet, with mixed forces of British regulars and American volunteers, moved westward from Albany and Pittsburgh, respectively, against little resistance. Gage, as he had been instructed, left the negotiation of peace to Sir William Johnson, whose stock with the British government had risen upon the fall of Amherst. The campaign of 1764 was arduous, but it was almost bloodless because the Indians had failed to destroy the garrisons at Detroit, Niagara, and Fort Pitt in 1763, and their small resources were nearly exhausted. Gage was able to put down the uprising more easily than expected.

The Indian problem did not disappear, however, with the end of the uprising. In fact, preventing another costly Indian war became more than ever a major concern to those responsible for British colonial policy, and the regular garrison in America figured prominently in their plans.

Prior to the French and Indian War, Britain had kept few regular troops in the colonies: several regiments to watch over a hostile population in Nova Scotia, and several more to curb slave insurrections in the West Indies. But, with the exception of a few undermanned companies in New York and South Carolina, the mainland colonies were completely dependent on their own militia for defense.[12] This arrangement seemed to break down in 1755, and Braddock's defeat brought thousands of regulars to America. At the end of the war it was decided to keep fifteen regiments on the mainland—three in Nova Scotia, four in Canada, four in Florida and along the Gulf coast, and the remaining four dispersed among the middle Atlantic seaboard, the Great Lakes, the Carolina and Georgia backcountry, and the Illinois side of the Mississippi. Gage was to command this army of about six thousand men, stretched across a thousand miles of wilderness.

The presence of a regular garrison led directly to the British attempt to raise a revenue in the colonies, but even now the mission of this military force is not altogether clear. Defense, properly speaking, was not a major consideration. The French population of Canada, and the relative emptiness of Florida and the transappalachian region, demanded a garrison for those areas. It was hoped that military posts in the backcountry could keep frontiersmen off Indian lands and bring some order to the fur trade, thus allaying the grievances that had led to the Indian uprising of 1763. New York City, New Jersey, and Philadelphia were convenient places for the rest and recuperation of units en route to other stations; these units would also be available, if needed, to act against smugglers. Finally, there was a vaguely expressed fear that troops might be useful to keep unruly Americans "in due subordination." No one, on the other hand, thought that a few thousand regulars could protect the whole frontier from another Indian attack, and everyone knew that sea power was the principal defense against France or Spain.[13]

Specifically, Gage was told to conciliate the Indians by:

1. "Restraining all unjust Settlement, and fraudulent Purchase of their Lands,"

and

    2. "Suppressing all unfair Practices in the free and open
       Trade to be carried on with them at the several [military]
       Posts,"

and to assist the customs officers in

    3. "The effectual Suppression of Contraband Trade in
       America." [14]

Privately Gage was warned of the general opinion within the
government "that the Indians have of late Years been too much
neglected, and that the . . . present Hostilities, have been in
great Measure owing to an apparent Contempt of their Consequence." [15] The message was unmistakable.

What thus appears on the surface to be a reasonable attempt
to improve the administration of the Empire soon gave rise to a
set of complicated, interlocking problems that were difficult
even to state clearly, much less solve. Gage himself was one of
the sponsors of the new plan to placate the Indians through
protection of their lands and regulation of the fur trade, but he
gradually came to understand that enormous obstacles stood in
the way. Frontier settlers and fur traders easily avoided the few
small garrisons in the back country, and when Gage tried to re-
strict their movements he often found himself caught between
rival pressure groups. His legal authority against civilians was
virtually nil, and colonial governors hesitated to cooperate with
the army against their own subjects, especially when they were
associated with land companies or commercial firms. Army post
commanders themselves could not be relied upon to refuse
bribes or to refrain from abusing Indians, nor could their behavior be controlled or checked easily when they were
hundreds of miles from headquarters. Although the British
government continued to fear the financial and political cost of
another Indian war, Gage and a few well-informed officials in
London were beginning to realize that the army could do little
to prevent it.

By the end of 1765, civil disorders along the seaboard
seemed to pose a more pressing problem for the army than the

danger of Indian uprisings on the frontier. During the riots over the Stamp Act in the autumn, no governor dared to call for military assistance, apparently because the troops nearby were too few to be employed effectively against the mobs in Boston, New York, Philadelphia, and Charleston. Gage began moving troops eastward, but was abruptly stopped when the Rockingham government decided to repeal the Stamp Act at the end of the year. Obviously the mission of the army in America was changing, but no one in an official position dared to articulate the change.

Confusion on the British political scene exacerbated the situation, making it difficult to adopt or pursue any coherent policy for the colonies or for the army in America. This confusion was only incidentally a result of trouble over American affairs. It was caused primarily by the successive political impact of the great but unorthodox war leader, William Pitt, and a new young king, George III, who was equally unorthodox in his view of politics, and by the collapse of a coalition that had ruled England for most of the century. The resultant bitterness among political leaders, coupled with severe economic distress in the postwar period, produced an instability at the cabinet level that is reminiscent of the Fourth French Republic.

From the American point of view, a "hard" Grenville ministry was succeeded in 1765 by a "soft" Rockingham government, which in turn was followed in 1766 by a coalition with Pitt at its head. Nominally "soft," this coalition steadily hardened in its approach to the American problem, becoming the "hardest" of them all when reorganized by Lord North in 1770. But Gage's immediate superior was the Secretary of State for the Southern Department, and the succession of men in that office did not quite conform to the general pattern of political change. The Earl of Shelburne, who served from 1766 to early 1768, was believed to be liberal in his approach to American grievances; the Earl of Hillsborough, who took the new office of Secretary of State for the American Colonies and served until mid-1772, was notoriously conservative. But Hillsborough was followed by the pious Earl of Dartmouth, North's step-brother, a man thought to be even more sympathetic than Shel-burne toward America. More important than any of these du-bious labels was the fact that, for a variety of reasons, no colonial secretary after the war held a strong position either in the cabinet or in the House of Commons. Under these circum-stances, American questions were buffeted by the rapidly shift-ing wind of politics. No question was more exposed to those winds than that of the colonial army, which was draining over £400,000 from the Treasury every year.

Gage responded to this instability with caution. During the past decade, British governments had dealt harshly with mili-tary commanders who had made mistakes: Admiral Byng had been shot, the Duke of Cumberland disgraced, three com-manders in America sacked in three years, Lord George Ger-main (who would direct the war against the colonies after 1775) court-martialed, and Amherst recalled. When Shelburne asked Gage for his opinion on desirable policies for the Indians, the unsettled West, and the American army, Gage sent back a long report full of information, but almost devoid of opinions that might later be used against him if things went badly. He knew that the historic antipathy in Britain toward a standing army would encourage a shaky government to make him the scape-goat if his advice turned out wrong.

Gage had opinions, however, and the men closest to him played on those opinions, drawing him toward a more active role in colonial affairs. A hint of what was in his mind came during the war when he wrote to his brother of the need to change the constitutions of Pennsylvania and Maryland. Sir William Johnson won Gage's official support for the plan to regulate the fur trade. And Lieutenant Colonel James Robert-son, Gage's principal staff officer and a Scot whose view of American disorder was unusually narrow, persuaded him in early 1765 to propose an Act of Parliament that would legalize the quartering of soldiers in private houses. The Ministry, under pressure from the agents in London of the colonial governments, revised the bill to allow quartering only in vacant buildings and existing barracks, though at colonial expense. Even as modified, the Quartering Act was a chronic source of trouble between Britain and her colonies.

More than anyone else, the Secretary at War, Lord Barrington, worked on and with Gage to help shape American policy. The office of Secretary at War was a secondary administrative post that constitutionally had nothing to do with either policy-making or the American colonies. Yet Barrington, who was at once a political hack and a charmingly honest fish in a sea of courtly hypocrisy, enjoyed the personal confidence of the king, serving him in the War Office from 1765 to 1778. Barrington had given up higher political ambitions, and the security of his position was due to a genuine zeal for the welfare of the army. Frequent visits to the royal closet on minor matters of military business gave Barrington an access to the king that even cabinet officers must have envied. It also gave Gage, one of Barrington's oldest friends, a line to the center of power if he cared or dared to use it.

In 1766 Barrington drafted a memorandum in which he proposed withdrawal of the army from the western posts and the middle Atlantic seaboard, and its concentration in Canada, Nova Scotia, and Florida. The West was to become a vast Indian reservation—"a desert," Barrington ignorantly called it—where no white settlement would be permitted to stir up another war. Withdrawal of troops from the West would facilitate their removal from the East, where there would no longer be any need for the Quartering Act. He appealed to the king and the army staff with the argument that a concentrated army would be better disciplined and better trained; he appealed to the cabinet with the prospect of eliminating the heavy cost of supplying troops in many remote garrisons. A few regiments, he suggested, might even be brought back to the British Isles.

Barrington showed his memorandum to Shelburne and Pitt (newly created Earl of Chatham), and sent a copy to Gage. At first Barrington thought that Chatham and Shelburne liked the plan, but he soon learned that his proposal to make the West "a desert" was drawing serious opposition to the plan as a whole. All those with an interest in western colonization or land speculation, including the postmaster general for America, Benjamin Franklin, were lobbying against it. General Amherst, who had returned to a position of influence on colonial and military questions when the Chatham government came to power, criticized Barrington's suggestion that small garrisons in the West (where Amherst had first put them) were useless against Indian uprisings. Amherst had never really understood what had gone wrong in 1763, and he never would, but his opinion carried weight. Shelburne vacillated. Chatham, meanwhile, fell ill and lost his effectiveness as a political leader. Thus, when the question of the cost of keeping the army in the transappalachian West came before the House of Commons, the leaderless cabinet divided. Parliament thereupon passed a new set of measures to raise a revenue in America—the Townshend Acts of 1767.

Barrington had expected that at least Gage would support him. For the most part, Gage did. But he objected to one key feature of Barrington's plan—the proposal to remove troops from the seaboard. Barrington had argued that troops in the colonial port cities were of little use, because by law only a civil magistrate could employ them against a mob, and few American magistrates, however loyal they might be to the Crown, had shown themselves willing to take this extreme step. Withdrawal of troops would remove an irritant and serve as a conciliatory gesture, Barrington reasoned, but they could quickly return from their bases to the North and South in case of a real rebellion. Gage disagreed. With more troops on the spot, he reasoned, magistrates would act more vigorously. Halifax, Quebec, Montreal, and St. Augustine were too far away for prompt action in the event of serious trouble. It is possible, and what is known of Mrs. Gage makes it rather likely, that Gage also did not want to move his headquarters away from the temperate, civilized atmosphere of New York City; he had already served one bleak tour in Canada, and had read enough dispatches relating the horrors of Florida to know what awaited the Gages at St. Augustine. Barrington deferred to the firsthand knowledge of his friend Gage for the time being, but the Secretary at War never gave up the hope of removing all regular soldiers from those colonies that had resisted taxation.

Whatever their disagreement over deployment of troops in the East, Gage and Barrington were as one on the need to get as many troops as possible out of the West—the soldiers stationed there were expensive, of no apparent use, and suffering from poor morale and inadequate supervision. The two men also agreed that the government ought to take a firm line toward American disorder. Both were ready to make minor gestures of conciliation, but they were unwilling to compromise on the basic issues of taxation, sovereignty, and obedience to law. In a fascinating private exchange of letters over the years, they alternately prayed for the government to stand firm and condemned its pusillanimity when it did not. In 1768, when another old friend of theirs, the Earl of Hillsborough, became Secretary of State for the American Colonies, their prayers and complaints stood in a fair way to be answered.

Hillsborough began by blocking Shelburne's plan for three new colonies in the West, and then gave Gage permission to reduce some of the western garrisons. Barrington was disappointed that withdrawal was only partial—troops remained in Illinois and at Fort Pitt for the time being, and there was no sign of the three Great Lakes posts (Niagara, Detroit, and Michilimackinac) being given up. But Hillsborough as Secretary of State would suffer the political consequences in case his orders and an Indian war happened to coincide, and so he was moving cautiously. Hillsborough was aware that he had already incurred the enmity of influential Englishmen and Americans who were interested in western colonization by his resistance to their plans; they would not miss a chance to attack him if he made a mistake. He next used a minor fracas at Boston in March 1768 as an excuse to order a regiment there, where troops had not been since the previous war. But before Gage received the letter, a real mob had run the customs officials out of town when they tried to seize John Hancock's sloop *Liberty* for smuggling, and Hillsborough told Gage to rush more troops to Boston.

Gage himself, confident as never before in the support of his two colleagues, dropped the mask of caution. "Quash this Spirit at a Blow," he wrote privately to Barrington, "without too much regard to the Expence and it will prove œconomy in the End." Later, in an official dispatch to Hillsborough, he stepped well outside the limits of his military duties; "I know of nothing that can so effectually quell the Spirit of Sedition . . . as Speedy, vigorous, and unanimous Measures taken in England to suppress it." Earlier he had warned Barrington: "If the Principles of Moderation and Forbearance are again Adopted . . . there will be an End to these Provinces as British Colonies." [16] For once even the Parliamentary Opposition, frightened by a series of riots in London and throughout the country during the year, seemed ready to acquiesce in "vigorous measures." By November, four regiments and part of a fifth had assembled at Boston; the crisis had come.

But nothing happened. Boston leaders kept the town quiet while the troops landed, and subsequent reports received in England, including one from Gage, who had paid a visit to Boston, suggested to the government that the *Liberty* riot might have been provoked and then exaggerated by royal officials in Boston. At home, the government found itself deeply involved in another crisis, unrelated to America, over the election of the radical leader, John Wilkes, to the House of Commons. The Opposition was taking heart, and the Ministry was losing its zeal for a crackdown at this time in Massachusetts. Only Hillsborough continued the fight, pushing for a set of measures similar to those adopted five years later. He would have altered the Massachusetts charter, bringing the province more directly under royal control, and military enforcement was implicit in such a step. But even the king had lost interest by February 1769, and Parliament disposed of the matter by passing eight fiery, ineffectual resolutions.

Gage thus had almost a third of his army in Boston to no apparent purpose. During the year that followed, he had a chance to learn a little more about the dynamics of a revolution. Bostonians found ways to harass the customs officers and the troops without breaking any laws. Magistrates, who were as afraid of not being supported by a fickle Ministry as they were of retaliation from their neighbors, refused to call for military aid. Gage, when he saw that troops were worse than useless, wanted to use the discretion Hillsborough had given him to withdraw them, but the Massachusetts governor, fearful of agreeing to any step that might be wrong, demurred. Two regiments remained in Boston during the next winter, 1769–70. With no one—the Ministry, the governor, or Gage—able to make a decision, and with Bostonians growing in their determination to get British soldiers out of their town, it was only a matter of time before an incident like the "Massacre" of March 5, 1770, took place. Under the direct threat of a massive uprising in the countryside on March 6, one regiment departed and the other moved to Castle Island in the harbor.

Gage, Barrington, and Hillsborough were sobered if not discouraged. Yet the experience left their belief unshaken that something drastic would have to be done about Boston; if anything, their belief was strengthened, because they could blame past failures on weakness in the government. Never in the next few years do they seem to have considered seriously whether military coercion was truly feasible.

Gage had his hands full during 1771–72 merely administering an army that was slowly deteriorating under the pressure of its American environment. Though regiments rotated across the Atlantic every four years or so, the chronic shortage of recruits forced Gage to permit men who wanted to stay in the colonies to transfer out of departing regiments. There proved to be hundreds of such men. Likewise, those officers most willing to remain at their posts in the colonies were the ones who had acquired American wives or American land or both, like Gage. The army gradually became a domesticated core of aging officers and men who were themselves virtually Americans, joined by a growing proportion of raw young subalterns (many of them sons of officers) and recruits (some illegally enlisted in America itself).

Away from the middle Atlantic coast, living conditions were unusually bad, even for an eighteenth-century army, and they were not getting any better. Gage had won respect from the government for his honesty and ability to cut costs, but human misery paid the price for part of his reputation. Being stationed at a post like Niagara was unpleasant to begin with, but it became unbearable when the roof was leaking, the bedding was filthy and falling apart, and the commander in chief asked for further information before agreeing to any expenditures. In the 1760's Gage had emphasized tactical training—marksmanship, for example—but little was heard of training in the early 1770's; sheer survival was task enough.

In 1772, Hillsborough fell from power when he refused to agree to a new colony in the Ohio Valley. Many speculators had merged to form this "Vandalia" project, as it was called, and they had managed to purchase a good deal of support even within the Privy Council. The whole affair was "an Infamous Jobb in every part of it," according to an undersecretary of state in a letter to Hillsborough's successor.[17] Gage was convinced that a western colony would mean an expensive and distracting war with the Indians, and he took up the fight that Hillsborough had lost. Barrington was now showing the king parts of his private correspondence with Gage, and the two friends worked together to delay royal approval of Vandalia until Gage could come home on leave. When he arrived in the summer of 1773, he succeeded in quietly getting the colony quashed, despite the powerful interests behind it.[18]

It is difficult to assess Gage's position with the government accurately at this crucial point in his career. His ability to block the Vandalia scheme suggests that he stood well with the king himself. But close association with the deposed Hillsborough and the fairly unpopular Barrington did not help him in the cabinet. Gage wrote in late 1773 from London to an old comrade, Lieutenant Colonel James Abercromby, who in turn reported as follows: "I am told General Gage is to go back to America. It seems they have offered him nothing on this side, and paid him but little attention." [19] It appears that Gage was seeking a better or an easier office—a major governorship or a sinecure. The Adjutant General of the British army, Edward Harvey, added another dimension to Abercromby's report: "Gage is come Home, it was thought not to Return, but the whisper now is, that M-d-m [Mrs. Gage] likes her Native Country better than Britain." There is evidence that the government had considered, even before he returned to England, replacing both Gage as commander in chief and Thomas Hutchinson as governor of Massachusetts with a single officer—Robert Monckton, a British general who had won great popularity in America during the last war.[20]

There is no clue as to whether the government was dissatisfied with Gage, or Gage had given the government some hint of being dissatisfied with his job. Despite his harsh private views on American resistance to British policy, Gage had been able to maintain an image of moderation within the colonies. Perhaps the strain of dissimulating toward Americans, of managing an army stretched over unmanageable distances, and of dealing with an erratic government, were proving too much for him. Five years before, an officer visiting headquarters, in writing to his commander in Florida, noted that Gage was so affected by his failure to get a clear statement of military policy from the government that "he is not the same Man he was when you left [New] York." [21] A reasonable guess is that Gage was indeed sick of his job, had thought seriously of giving it up, but changed his mind when Margaret Kemble Gage began longing for what they had left behind in New York and New Jersey.

Whatever the truth about Gage's motives and position, his situation changed abruptly in early 1774 when news of the destruction of the tea in Boston harbor reached London. Within a week Gage had had an interview with George III, and the king's report to Lord North is worth quoting at length:

> Since You left me this day, I have seen Lieutenant General Gage, who came to express his readiness though so lately come from America to return at a day's notice if the conduct of the Colonies should induce the directing coercive measures, his language was very consonant to his Character of an honest determined Man; he says they will be Lyons, whilst we are Lambs but if we take the resolute part they will undoubtedly prove very meek; he thinks the four Regiments intended to Relieve as many Regiments in America if sent to Boston are sufficient to prevent any disturbance; I wish You would see him and hear his ideas as to the mode of compelling Boston to submit to whatever may be thought necessary.[22]

Years later, in reply to the question of an historian, Gage recollected that he had said something quite different:

> The General [Gage referring to himself] not long from his command by leave, and still holding it, made no objection to return to his duty, but was averse to taking the Government of the Massachusetts Bay. He desired at length that a much larger force than four weak regiments might be sent out, and the Town of Boston declared in rebellion, without which his hands would be tied up.[23]

About the same time, James Paterson, who had been a colonel in 1775 and became a major general in the American war, told Frederick Haldimand, who had been one of Gage's brigadier generals, that "he was present when the general told the King (speaking of Boston) that he had sufficient troops to bring these people to reason." [24] The presumption must be that Gage, who had been gradually becoming more outspoken in his opinions on America, made promises to the king that both men would live to regret.

For Gage, regret may have begun as soon as he stepped out of the royal closet. He had promised to ram the policy of the government down American throats before he (or anyone else) even knew what the policy would be. Anxiously he sought to strengthen his legal position by asking the cabinet if he could use troops against civilian disorder. As commander in chief, he had no power to do so, and when made governor, he was constitutionally required to seek the advice of his Council. The cabinet, with some equivocation, said that he could.[25]

So far as is known, Gage played no part in drafting those "Coercive Acts" of the spring of 1774, which closed the port of Boston, made the Council of Massachusetts appointive, and curbed the power of town meetings. He certainly had a hand in new laws for the trial of accused persons outside the province, and for the quartering of soldiers wherever they were needed; both were intended to prevent some of the problems the army had had previously with juries and quarters in Boston. It is also likely that he supported the Quebec Act, which among other things provided for a clear legal authority in the transappalachian West.

When Gage had departed New York in 1773, the mayor and council had tendered him the freedom of the city and a flowery address. When he returned to America a year later, Boston welcomed him with dignity and even a touch of warmth. As one intelligent Bostonian reported, Gage was proclaimed governor "amid the acclamations of the people. He express'd himself as sensible of the unwelcome errand he came upon, but as a servant of the Crown, he was obliged to see the [Port] Act put in execution: but would do all in his power to serve us." At an "elegant entertainment" afterward at Faneuil Hall, Gage toasted the prosperity of Boston.[26] Since he had intervened to prevent bloodshed during the Stamp Act riots at New York in 1765, Gage had been surprisingly popular in the colonies. He had run his army with evident care and common sense, avoiding disputes whenever possible, and he had behaved himself with tact and sobriety. Late in 1774, Dr. Joseph Warren, a leader of the Boston radicals, still considered Gage as "a man of honest, upright principles" who would work for "a just and honourable settlement."[27] Americans looked to him as their last hope for some reasonable solution of the tea controversy, while his own government believed that he was the man who could bring Boston to its knees without a civil war. He could not possibly satisfy both at once, and he was doomed to satisfy neither.

His first dispatches home were fairly optimistic. With the help of the navy, he had closed Boston port, and had shifted the capital to Salem. There was little that rebellious spirits could do about a blockade, and they were less daring as regiment after regiment moved into Massachusetts. But with the announcement of the Massachusetts Government Act, which virtually annulled the charter of the province, effective August 1, the situation began to change. On September 7, the British government heard from Gage that trouble was likely; by October 1 it was learned that trouble had occurred—the new Crown-appointed members of the council had been terrorized into resignation, courts had been closed by mobs in the interior of the province, and "Civil Government is near its End . . . Conciliating, Moderation, Reasoning is over, Nothing can be done but by forceable Means." Gage complained that his troops were too few, and he promised to "avoid any bloody Crisis as long as possible" while "His Majesty will in the mean Time Judge what is best to be done."[28] The government, believing that it had already decided "what is best to be done" when it

sent Gage to Boston, was apparently thunderstruck; it took sixteen days to write an answer to his letter.

Even more incredible, Gage did not send off his next dispatch for another three weeks. As autumn storms lengthened
the time-distance between Boston and London, the government heard nothing from him until November 18. Throughout
this seven-week interval Gage's stock had been dropping; it
dropped lower still when the government read his next bundle
of dispatches. He reported that all the northern colonies were
supporting Boston to a degree "beyond the Conception of most
People, and foreseen by none. The Disease was believed to
have been confined to the Town of Boston . . . But now it's so
universal there is no knowing where to apply a Remedy." Only
the conquest of New England would be effective. To accomplish this end, he proposed, in a private and round-about
way, suspending the Coercive Acts, withdrawing all troops,
blockading the coast, and returning only after a much larger
army, including German mercenaries, had been raised. From
that time on the government stopped listening to Thomas
Gage.[29]

Gage seems not to have realized what was happening to his
reputation at home. Toward the end of October he was reading warm praise in a private letter from Secretary of State Dartmouth for his prudent conduct under "the nice and delicate
circumstances" which existed in Massachusetts.[30] But that letter
had crossed those dispatches of his own that would cause his
supporters in the government to lose faith in him. As early as
September they had been irritated by the infrequency of his
letters and their lack of detailed information. By December,
both of the undersecretaries of state for the colonies, men who
had supported the hard Hillsborough line toward colonial disorder, were writing to Dartmouth of Gage's "timidity and
weakness," and the "Inactivity and Irresolution of his Conduct," which "astonished and alarmed" everyone because it

seemed "devoid of both sense and spirit." [31] Even his friend, the tactful and cautious ex-governor of Massachusetts, Thomas Hutchinson, warned him that his proposal to suspend the Acts and to raise German mercenaries had not been well received.[32] Only Barrington continued to write encouragingly.

The government went on listening to messages from America, if not to those of Gage. When he had decided in late August that the next move was up to the king and his ministers, he had withdrawn himself and his army to the Boston peninsula and had begun buttoning up for the winter. Boston had a population of less than 20,000 and it was now occupied by over 3000 officers and men who had come to police the whole province. Little imagination is required to see what was likely to happen. The townspeople were angry and afraid, the army—especially its officer corps—was bored and humiliated, and everyone was tense and crowded. Gage, as governor, was determined to prevent trouble. If trouble came despite his efforts, he was determined that he, his army, and the home government would not be caught on the wrong side of any dispute or incident. He negotiated an agreement with a committee of the town in which he promised to keep his troops on a tight rein and to listen sympathetically to all complaints concerning their behavior. He kept his promise to Boston, but it cost him the morale of his men and the confidence of his officers.

Not all the officers attacked Gage; there were a few who understood his predicament. But there were many more who sent home disparaging comments about their general. Young John Barker of the 4th Foot, for example, was an immature officer who might have criticized any commander under whom he served, but Barker's complaints of "Tommy" who favored the Yankees over his own soldiers were the sort of news from Boston that had made Gage's timidity a subject of coffee-house gossip in London by the end of the year.[33] Far more weighty with the government, however, was a letter like the one from Lieutenant Colonel James Abercromby, a respected officer who had served with Gage during the last war and who had been sent to Boston especially to serve on his staff. Soon after Gage withdrew to the Boston peninsula, Abercromby wrote that "he likes his Colonel [that is, Gage] as a gentleman, but would never employ him on a forlorn hope." [34] Even Bostonians knew that his army was calling Gage "*Old Woman.*" [35]

In eighteenth-century England, where a small aristocracy both ruled the country and officered the army, such complaints struck resonant chords. For those at the highest levels of government, policy and honor were becoming hopelessly confused with one another. The honor of the army, virtually penned up inside Boston by fear of a rabble that had proved its cowardice and indiscipline during the last war, was at issue; thus, by extension, the honor of the king (commander in chief of the whole army), of the nobility (whose sons led it), and even of the "nation" (which the army represented in the eyes of the world), was involved. Though the Boston crisis required the most careful calculations of power and interest, the king seemed more upset by the shameful rate of desertion from his regiments in Boston than by the prospect of war; reportedly he wept on General William Howe's shoulder when they heard how fast soldiers were running off into the Massachusetts countryside. By the end of 1774, there was no more calculating of the evidence at Whitehall, Westminster, or St. James's. The king had told Lord North, "Blows must decide"; the government had ceased to think—it was merely reacting.[36]

Only a few men in the government had both the knowledge and the self-control to realize that Gage was right, however unpleasant the realization might be. Barrington and Adjutant General Harvey believed him when he said that Americans would fight rather than submit. They understood also how nearly impossible it would be for Britain to carry on a land war across an ocean against an armed population. Both men thought that pacification had to be achieved by naval blockade. At Boston itself, Frederick Haldimand, a capable Swiss officer

and a veteran of the last war in America who had served as
Gage's second in command, was not impressed by those who
dismissed the colonial militia as a rabble in arms. "The Americans," Haldimand noted, "would be less dangerous if they had
a regular army." [37] A later generation of Americans, learning
lessons of their own about revolutionary wars, can readily understand what Haldimand meant.

But the government had already made up its mind. Gage
would have to be superseded, though the king was unwilling to
recall him in disgrace. General William Howe would go out to
Boston, nominally as second in command, but all would understand that Howe was to be the "acting officer." [38] Howe would
take with him as lieutenants Henry Clinton and John
Burgoyne. While Howe, Clinton, and Burgoyne were gathering
together their baggage and the reinforcements they would take
with them, Gage himself should do something to salvage the
situation. Dartmouth accordingly signed a long, secret letter
which first rejected Gage's appreciation of the situation and his
proposals for action, and then ordered him to go out into the
countryside and arrest the leaders of the Massachusetts Provincial Congress. In case there was any doubt about what the government expected of him, Barrington also wrote to say that he
was organizing a hospital for the army in America "on a large
scale." [39]

The action at Lexington and Concord, like that at Bunker
Hill, has been exhaustively studied, but it raises more questions
about Gage than have ever been answered. He had known in
February that spring would bring some positive order from the
government, and that the order would probably mean war.
Through an excellent spy system, he also knew what was going
on in the countryside, that the Americans were training troops
and gathering supplies at Concord, Worcester, and elsewhere.
By early April, he had begun to get unofficial news of the
measures adopted by the British government. At the same
time, one of his spies informed him that the Provincial

Congress had been greatly alarmed by the recent march of a brigade of British regulars out of Boston. A committee of the Congress had reported its opinion "that should any body of troops, with Artillery and Baggage, march out of Boston, the Country should instantly be alarmed and called together to oppose their March, to the last extremity." Towns around Boston had petitioned Congress to the same effect. Gage had seen the militia rise on several previous false alarms, and he had no reason to think these words were an empty threat.[40]

Gage had already started preparations for an offensive move into the countryside when he received the secret orders from Dartmouth on April 14. The Massachusetts leaders were as well informed about his preparations as he was about their activities, so there was little mystery on either side. More obscure is the question of why Gage organized the expedition as he did. He must have known that the colonists would resist if he marched to destroy their munitions or arrest their leaders, yet his plans suggest that he counted on avoiding hostilities. He knew the sort of broken terrain his troops would be marching through, and he could not have forgotten the difficulties it posed for a column of regulars, but there is no hint that he was seriously concerned about tactical problems. He sent an improvised brigade made up of twenty-one grenadier and light infantry companies—the elite troops drawn from each regiment, about 800 men. Every man carried one day's ration but no knapsack. No artillery or baggage accompanied the column. Its commander was the senior field officer on duty, "a very fat heavy Man," seconded by a major of Marines. One can only guess that Gage hoped to make up in speed of movement what such a force lacked in weight and cohesion. Its mission was to destroy the American supplies at Concord and return to Boston, thirty-two miles round trip.

There was a brief skirmish at Lexington, ten miles out, a fight at Concord, and a running battle all the way home in which the British suffered over 250 casualties. In what seems to have been an afterthought, Gage ordered a brigade to set out with two light artillery pieces ten hours later in support of the first column. The grenadiers and light infantry probably would have been wiped out except for meeting this relief force with its cannon near Lexington on the journey back. Numerous details of the whole operation—its conception, the security measures surrounding it, and its execution—indicate that either Gage did not really believe the militia would fight (which would have contradicted what he had been telling the government), or he did not do even a routinely competent job of planning and supervision. As far as the historian can tell, he had learned nothing from the last war about ambush and tactical marches in America.

Although Gage was henceforth literally besieged in Boston by thousands of New England militia, he obviously continued to hope that Lexington and Concord were not the beginning of a civil war but only an incident that might somehow be smoothed over. He disarmed the people of Boston, and severely restricted civilian movement over Boston neck, but he did not declare martial law. There was talk, at least, of conciliatory measures in both London and Philadelphia, and Gage did not want to jeopardize even a slim chance for peace. Admiral Samuel Graves, who commanded the small fleet in Boston harbor, wanted Gage to seize and fortify Charlestown and Dorchester peninsulas which, like Boston, commanded part of the harbor from their heights and were connected to the mainland by narrow, easily defended causeways. But Gage refused. He was convinced that his army of 4000 effectives was too weak. Moreover, he was unwilling to begin offensive operations before all political remedies were exhausted. Nor did Graves himself employ the navy on offensive missions. In the end, both men suffered from criticism for their inactivity.

With the arrival of Howe, Clinton, and Burgoyne in late May, Gage, though still commander in chief, all but disappears in a fog of collective responsibility. How he finally came to declare martial law on June 12 is unknown, but it is certain that Burgoyne wrote the bombastic proclamation. In a leisurely manner, the generals began to plot how they might pursue Graves's sound proposal to occupy Charlestown and Dorchester, clearly a necessity if Boston were to remain tenable. But they do not seem to have spent much time discussing broader questions of strategy, such as why an army should be in Boston at all. Gage had asked for help from Governor Guy Carleton of Canada, and he had authorized Lieutenant Colonel Allen Maclean to raise a corps of Scottish Highland immigrants in the Carolina backcountry; otherwise the commander in chief waited for reinforcements, further orders, and the next American move.

That move came, of course, with the appearance of fortifications one morning in mid-June on a spur of Bunker Hill, on Charlestown peninsula. General Clinton wanted to cut off the American forces by landing behind them on Charlestown neck, but his colleagues decided that the militia should be taught a different kind of lesson. Some insight into the mind of the British council of war, which decided to make a frontal assault, can be gained from a letter written by Burgoyne two months after the ensuing battle:

> I believe in most states of the world as well as in our own, that respect, and control, and subordination of government . . . depend in a great measure upon the idea that trained troops are invincible against any numbers or any position of undisciplined rabble; and this idea was a little in suspense since the 19th of April.[41]

In short, the attack at Bunker Hill, which cost the British over 1000 casualties, was to be understood on psychological rather than tactical grounds.

Once again, as at Lexington and Concord, neither the plan nor its execution does Gage any credit, though not all the blame can justly be laid to him alone. But, as at Lexington and Concord, he seems to have learned nothing from his own previous military experience. The unsuccessful assaults at Ticonderoga in 1758 and at Niagara in 1759 were basically similar to the situation at Bunker Hill in 1775, with one exception: at Bunker Hill the *militia* stood behind the fieldworks. Gage apparently thought that the one difference made all the difference, for his post-mortem lament to Barrington shows that he finally understood:

> These People Shew a Spirit and Conduct against us, they never shewed against the French, and every body had Judged of them from their former Appearance, and behaviour . . . which has led many into great mistakes.

And, at last, he had begun to grasp the strategic problem as well:

> We are here, to use a common expression, taking the Bull by the horns, Attacking the Enemy in their Strong parts, I wish this Cursed place was burned . . . its the worst place to act Offensively from, or defencively. I think if this Army was in New York, that we should find many friends, and be able to raise Forces in that Province on the side of Government.[42]

Boston was a trap; New York was the key. But by then everyone saw it (Howe had seen it as early as June 12), and it was too late to move the army until 1776. Gage could only wait gracefully for his recall, which arrived in September.

Thomas Gage lived twelve more years, to the age of sixty-seven, never doing or saying anything to attract special notice. He made few excuses and blamed no colleagues, which is remarkable among disgraced leaders in any age. Equally remarkable was the agreement among his contemporaries in their estimate of him. Burgoyne had begun a tortuous description of his chief with the following words:

> I have a most sincere value for his private character which is replete with virtues and with talents. That it is not of a cast for the situation in which he is placed I allow; and hence many, tho' far from all, of our misfortunes.

Major James Wemyss, on the other hand, wrote incautiously, but he said the same thing about Gage:

> Of moderate abilities, but altogether deficient in military knowledge. Timid and undecided in every path of duty, was unfit to command at a time of resistance, and approaching Rebellion to the Mother Country.

Almost every other estimate of Gage points in the same direction: pleasant, honest, sober; a little dull; cautious, even timid at times; no talent at all for making war.[43]

Despite his comparatively simple personality, and the contemporary consensus about him, it is difficult to reach a satisfactory judgment on Gage's role in the outbreak of the American Revolution. Without the Revolution smoldering beneath him, he would have been the ideal peacetime military administrator. Before 1774, he was generally liked and respected, both by his troops and by the colonists. He had gone far to keep the army, as such, from being an important grievance to Americans. Unlike some other British officials in the colonies, Gage never played with a high hand, nor was there ever a sign of scandal in his conduct of business. Finally, he was tied to America by marriage, property, and length of service on this side of the Atlantic.

His administrative record is balanced by his combat record. Americans could count themselves fortunate to have been opposed in the beginning by a general with so little ability as a fighter. Perhaps, as has been said about other British leaders in the Revolutionary War, he had no heart for the fight against fellow Englishmen. Or perhaps, as Dr. Huck had said, Gage was unlucky—"none of the Sons of Fortune." But chance ought to have given even an unlucky man, provided he had a modicum of skill, some small success in the course of two wars.

Gage the military administrator and Gage the combat leader were, however, incidental to his third role—Gage the imperial statesman.[44] Nothing in his commission as commander in chief required that he play such a role, and a great deal in his personality indicated that he would not, but circumstances thrust him into the part. His particular interest in finding a policy for the transappalachian West, and his strong personal ties to Barrington and Hillsborough, tended to erode his self-protective reserve. The king's special concern with the army offered Gage a better chance to be heard, and the coincidence of his presence in London with the Boston Tea Party brought all circumstances to a focus. Gage encouraged the king and his government to make him the last major link between Britain and America.

Unfortunately, Gage was a weak link: his understanding of the situation in the colonies was surprisingly feeble. There were those who thought that Gage, despite almost twenty years' service in America, had permitted a few personal associates to insulate him against the facts of colonial life. Whatever the explanation, his poor understanding of the problem was responsible for the government's resting its policy on a false premise: that the main obstacle to the use of military force in America was legal, not practical; that Britain actually could coerce the colonists whenever it decided to pass the necessary laws. The ministers managed to slight the fact that Americans, unlike Englishmen or Irishmen or Scots, were armed. In playing his political role, Gage did not remind them early or forcibly enough to make them reconsider. Only at the end did he himself see the great difficulty of coercing thousands of armed men, and even then, through another kind of weakness, he failed to make himself heard.

This other weakness, weakness of temperament rather than of understanding, led him to support a second false premise of British policy: that Boston was the source of revolutionary infection, and that Boston could be isolated. He must have known better as early as 1769, when New York and South Carolina gave Massachusetts vigorous support against military occupation. But he also must have been temperamentally unable to tell Barrington, or Hillsborough, or the king, anything except what they wanted to hear and he wanted to believe—until it was too late.

The obverse effect of temperamental weakness was the kindly face he presented to the colonists themselves. Even as he arrived at Boston to enforce the Coercive Acts, he exuded easy-going charm and gave Americans a feeling that he, and the government he represented, would never push matters to civil war. A Boston radical read the smiling face and solicitous manner as weakness in the man and in the government behind him. It is only fair to admit that Gage was indeed unlucky, that he was caught up by forces no one could direct or deflect. But it is also fair to conclude that he was a modest force in his own right, and that his impact served to increase miscalculation by both sides.

CHAPTER FIVE

American Society and
Its War for Independence

The American Revolutionary War ended, for all practical purposes, at and around West Point, New York, one of the most remarkable bits of American scenery, and today the site of the U.S. Military Academy. Appropriately, the Academy in April 1976 sponsored a symposium on the military history of the Revolution. This was my personal Last Hurrah of the Bicentennial, and, with an audience of military historians and military professionals, the time and place seemed right to reverse the emphasis of other essays in this volume on how war had affected society, and instead to specify the ways in which the structure of eighteenth-century American society had given the Revolutionary War its particular pattern. That perspective also seems the proper way to begin the consideration here of the subject of the war itself.

The British seem to enjoy celebrating their military disasters more than their victories. A best-selling book on the charge of the Light Brigade was made into a popular film. The Department of War Studies at King's College, University of London, offers as a special subject for advanced students a course on the Gallipoli campaign. And every year the evacuation of Dunkirk is celebrated by BBC television and vacationing British veterans, while the anniversary of Waterloo, not many miles away, is relatively neglected. True to form, the British have celebrated the Bicentennial of the American Revolution as enthusiastically as have the Americans, and perhaps even more effectively. In April 1976 the queen personally opened an outstanding Bicentennial exhibit at Greenwich, and during the previous autumn the British Museum mounted not one but two simultaneous exhibits devoted to the American Revolution.

The two exhibits at the British Museum were especially good and interesting. One, called "The World of Franklin and Jefferson," concentrated on the highest ideals and noblest rhetoric of the Revolution; its subject matter was very edifying. The other concentrated on the War of American Independence; while many items in the latter exhibit were delightful to look at—beautifully drawn and colored maps, fine portraits—its subject matter, dealing as it must with death and destruction, was not so edifying. In effect, the British Museum split the American Revolution into two parts: the constructive part of the political revolution upstairs, and the Revolutionary War downstairs.

Splitting the Revolution into two halves—one political and social history, the other military history—is not peculiar to the British Museum; rather, it has been a characteristic tendency for a long time of almost everyone who has studied the subject. But this characteristic tendency of historians is essentially false to the historical event, because people living through the long, hard years from 1775 to 1783 made no such artificial division.

To cross this dividing line, and to restore some of the unified reality of two hundred years ago, is the self-imposed task of this essay. In particular, it explores the ways in which the nature of American society on the eve of the Revolution shaped the armed struggle and would affect its outcome.[1]

Because much of what follows has to be stated in generalities, it may be useful to begin with two concrete bits of revolutionary history. In 1775–76 General Washington was criticized because he had let the British evacuate Boston without attacking the town. Washington was defended by Charles Lee, his third in command and an able if highly eccentric ex-British officer who would eventually ruin himself by engaging in open controversy with Washington. But in the beginning Lee strongly backed Washington against his critics, contending that they simply failed to understand the American soldier. If Washington had commanded an army of Russians, Lee wrote, he would have assaulted Boston's fortifications. But Americans were not Russians, and Washington correctly did not try to misuse the excellent human material that made up his army. Lee did not bother to defend American courage; instead, he implied that American soldiers, fresh from their farms and their families, were not stupid enough, or docile enough, to assault strong field works in close-order formation.[2]

The other concrete bit of revolutionary history happened later in the war and takes us to the other side of the hill. In 1780 the British had virtually conquered Georgia and South Carolina. One American army had surrendered at Charleston in May, and a second had been destroyed at Camden in August. As British forces deployed through the lower South and tried to restore royal authority, Lord Rawdon, an energetic young British officer, was given command in the South Carolina back-country. Rawdon's own regiment was the Royal Volunteers of Ireland, a tough, well-disciplined unit, made up almost entirely of Scotch-Irish deserters from the American

Continental army. Rawdon decided to post the Royal Volunteers of Ireland in the Waxhaws district, on the border between North and South Carolina. The inhabitants of the Waxhaws district were recent Protestant immigrants from Ulster in Ireland, and Rawdon expected that his regiment, with a similiar ethnic and religious background, would win the civilians over to the royal cause. But the opposite actually happened. Within a short time, desertion among the Royal Volunteers of Ireland had risen sharply, and Rawdon felt compelled to issue an exceptionally harsh manifesto. In it, he threatened to flog or ship to the West Indies any civilian who aided a British deserter, and he offered a reward for the return of any such deserter—£5 if brought in alive, £10 if only the head were turned in.

This extraordinary document soon reached Washington, who used it to embarrass the British government and high command. When Rawdon's commanding general demanded an explanation, Rawdon tried to pass the matter off as a joke—a bluff intended only to frighten, not a serious threat. But he also complained that the Waxhaws district people had been "universally disaffected," that he had hoped to pacify them by stationing the Royal Volunteers of Ireland among them, but that the people had done everything "to debauch the minds of my soldiers" and had succeeded to "a very alarming degree." He pleaded with Cornwallis, his commander, to recall how the army had been "betrayed on every side by the inhabitants," how people who acted like friends in camp were firing on the British an hour later, and how supposedly "loyal" American militia actually supplied the enemy with arms, horses, and information. Clearly, the matter was no joke.[3]

These two incidents illustrate a simple point: the military operations of the American Revolution make sense only when they are placed in their political and social context. The nature of American society profoundly affected the character and the outcome of the Revolutionary War. Let us turn to a more systematic examination of this simple but neglected point.

The first step is to look at American society on the eve of revolutionary troubles, in about 1760—not at political conflicts with Britain, which usually get most of the attention, but at the people, how they lived and what was happening to them. Colonial America was highly diverse, with little natural unity before the Revolution. Only our knowledge that the United States would soon emerge from these diverse and disunited colonies leads us to see an artificial unity where in fact there was very little, except the common, though tenuous, bond to London. But it is possible to identify certain social character-istics, common to most or all colonies, that would strongly affect the armed struggle for independence during 1775–83.[4] At least six of these characteristics can be specified.

First, the population of colonial America grew very rapidly during the first three-quarters of the eighteenth century, more rapidly perhaps than any other society had ever grown up to that point in recorded history. It had grown tenfold in only seventy-five years, from about 250,000 in 1770 to 2.5 million at the outbreak of the Revolutionary War. As might be expected, this rate of growth caused some problems, which are discussed below.[5]

Second, the availability of a virtually unlimited supply of land eliminated the periodic starvation, chronic malnutrition, and much of the epidemic disease that were still evident in Europe and kept the European population growth rate close to zero. For example, it is estimated that 400,000 people died during the Irish famine of 1740–41.[6] Although colonial America occasionally suffered the effects of epidemic diphtheria or yel-low fever, an adequate food supply made an enormous differ-ence; by cutting infant mortality to a fraction of the Europeon rate, adequate nutrition explains most of the spectacular growth of the colonial American population.[7]

Third, and closely related to rapid population growth and natural prosperity, was a very high rate of immigration after 1700. Not only did thousands of immigrants, attracted by American land and prosperity, increase the population, but they made it much more diverse. To the relatively homogeneous English population of the seventeenth century were added about 200,000 Scotch-Irish and almost 100,000 Germans in the four decades after 1715, while as many as a quarter of a million black Africans were forced to migrate to the Continental colonies between 1700 and 1775. By 1760, British North America was a very different society from what it had been at the turn of the century. Blacks, who had done so much to solve the chronic labor shortage, caused a growing fear of bloody insurrection, especially after about 1740, when New York City and South Carolina had each felt the terror of slave uprisings. The Scotch-Irish, hardly distinguishable from other English-speaking people today, were widely regarded in the eighteenth century as dirty, lazy, disorderly, and generally undesirable. And Germans, more orderly and diligent, were disliked for being non-English-speaking, remaining clannish, and practicing some of the more bizarre forms of Protestantism.[8] Immigration, as well as increasing and diversifying the population, was a primary factor in spreading people over the land; if population increased tenfold from 1700 to 1775, a rough guess is that the area under settlement increased fivefold in the same period.

Fourth was an emergent social elite. Prosperity naturally gave a minority of early settlers the chance to acquire wealth and status, so by 1760 there was a clearly recognizable group of families in every colony who, in effect, ruled. This was as true of New England as of the middle and southern colonies. But the position of this colonial elite was precarious, for several reasons. It ruled only by consent; the right to vote was widespread in the America of 1760, so most voters simply "deferred" to their social and economic superiors. Too, it depended on British government *letting* it exercise power, in the elective provincial assemblies and in local government. And, finally, it was threatened by the rapid growth, the diversification, and the dispersion of population; the traditional face-to-face methods by which the elite had governed earlier in the century simply ceased to be effective when people became too numerous, too distant, and too different as they were by 1760.[9]

Fifth is a negative characteristic that may be labeled "institutional weakness." Underscoring the increasing problems of controlling this exploding society and the precarious position of its governing elite was the lack of European-type structures for the maintenance of order. The elite itself was simply the wealthier and better educated people, not in any sense a legally privileged aristocracy. The colonial militia was a universal military obligation, but not a standing army—there was no specialized armed force to police the colonies. The churches, even where they were legally established (like Anglicanism in the South and Congregationalism in New England), were themselves unable to impose their will on people: the Anglicans looked much like Congregationalists in practice, and the Congregationalists were split by the great mid-century revival. All colonial churches by 1760 were in considerable disarray. There was no governmental bureaucracy. Even slavery, presumably a strong institution, was looser in practice than in law; the tightening of slavery came *after* the Revolution. In other words, American society was much freer than contemporary European societies. But to many it looked not so much free, in any positive sense, as dangerously anarchic. And there was ample evidence for fear of anarchy; there were outbreaks of violence after mid-century from present-day Vermont to the back-country Carolinas, making civil war seem as likely as a war for independence.[10]

Sixth and last, late colonial American society had a special quality that may be called "provincialism." It was a basic attitude, toward themselves and the outside world, that set

Americans off from European societies. Although filled with contradiction, this attitude is characteristic of people who are weak and dependent, yet also energetic and troubled by the internal effects of dynamic growth. Simply defined, "provincialism" meant a love-hate relationship with Britain and with European civilization generally. Americans, especially the colonial elite, admired Britain and Europe, taking them as models for their own lives and seeing them as standards against which to measure a more primitive America. But Americans also feared and resented European strength and superiority. Americans felt morally superior to Europe and never tired of saying so; but they also knew that America was inferior. Nothing better illustrates American "provincialism," with love increasing at least as rapidly as hate during the early eighteenth century, than George Washington's vain efforts to get a regular commission in the British army.[11]

These, then, were the peculiar and defining characteristics of colonial American society on the eve of the Revolution: (1) rapid population growth, (2) basic prosperity, (3) increasing diversity and dispersion, (4) an emergent social elite in a precarious postion, (5) institutional weakness, and (6) provincialism. The question is how these characteristic features of late colonial American society impinged on the waging and outcome of the Revolutionary War. What impact did the society have on the war?

At the outset—from the crisis of 1774 caused by the Boston Tea Party, through the outbreak of fighting in April, 1775, to the end of 1775, when the British decided to evacuate Boston—it was the sheer size, prosperity and energy of American society that shaped the war. Moreover, new British policies after 1763 had directly threatened the economic and political position of the American elite, and that elite—itself heavily dependent on popular support—had skillfully mobilized public opinion behind it and against British authority. In New England towns, in seaboard cities where most people were dependent on the merchants, in the southern colonies where a single crop united the interest of all white men, and in the Scotch-Irish settlements of New Hampshire, western Pennsylvania, and the Carolina back-country (where hostility to Britain came naturally), the elite had mobilized whole communities, first to offer a wall of unified resistance and then to fight a war. Towns, not individuals, decided to fight, and almost every male over sixteen headed for Boston.[12] The lack of any specialized military organization meant that virtually everyone went to war. And "everyone" meant a great many; within days after Lexington and Concord, 20,000 armed Americans had penned the British Army inside Boston. This was possible in 1775, when the population of New England was over 600,000; it would have been impossible in 1700, with less than 100,000 in the same area. Numbers as much as anything were the backbone of American strategy in the beginning.[13]

Considering the problems Britain had in operating at the end of a 3000-mile-long line of communications, as well as the sheer number of Americans, mobilized and led by the colonial elite, one might see in this situation a surefire social formula for waging and winning a revolutionary war. But two other social factors soon began to create a new strategic picture.

First, the "provincialism" of American leaders, especially Washington, led American strategy away from reliance on popular military forces—on militia—and toward the organization of something like a regular army. From the outset, Washington said that the militia was worse than useless, and that the creation of a European-style, long-service, tightly disciplined force was essential.[14] Maybe so; historians still argue the question. But one shrewd, experienced British officer thought American rebels would have been *less* dangerous if they had had a regular army; and it was ex-British officers in American service (Lee, Gates, and Montgomery) who seemed to have the best appreciation of what popular forces might accomplish in an unconventional war.[15] Washington and other native American leaders stressed a regular army, I suspect, because they felt a need to be seen as cultivated, honorable, respectable men, not savages leading other savages in a howling wilderness. So a Continental army was formed with enlistments for three years or the duration, harsh discipline, and Prussian drill as modified by Steuben. It was never a very good army by European standards, it never won a battle in open field, and it was never very large because most Americans simply would not join that kind of un-American institution. In this respect, Lee's observation that Americans were not Russians (who in 1776 could be—and were—marched off to serve in the czarina's army whether they liked it or not) takes on a new meaning. But the Continental army did keep the British army pinned down and concentrated, leaving most of the country free to be contested between Americans; it did give the Revolution a kind of respectability that was politically valuable; and it created a chance for men, as officers, to achieve a reputation on a national scale. Out of the Continental army officer corps would come much of the cadre of what would a decade later be the Federalist party.[16]

The second thing that happened to the original American strategy was that the popular enthusiasm of 1775 began to give out rapidly in 1776 and became hardly visible by 1777. The internal divisions and conflicts of late colonial America re-emerged to weaken the war effort. Everyone was suspicious of New England; domestic instability kept both New York and Pennsylvania from mobilizing anything near their full potential; and southern states, fearful of slave insurrection, had trouble recruiting men to fight in the North. The lack of any effective institutional mechanism to mobilize manpower for war, once local and popular pressure had begun to weaken, forced the Revolutionaries to fall back on other means—mainly economic incentive.

Though revolutionary America had what looks like a military draft system, operating through the militia, in fact, down at the grass roots, men were almost never drafted; instead, the town or the militia unit, faced with the need to fill a quota, found some way to hire men to do it.[17] The men hired were in general those most in need of money, that is, at the economic bottom of society, men like the poor Scotch-Irish deserters from the Continental army who made up the Royal Volunteers of Ireland. The process over a period of years was one of economic differentiation between those who served actively for long periods in war and those who did not. Thus, prewar social differences were reflected in the way the war was fought, and in turn the war sharpened those social differences.[18] This method of raising an army had several important effects: it further weakened the role of higher kinds of motivation in waging the Revolutionary War; unlike the two world wars, most men were not serving because it was their unavoidable duty to do so imposed on (almost) all alike, but because they were the ones least able to resist a crass economic appeal. It contributed significantly to the bankruptcy of the war effort so evident by 1778. The financial demands of a centralized army recruited in this way were simply too great for the fiscal system to handle; it was *not* a problem of war being too much for available resources.[19] And, finally, weak personal motivation and governmental bankruptcy combined to produce the real crises of the latter part of the war: the mutinies, the high rates of desertion, the defection of Arnold and others, and virtual collapse of the war effort from central control back onto state and local levels.

All in all, it was not a pretty picture, and it was not militarily very effective; battles were lost, and fear grew of the collapse of the Revolution itself. The method of waging war seemed a perversion of revolutionary ideals.

To sum up: the sheer size and wealth of late colonial America, plus the ability of its leadership group to mobilize the society, made initial resistance possible. But the "provincialism" of most leaders, plus the lack of strong institutions and the prewar weaknesses and internal social conflicts, led to a serious degeneration in the quality and strength of the war effort. This begins to sound as if the Americans could not possibly have won the war; and yet they did. To understand why they did, we must once again cross to the other side of the hill and consider the effect of social factors on British strategy.

Throughout the war, the nature of American society caused British leaders to misread their strategic problem, misread it so badly that it became a major factor in the way the war turned out. In the beginning, British leaders saw clearly enough certain characteristic features of American society, but they drew the wrong conclusions. What they saw especially was the colonial elite, which made America resemble England with its aristocracy and gentry. They also saw the prosperity; from this, as well as from their experience during the colonial wars, they concluded that the American population was "soft," like the more prosperous farmers and artisans of England and Europe, little inclined to active military service. In other words, they saw that the American masses were not Russian peasants. From this one-sided social analysis the British concluded that it ought to be possible to neutralize the leaders of rebellion, causing the enthusiasm of the people to subside quickly. This kind of thinking lay behind the attempts at Boston in 1775 and behind the conventional warfare waged in 1776 and 1777. The British badly underestimated the degree to which broad-based public opinion sustained the initial rebellion, more or less independently of leaders who had mobilized it, making Americans better fighters than they had been in colonial wars. The British failed to think through the way in which their military strategy could be *politically* effective; they simply assumed armed force could "work" in America as it did in Europe or in Ireland.

In the latter stage of the war, British leaders overcorrected early errors; they tended to see and emphasize other characteristic features of American society and to build a new strategy on these. What they saw and stressed were institutional weakness, internal conflicts, and "provincialism" (which often looked to them like pro-British feeling). The British by 1778 tried to exploit these features to create a Loyalist base on which to build a pacified America, and their effort was informed by reports of extensive loyalism (that is, dislike of, or resistance to, revolutionary leaders) everywhere. Building such a base was what Rawdon and his commanders were doing in the South in 1780; Rawdon's interest in the political situation around the Waxhaws was typical of this new strategy.[20]

It is more difficult to say what was wrong (or went wrong) with the new British strategy based on this analysis of American society. But what happened is that instead of restoring law and order, Britain fomented a civil war—not only a civil war, but a war their side (British and Loyalist) seemed never able to win. Perhaps the main reason they could not win was that it was too late—too many Americans were already disillusioned by the previous lack of British success. But they also could not win because those Americans who *would* fight for them were bitterly angry people, bent on vengeance, not on restoration of law and order. Moreover, these Loyalist allies were often minorities who turned to the British side, not out of principle, but because they were socially and numerically weaker. As soon as British military support was withdrawn, the Loyalists were usually overwhelmed by an armed majority.[21] For example, Rawdon failed to pacify the Scotch-Irish in the Waxhaws district at least in part because of British *success* in arming and organizing some neighboring areas, settled by Germans—a back-country minority intensely disliked by the Scotch-Irish.[22] British arming of the Cherokee Indians, and British calls for black slaves to turn against their masters, had the same kind of ultimately counterproductive effects. In other words, British leaders and army may have stepped into the

middle of a great issue in American history: Tocqueville's
"tyranny of the majority." Nothing did more in the later
stages of the war to keep the Revolution alive than the British
effort to arm and activate militarily these "loyalist" minorities.

To reach some sensible overall conclusions about how
American society shaped the Revolutionary War, something
must be said of French intervention. Without a French army
and navy, and without France turning a colonial war into a
global war for Britain, the Revolution could not possibly have
ended *when* it did and in the *way* that it did. In the long run,
politically speaking, French intervention may have made the
difference between American success and American failure.
But it did not make the difference between Britain's winning
and losing; American society itself almost guaranteed the military outcome and powerfully affected the political outcome.
The size of the society, combined with an elite running scared
from American public opinion as well as from British interference, explains massive initial resistance; Britain functioned
beautifully as a scapegoat against which to focus otherwise
centrifugal social energies. Lee saw it: if Americans fought, it
could be only because they wanted to fight—they were not
Russian peasants. The "degeneration" of the American war
effort from 1776 onward—a predictable process if the social
situation is understood—encouraged the British to exploit the
internal weaknesses of American society. After fatally underestimating the importance of public opinion in 1774-75, the
British went to the opposite extreme, thereby providing the
motivation for continued American resistance when the initial
enthusiasm seemed to have burned out. Rawdon failed to see
that the positive persuasion of one Scotch-Irishman by another
had become much less important than the negative effect of
Indians, blacks, and some "Dutchmen" (that is, Germans)
fighting for the king. And finally, the "degeneration" of the
American war effort produced a new realism, almost a cyni-

cism, about human nature that is one key to American political survival after 1783: the harsh realities of a protracted war,
more than anything else, explain the difference between the
euphoria at Philadelphia in 1776, when Congress declared independence, and the hard-headedness of many of the same
men, when eleven years later, in the same city, they hammered out a federal constitution.[23] It is at just this point that
Upstairs at the British Museum—the ideals and ideas of the
Revolution, the constructive achievement of the Founding Fathers—comes Downstairs and there confronts the grim but instructive experience of a long, dirty war.

CHAPTER SIX

American Strategy:
Charles Lee and the Radical Alternative

Before George Billias asked me to contribute to a book on George Washington's generals, I had found the causes of the American Revolution a more interesting subject than the war itself, which seemed worked to death by generations of military historians, who had painstakingly refought every battle from Bunker Hill to Blue Licks. Ignorance, as usual, was the real reason for my apathetic attitude, and the challenge of writing an essay on Lee gave me a chance to educate myself in the war. Almost all the surviving Lee Papers were published by the New-York Historical Society late in the last century in four volumes, so research was less arduous than it often is. No doubt writing a short book, with Peter Paret, on modern guerrilla warfare, a few years before had sensitized me to certain things in Lee's letters, but I began with no intention of finding in this notoriously wild character some Anglo-American precursor of Mao Tse-tung. In fact, I had no idea what I would find. His radicalism, both political and military, fairly leaped out of the four volumes. In revising the essay, I went back to see whether the essay might have exaggerated either his radicalism or its coherence; I concluded it did not, and the essay here offered is only a slightly revised version of the original, published in George Washington's Generals *(New York, 1964).*

The reputation of Charles Lee has long suffered by comparison with that of George Washington. Lee is traditionally remembered as a troublemaker—one who confounded Washington by disobeying orders, intriguing for the position of commander in chief, and calling for a court-martial with the hope of casting his superior into oblivion. Lee may have even betrayed the Revolution itself because of his malice toward Washington. His conduct has been debated so long as a political, not a military, question that Lee's modern biographer has subtitled his book *Traitor or Patriot?* [1] The result has been to judge rather than to understand an extraordinary human being.

To understand Lee the insights of psychology are as useful as the skills of the historian. Certainly he needed some sort of psychiatric help, had such a thing been available in eighteenth-century Anglo-America. Born as the youngest child of a prominent family near Chester, England, he grew up in a home environment created by the early deaths of five out of seven children. The only other survivor was his elder sister Sidney. Disliked by his mother, he lavished much of his affection on Sidney, who like himself never married. He grew to be a tall, skinny, ugly young man, remarkable for his slovenly personal habits and coarse speech. His sex life seems to have been of the transient kind, and in those instances where he became seriously interested in some woman he seems to have been rebuffed. There were hints, but no more than that, of homosexuality.[2] Aside from his sister, the only serious rivals for his affection were his dogs. It may be that Lee's love for dumb animals was the only kind of uncomplicated relationship of which this most complex personality was capable.

If Charles Lee conversed as he wrote, then the mid-twentieth-century label for him would be "compulsive talker." It appears that Lee would say almost anything. He was equally unrestrained in his letters. Rarely did he include a request that his views be kept confidential; more often than not, he suggested his letters be printed. His published attacks on Washington after the court-martial caused even Lee's remaining friends to turn away in disgust. When Lee turned sour, and the frenetic energy that had helped sustain the American cause in 1776 was turned against the commander in chief two years later, then another modern label is suggested: the "true believer," the fanatic whose very strength lies in his lack of balance, judgment, and self-restraint.[3]

Washington, with all the understatement of a Virginia gentleman, called Lee "fickle" long before he knew the worst about him. Washington's biographer, Douglas Southall Freeman, another Virginia gentleman who understood perfectly the vocabulary of his subject, hated Charles Lee with a passion that he had some difficulty in controlling.[4] At best, Freeman ceased to take Lee seriously, treating him as a two-dimensional, unbalanced man. Many historians, led on perhaps by Lee's own admission of "the distemper of my mind," have been willing to do likewise.[5]

Members of the Continental Congress took Lee with utter seriousness, however, when the time came to organize an American army in June 1775. For a man of forty-three, and a citizen of an empire at peace for more than a decade, he had an impressive military record. At the age of fourteen he had received a commission in his father's regiment. While still in his early twenties, he served as lieutenant in one of two British regiments sent to America from Ireland in early 1755 under the command of Major General Edward Braddock. Scanty evidence suggests that Lee first met Washington that spring on the disastrous expedition against Fort Duquesne, when Lee's regiment was shot to pieces and Braddock killed in an ambush by French-led Indians.[6]

Lee's regiment, the 44th Foot, moved northward into New York as Britain's war with France expanded in North America. Vigorous recruiting, by Lee and others, brought the 44th back to strength, so that it soon was composed primarily of native

Americans. The regiment was in the Albany area during 1756, where Lee had time to study Iroquois culture, acquiring an Indian consort and a Mohawk name—"Boiling Water"—in the process. In 1757, he went on the abortive expedition against Louisbourg, but service the next summer was more rugged. By then a captain and company commander, Lee had two ribs smashed by a musket ball before the French earthworks around Ticonderoga. He was several months recovering from his wounds, but spent some of his convalescence criticizing his superior for the conduct of a campaign that ranks with Braddock's march for misfortune and bloodshed.

The last two campaigns in which Lee participated brought about the fall of Canada. He was at the siege of Niagara, went on a hazardous mission from Niagara to Fort Pitt, and then accompanied the main attack in 1760 down the St. Lawrence which ended with the taking of Montreal. With the capture of Montreal, fighting came to an end on the American mainland.

Lee got leave to go to England, rather than vegetate with his messmates in the American wilderness, and soon was promoted to major in a newly raised regiment. When Spain jumped into the war in early 1762, the British response was an expedition to the Iberian peninsula. Lee served there under Brigadier General John Burgoyne, and each won his brightest victory when Burgoyne ordered and Lee led a daring and successful raid upon a Spanish encampment.

Peace came to Britain in 1763, but by 1765 Lee was off to other wars. He went to Poland, where civil strife threatened, carrying letters of introduction to Stanislas Poniatowski—king of Poland, onetime lover of Catherine the Great, and reputedly one of the most enlightened and liberal minds of his age. Though Lee became royal aide-de-camp, he saw no action and, after a visit to Constantinople, returned to England. In 1769, when Stanislas lost control of his kingdom as the result of a revolt, and Russian armies began moving into Poland to give him "support," Lee returned to Warsaw. Commissioned a Polish major general without command, he joined the huge Russian army in Moldavia, and watched it grapple with an even larger Turkish army. Then, sick and disgusted, he went slowly home to England by way of Hungarian spas and Italian beaches. He had seen in his travels through Poland what civil war could be: rebel bands so active that "it is impossible to stir ten yards without an escort of Russians," and vicious fighting methods "about as gentle as ours was in America with the Shawenese and Dellawars." [7]

During the years after 1755, while Washington was patrolling a comparatively quiet Virginia frontier and worrying about the price of tobacco, Lee had been exposed to a variety of military experiences. More important, his experience had profoundly affected him, because he was that rarity in any age—the soldier who is also an intellectual. He had attended good schools, knew classical and modern languages and literature, and was especially fond of Shakespeare. But above all, he had studied military theory and tactics. John Adams, who came to know Lee "very thoroughly," modestly admitted that Lee was the only American officer who had read more than he had on the history and art of war.

If the active service which guided his military study was deficient in any respect, it was in its comparative lack of experience with the "conventional" warfare epitomized by Frederick the Great. Lee had seen the highly disciplined Prussian battalions move slowly through their intricate linear tactical formations, but no document records that he was especially impressed. On the contrary, he expressed contempt for "Hyde Park tactics" and recollected that British regulars became effective in the French and Indian War only after they had forgotten everything they had learned on the parade ground at home. His less studious and stay-at-home contemporaries were apt to regard Prussian military methods as the proper models for warfare, but Lee knew better. Between his books, travels, and combat experience in irregular warfare, he had become something of a military radical, prone to doubt the accepted practices of his day.[8]

His radicalism was not solely the product of experience and study, nor was it confined to military affairs. By temperament he was disposed to attack or question the assumptions and conventions that most men lived by. Quiet loyalty did not stand high in his scale of values and three British commanders in America had felt the sting of Captain Lee's tongue and pen. The king of England himself was not immune. When George III granted Lee an audience in order to receive a letter from Stanislas of Poland, and began to apologize for his inability to offer Lee military preferment, the latter stopped him short by coolly observing: "Sir, I will never give your Majesty an opportunity of breaking your promise to me again."[9]

Some have used this broken promise to explain Lee's readiness to serve on the American side in the Revolution. But the truth lies deeper. Lee's personal and family connections were with the Whig politicians who opposed the policies of young King George in the 1760's. He was not satisfied, however, with the narrow ground of opposition taken by the Whig aristocrats. Instead, Lee repeatedly attacked the very principle of monarchy itself. He called Switzerland "those bless'd regions of manly Democracy" (when *democracy* was still a dirty word), and darkly alluded to making himself a good soldier "for purposes honest, but which I shall not mention."[10] It was not only a disgruntled half-pay officer who tendered his services to Congress in 1775, but a man whose whole life seemed preparation to fight against arbitrary, corrupt monarchical authority in the name of American freedom.

Members of Congress were impressed by Lee, for political as well as military reasons. Shrewd, learned men like John Adams would almost surely have detected a mere military adventurer. But Lee talked to them earnestly and knowledgeably about Rousseau and the rights of man; he shared their fondness for the now-forgotten Whiggish historian, Catharine Macaulay;

and he wrote a biting pamphlet explaining why American militiamen could fight more effectively than British regulars. Once Virginia had been placated with the appointment of Washington as commander in chief and Massachusetts was satisfied by the naming of Artemas Ward, some delegates from these two provinces proposed Lee as third-ranking general. When Congress hesitated, Washington himself requested Lee's appointment and the issue was settled in June 1775.[11]

From that time until the early fall of 1776, there can be no question that Lee lived up to the highest expectations of his supporters. To the Boston siege in the summer of 1775 he brought the organizational, tactical, and engineering skills that were so badly needed. There are glimpses in the records of Lee working tirelessly to improve the new American army—riding, observing, writing, correcting, and commending. James Warren, who was disturbed by Lee's lack of conventional manners, described Lee's activity for Sam Adams: "[Lee] came in just before dinner, drank some punch, said he wanted no dinner, took no notice of the company, mounted his horse, and went off again to the lines." [12]

Washington, dividing his army into three divisions, gave Lee the northernmost command, facing the Charlestown peninsula and British position on Bunker Hill. Lee's brigadiers were Nathanael Greene, of Rhode Island, and John Sullivan, of New Hampshire. In late July, he was exhorting Sullivan to use all his manpower to complete the fortifications, adding: "For God's sake finish and strengthen the abattis." By late August, when a British attack over the Charlestown neck against Lee's position seemed imminent, the Americans were able to move first. With 1200 men as a work party and twice as many to cover them, Sullivan moved forward and in a single night entrenched Ploughed Hill, within pointblank range of Bunker Hill. The British countered with a violent artillery and naval bombardment, but the work had been done too well; Lee's division stood fast.[13]

Confidence in Lee's abilities soon spread throughout the army. Greene wrote of Lee's "genius and learning," and William Thompson, colonel of riflemen, reported that he was "everyday more pleased with General Lee." [14] As winter came on and the likelihood of British naval raids on American ports grew, Washington ordered Lee to Rhode Island to lay out defensive positions, and later to New York on a similar mission. It is clear that Lee was a trouble shooter, a key man to be sent to points where danger threatened.

When it became apparent in February 1776 that the American expedition against Canada had failed, and that the British soon would withdraw from Boston to attack somewhere to the southward, American leaders were in a quandary as to what to do with Lee. "We want you at N. York—We want you at Cambridge—We want you in Virginia—" wrote John Adams. "But Canada seems of more Importance than any of those places," he continued, "and therefore you are sent there." [15] But the estimate of the situation changed almost before Lee received this letter, and Congress ordered him south instead. At Baltimore, Williamsburg, and Norfolk, Lee did all he could to strengthen defenses. Then in May came definite word that a British fleet was moving off the Carolinas, probably toward Charleston. Lee set out immediately for that city.

From Boston to Norfolk, Lee had contributed his military expertise at the crucial, formative stage of American resistance. The defenses that he had planned and begun at Newport and New York would later crumble before determined British attacks, but he had made those places far stronger than they had been before. Of greater importance, however, was his political activity between December 1775 and May 1776. During those trying months, people on the American seaboard outside Boston were wavering. There had been little fighting and many people, caught up in the shadowy state between war and peace and loyalty and treason, made small compromises with British officials. There seemed to be a tendency to listen more closely

to loyalist neighbors now that an abstract argument had become immediate and concrete, and to postpone any violent or
decisive action as long as possible. Lee moved through this
murky world of indecision like a flame. In Newport and New
York, he made suspected Tories swear an elaborate oath.[16] In
New York and Virginia, he disarmed them or moved them
from militarily sensitive areas. When fence-sitters living under
the guns of British ships used their vulnerability as an excuse
for inaction, Lee told them to move out where they could not
be threatened. He demanded that the Revolutionary authorities in New York, Maryland, and Virginia stop communicating
with their royal governors, and make a clean break.

Lee antagonized and upset civil officials wherever he went,
but he also shocked them out of their lethargy. He had been an
outspoken advocate of an immediate declaration of American
independence since October 1775. Lee supported the idea of
independence partly for diplomatic reasons, but primarily as a
means of crystallizing the popular will to fight before it was
eroded by confusion and delay. He saw clearly that a successful
revolution needed much more than an army in the field; it
required action at the grass-roots level—determination and efficiency among its supporters, and firm control over its enemies. The extralegal political bodies that had sprung up since
1774 were to provide the basis of this action, but their members
in general had been unwilling to usurp the essential function of
government by using coercion in a systematic way. Everywhere
he went, Lee pushed the new holders of power toward this last
and decisive step—the step that meant treason and no turning
back.[17]

He made an effort to be tactful in his direct dealings with
Revolutionary officials, but he let himself go in his reports to
Congress and to Washington. Wherever he saw vacillation, or
interest in conciliation with the British government, it sickened
him and he said so. When he could not obtain civilian cooperation in New York, he moved against Tories and suspects on his

own initiative and justified his conduct on the basis of military necessity. Congress, frightened by any encroachment of the military on civil authority, reprimanded him gently.[18]

What Washington thought about Lee and his behavior at this time is more interesting. When he sent Lee to New York, he had accurately predicted that Congress would not support Lee, but would be "duped" by the lukewarm New York government. Two months later, as if in response to Lee's rhetorical question, "Are we at war or are we not?", he wrote: "It is a great stake we are playing for, and sure we are of winning if the Cards are well managed. Inactivity in some, disaffection in others, and timidity, in many may hurt the Cause; nothing else can. . . ." And of Lee himself: "General Lee . . . is the first Officer in Military knowledge and experience we have in the whole Army. He is zealously attach'd to the Cause, honest and well meaning, but rather fickle and violent I fear in his temper. However as he possesses an uncommon share of good Sense and Spirit I congratulate my Countrymen upon his appointment. . . ."[19] Whatever his doubts, Washington was equally uncompromising in the face of fear and uncertainty.

When Lee arrived at Charleston in early June 1776, he found less trouble with Tories and more preparation for defense than he had elsewhere. But Charleston was not ready to resist the British force that had appeared on the horizon almost as Lee rode into town. Islands, rivers, marsh, shoal and deep water created a problem for the defender nearly as complex as the one Lee had met in fortifying New York.[20] There was a half-finished fort on Sullivan's Island, east of the city and commanding the entrance to the harbor. Both Lee and the British commanders saw its weaknesses: it could not protect the city from a determined attack, could be flanked by sea from the west and by land from the east, and might well be a trap for its garrison. Lee wanted to abandon the fort, but too much labor and prestige were invested in it. The hour was late and he finally agreed to complete the fort and to make it as defensible as possible, though he was still dubious about its strength. By erecting batteries, building bridges, digging trenches, and clearing fields of fire, he managed to keep pace with the slow-moving councils of the invaders.[21]

Lee angered more than one Charleston worthy with his "hasty and rough" manners, his demands for speed and obedience, and his insistence that white men do work usually reserved for Negro slaves. He made life miserable for Colonel William Moultrie, the easy-going commander of the fort, and alienated William Henry Drayton, future chief justice of South Carolina. When the British finally launched their attack on June 28, it came in the form of a naval assault on the fort itself. The enemy plan was both unimaginative and badly executed. In part, this was because Lee had managed to eliminate most other tactical choices. Moultrie's men drove off the attackers with heavy losses and suffered few casualties themselves.

In the report he submitted after the battle, Lee gave full credit to the Carolinians for the victory. He admitted he "had once thoughts of ordering the Commanding officer to spike his guns," but that the "cool courage" of the garrison, which "astonished and enraptured" him, had made it unnecessary. Moultrie, he concluded, "deserves the highest honors." [22] Lee, in fact, had been on the verge of replacing Moultrie when the attack began, and after its repulse continued to harass the colonel with directions and questions—"Is your Gate finish'd? How is the Bridge? I beg you will inform me. . . ." [23] After Lee's disgrace and death, Moultrie and Drayton's son each wrote memoirs of the Revolution, and one might expect to find in them two hostile witnesses. But John Drayton thought that "however disagreeable General Lee's manners were, . . . there is much reason for being thankful, that he was sent on to command. . . ." [24] Moultrie concurred: ". . . his coming among us was equal to a reinforcement of 1000 men . . . he taught us to think lightly of the enemy, and gave a spur to all our actions." [25]

Lee was at the peak of his career when Congress ordered him, on August 8, to return to New York. The war was going badly. Before Lee arrived, Washington suffered a sharp reverse in the Battle of Long Island in late August and was forced to evacuate his position. Many in the American army began comparing Washington's dark defeat with Lee's shining victory in Charleston. Washington's army was then driven from New York City and lower Manhattan. The army retreated to Harlem Heights, where it was exposed on both flanks to envelopment by British amphibious attack, and Congress was directing the commander in chief to hold the forts located near the ends of the present George Washington Bridge. More than one American officer looked to Lee's arrival as the only salvation of the army.

When he finally reached New York and saw the situation, Lee responded to it just as he had responded to every new turn in his life—sharply. He wrote to Horatio Gates that he disliked the position of the army and that Congress was a herd of stumbling cattle. Washington, said Lee, was wrong to let the legislators interfere with military strategy.[26]

As at Charleston, Lee seemed to appear just in the nick of time. In a well-executed amphibious operation, Howe landed most of his force on the north shore of Long Island Sound on October 12, threatening Washington's left flank and rear. Lee took command in that sector on the fourteenth. Tench Tilghman, one of Washington's aides, described the effect: "You ask if General Lee is in Health and our people feel bold? I answer both in the affirmative. His appearance among us has not contributed a little to the latter." [27] The troops in Lee's command fought a skillful delaying action, Howe cooperated by not pressing too hard, and Washington was able to extricate most of his army from Manhattan and march safely to White Plains.

As soon as Lee joined Washington at White Plains, the two generals reconnoitered the lines together. Lee saw serious flaws in the position and recommended a movement northward to the next ridgeline. Washington agreed, but immediately received a report that British troops were preparing for an attack. There was no time to deploy, and Washington could only alert his command and tell his generals, rather lamely, "do the best you can." [28] Their best was not good enough to hold a faulty position, and the American army was again driven back.

There was a lull in the fighting in early November until Howe suddenly turned southward to swoop down upon the American garrison at Fort Washington, which had been left as a pocket in the British rear on upper Manhattan. When Washington was sure that Howe had left White Plains, he crossed the Hudson with all the troops who came from states south of that river, leaving Lee with about 7500 New Yorkers and New Englanders on the east side. From that day—November 12—there was never again a meeting of the minds between the two men, and Lee's career began its downward run.

It may well be that their minds had never met at all. When they had first inspected the troops around Boston in June 1775, both had agreed that the officers as a group were woefully incompetent. But their reports showed a significant difference in evaluating the rank and file. Washington seemed to doubt whether Yankees could ever be good soldiers; ". . . an exceeding dirty and nasty people," he wrote to Lund Washington, and to Richard Henry Lee he described "an unaccountable kind of stupidity in the lower class of these people." [29] Nothing comparable is to be found in Lee's correspondence.

Lee explained in one letter that British officers were fatally underestimating Yankee soldiers as a result of the French and Indian War. In that conflict, "the regulars attributed to a difference of materials in their men what, in fact, ought to have been attributed solely to ignorance of method." [30] This letter to Edmund Burke was admittedly propaganda, but his reports to Benjamin Rush can be trusted. In one of them, he stated his belief in a close connection, not separation, between military and civil affairs: "Duke Ferdinand," who reportedly had cri-

ticized the American failure to assault the British garrison inside Boston, "is beyond dispute a very great soldier," wrote
Lee. "But if he is at the same time a Philosopher he wou'd not
dictate the same measure to different Troops—if the Army
before Boston had been Russians, Boston must have been ours
. . . but They are not Russians . . . the men (as I observ'd
before) are excellent materials. . . . Our new Army will I hope
and believe be good." [31] The military virtues of a free people
were different in kind from those of a peasant army, he ob-
served, and military organization and tactics had to take account of the differences. Among the American troops, Lee had
doubts only about the southern soldier because Virginians and
Carolinians seemed not quite ready for republicanism; but
even on this point he had soon changed his mind. [32]

Nearly every step taken by Lee as general in the American
army had shown a consciousness of the political aspects of the
war. He was obsessed with the idea of maintaining the morale
of his men and creating the proper attitude among the civilian
population. He even capitalized upon his own eccentric behavior in order to gain these ends. Whether recommending that a
pro-American Jesuit be sent to the army in Canada, or suggesting that unarmed Virginians be trained in the use of spears,
Lee constantly emphasized the psychological aspects of warfare. [33] Washington, on the other hand, was far more in tune
with the mid-eighteenth-century concept of warfare—an era in
which war and society were carefully separated and the soldier
fought primarily because he was more afraid to disobey than to
die. Washington and Lee looked at the same troops, but where
the Virginia planter saw only surliness and disobedience, the
British radical saw alertness and zeal.

If the war had not gone badly, perhaps the divergence of
their views never would have been of any consequence. During
the first year of the Revolution, when the two men played com-
plementary rather than clashing roles, their assignments were
nicely suited to their respective attitudes. But Lee's success and

rising reputation, coupled with Washington's record of failure from August to November, were bound to bring a change. Relations between the two had remained friendly, and Lee's barbs had been aimed only at Congressional interference with Washington. It is likely, however, that the incident on the lines at White Plains in late October had shaken Lee's confidence in his commander. By the end of November, it is certain that this confidence was destroyed.

On November 16, Lee expressed an opinion which he directed to Joseph Reed, Washington's adjutant general: "I cannot conceive what circumstances give to Fort Washington so great a degree of value and importance as to counterbalance the probability or almost certainty of losing 1400 of our best Troops." [34] Washington had decided not to evacuate Fort Washington when Nathanael Greene convinced him that the fort was defensible, and that the troops could be withdrawn across the river whenever necessary. Greene was soon proved wrong on both points. On the day that Lee wrote his letter to Reed, Howe assaulted the fort, capturing not 1400 but 3000 men, and inflicted one of the worst American defeats of the Revolution. Several years later, Washington confessed there had been "warfare in my mind and hesitation which ended in the loss of the Garrison." [35] Lee, when he heard the news, by all accounts went wild. Someone told Benjamin Rush that he cried out in anger and grief, ". . . had it been called Fort Lee, it would have been evacuated long ago." [36] His first letter to Rush after the loss was certainly indiscreet, though a close reading reveals that the principal target of his wrath was Congress, not Washington.

Before Lee could recover from this shock, he learned that the garrison of Fort Lee, on the New Jersey side, had almost been surprised by a similar attack. Washington at this time was known to be fleeing across the Hackensack River. On the heels of this news Lee received an incredible reply from Joseph Reed, dated November 21: "I do not mean to flatter," wrote

Washington's most trusted staff officer, "nor praise you at the Expence of any other, but I confess I do think that it is entirely owing to you that this Army & the Liberties of America so far as they are depending on it are not totally cut off. You have Decision, a Quality often wanting in Minds otherwise valuable. . . ." [37] There was more in the same vein, including the hint that Reed was speaking for the whole army. It is hardly surprising that Lee, upon reading these words, lost his equilibrium, never to regain it. From the time he received Reed's letter until his capture by the British on December 13, Lee was no longer the subordinate ready to give unquestioning obedience to his commander.

The events of Washington's retreat across New Jersey are usually treated as the prelude to the Trenton-Princeton campaign—the most brilliant stroke of his military career. In this context, Lee's failure to join him becomes just one more gloomy aspect of a situation so dismal that it provoked Thomas Paine to begin a pamphlet with the words, "These are the times that try men's souls." It is as difficult to quarrel with success as it is with some traditional ideas about George Washington. But the traditional view does less than justice to the actual course of events.

After the fall of the Hudson forts, Washington repeatedly urged Lee to move west of the river and join him, although the wording of these orders was more or less equivocal. The truth is that Lee did not want to move, and he used every possible excuse to delay. Some of the excuses seemed good ones: enlistments throughout the American army expired at the end of the year, but Lee's troops, unlike Washington's, would be marching farther from home rather than closer to it. Lee was afraid, with reason, that his army would simply fall apart. It was winter, many of the men were sick and some were literally naked, and there seemed little chance to find adequate shelter on the other side of the Hudson. Washington's retreat was along the main road between New York and Philadelphia, but

Lee would have to follow a longer and rougher route and perhaps expose his army to capture. Was Washington's order militarily sound? He justified it by expressing fear that Howe's objective was Philadelphia; Lee disagreed, and thought that Howe wanted no more than to clear East Jersey for use as winter quarters. We know now that Lee was right in his estimate, Washington wrong.[38] The excuses make an impressive list, but the fact remains that Lee disobeyed.

Lee had never before allowed obstacles to stand in his way when he thought some course of action was necessary. In fact, he took pleasure in overcoming such obstacles. In this case, the explanation is that he considered the orders given by Washington not only unnecessary but unwise. When Washington scuttled back across New Jersey, resistance in the state collapsed. British observers were delighted by the submissiveness of the inhabitants, Loyalists came out of hiding everywhere, and there were even reports of Tory militia units rounding up known "rebels." Washington himself knew why this had happened; he had written to Lee that the people of New Jersey "will expect the Continental Army to give what support they can, or failing in this, will cease to depend upon or support a force, from which no protection is giv'n to them." [39] But the need to maintain popular support by protecting people and property, and the need to keep a Continental army intact and united, had become conflicting demands on American strategy. It was obvious to Washington that, however painful the choice, the army was more important than the people if the war were to be won. To Lee, it was not at all obvious. He had a different conception of what to do with a revolutionary war on the brink of failure, and being no longer willing to trust Washington's judgment, he intended to be guided by that conception. Lee meant, as he so incautiously phrased it, to commit a "brave, virtuous kind of treason," and "to reconquer . . . the Jerseys." [40]

His plan for doing so, from all indications, was based on the use of militia forces. The militia was the last line of local defense. When militiamen did not fight to defend their locality or at least to make existence there dangerous for small bodies of the enemy, then the rest of the people were sure to submit, hoping for gentler treatment at the hands of the British and Germans in return for good behavior. But militiamen would not automatically spring to arms in time of danger. They were afraid. They lacked the confidence that comes with training and experience, and their companies and regiments were much too small to fight without help. Militiamen had to be encouraged, they had to be organized, and they had to be supported by Continental troops until there were enough active militia units to support one another. Lee would cooperate with Washington, but he would do so by creating zones of resistance that could deny General Howe the fruits of his recent victories. As the end of the year approached and one-year soldiers prepared to go home, Washington damned the militia and called on Congress for a professional army of long-service volunteers.[41] Lee was doing the opposite. Forget long-service enlistment, he wrote Benjamin Rush, and get soldiers on any terms you can. Draft every seventh man from the militia, Lee begged James Bowdoin of Massachusetts, and he praised a "people" who had "virtue enough to . . . oblige every citizen to serve in his turn as a soldier." [42]

Lee knew on November 21 that he was supposed to join Washington. From his camp north of White Plains, he could have had his whole command across the Hudson at Peekskill no later than November 26. He actually completed the crossing nine days later, on December 5. He was at Morristown, about fifty miles away from the crossing, on December 8—not an unreasonable rate of march for men "so destitute of shoes that the blood left on the rugged frozen ground, in many places, marked the route they had taken." [43] The delay east of the Hudson had been used to re-enlist soldiers, to clear upper Westchester of Tories and irregulars like Robert Rogers and his "Queen's Rangers," and to give Massachusetts and Connec-

ticut time to replace the departing Continentals with militia. As
Lee moved through New Jersey, he arrested Tories and called
out the militia. He established a base for the militia in the Morristown area. Some successful raids were conducted and the
New York militia under George Clinton started moving to join
him. Northern New Jersey began to present a considerably different picture from the one Washington had seen as he retreated south to the Delaware leaving the state to the mercy of
the British.

Three times—on December 3, 5, and 7—Washington sent
messengers to find Lee. There can be no doubt that the commander in chief was exasperated by the tardiness of his subordinate. But there was once good evidence, of which only traces
remain, that Washington was not sure himself of just what he
should do next. Unfortunately, the letters have disappeared
that could prove this indecision beyond a doubt. On December
8, Lee wrote a reply to accompany the messenger sent by
Washington on December 5. In his letter, Lee said he had
learned that Washington was "considerably reinforced," and he
referred to "your Excellency's idea of surprising [New] Brunswick." If such a letter was sent to Lee with the messenger on
December 5, it no longer exists. The implication that Washington had proposed or agreed to some plan of raids on the British flanks and rear is borne out by a second letter from Lee, on
December 8. The third messenger, sent by Washington the day
before, had just arrived, and Lee expressed surprise that his information about reinforcements had been wrong. Lee then
wrote: "Your last letters proposing a plan of surprises and
forced marches convinced me that there was no danger of your
being obliged to pass the Delaware; in consequence of which
proposals I have put myself in a position the most convenient
to cooperate with you by attacking their rear."

Lee had referred to "letters" from Washington. These may
have been the letters of December 2 and 3, which Washington
said he wrote but which no longer exist, or the letter of Decem-

ber 5, if there ever was one. Likewise the letter sent by the messenger on December 7 is not to be found. But the internal evidence is unmistakable; some or all of these missing letters must
have presented to Lee an image of a commander still unsure
and wavering between alternatives.[44]

None of this, of course, can excuse Lee. After he received
the peremptory order on December 8 to make haste, he remained near Morristown. In his last letter to Washington before his capture, he revealed himself in the final sentences:
"The Militia in this part of the Province seem sanguine. If they
could be assured of an army remaining amongst 'em, I believe
they would raise a considerable number." [45] Apparently he
tried to swing Washington around to his view, and failing, he
was ready to disobey. On December 12, he unwisely accepted
an invitation to stay at an inn at Baskingridge, several miles
from his camp. That night, he complained about Washington
to his old comrade, Horatio Gates: ". . . *entre nous,* a certain
great man is most damnably deficient—He has thrown me into
a situation where I have my choice of difficulties—if I stay in
this Province I risk myself and Army and if I do not stay the
Province is lost for ever." [46]

The next morning Lee was taken prisoner by a patrol of
British cavalry. Ironically, he was captured by members of a
unit he had once commanded in Portugal. For a time, there
was danger that he would be hanged as a British officer waging
war on the king. Instead, he was finally exchanged in April
1778. Had he been put to death, he probably would have gone
down in history as one of America's heroes.

But it was not to be. In the mid-nineteenth century, a document was found, unquestionably in Lee's handwriting, dated
March 29, 1777, in the family papers of one of the British commissioners then in New York. It called into question Lee's
whole career in the Revolution because it was a plan to end the
war. The document began by expressing concern for continued
bloodshed on both sides. It then proposed that British sea

power be used to support an army controlling a line from the
upper Chesapeake Bay to Narragansett Bay, or Alexandria-An-
napolis-Philadelphia-New York-Newport. Such a deployment
was supposed to rally the Tories, to "unhinge and dissolve the
whole system of defence," and to end the war two months after
its execution.

The discoverer of the plan believed it proved Lee's treason.
His chief biographer, however, is of the opinion that it was intended to trick Howe into his fruitless expedition to Philadelphia in 1777.[47] Curiously enough no reference to the plan has
ever been found in any other contemporary document. But
Lee's recommendations to Congress after his release were
based on a similar analysis of the strategic situation, so there is
little room to doubt its authenticity. The plan itself seemed
sound, though rather ambitious for the forces available to
Howe. It was characteristic of Lee to argue that encouragement
and protection of Loyalists were the true keys to pacifying
America. From the American point of view, the plan was fairly
humane, for it proposed no raids or harsh policies. One can
only guess why Lee wrote it: to save his neck, to mislead Howe,
to strike at Washington, perhaps simply to become a participant again instead of a bystander—it would have been perfectly
in character for Lee to do such a thing.

Upon his release, Lee had another plan ready, this one for
Washington and Congress. In it, he proposed a reformation of
army organization and tactics, and analyzed the strategic
choices for the campaign of 1778. His discussion of tactics and
organization showed that his ideas had not changed. He
stressed the value of simplicity and the need for American warfare to fit the American genius. "If the Americans are servilely
kept to the European Plan," he wrote, "they will make an Awk-
ward Figure, be laugh'd at as a bad Army by their Enemy, and
defeated in every Rencontre which depends on Manoeuvres."
The exact meaning of these ideas became clearer when he discussed strategy. He believed that it was madness to think of

fighting British regulars on their own terms; to do so would be to forsake the natural advantages of the American position. The idea "that a Decisive Action in fair Ground may be risqued is talking Nonsense." Instead, "a plan of Defense, harassing and impeding can alone Succeed." If necessary, the Americans could base their operations on the rough country west of the Susquehanna, where British regulars would not dare penetrate. In short, Lee had driven his earlier thinking toward its logical conclusion, and was proposing a war waged along guerrilla lines.[48]

Nothing could have been further from Washington's mind. Throughout the winter and spring at Valley Forge, he and Steuben had planned and trained the army according to the "European Plan," as Lee had put it. Steuben has often been quoted on the difference between Europeans and Americans as soldiers, but if he learned to explain to Americans why they were being trained, it was only to shape them better to the conventional European form of tactics. It is likely, in fact, that Lee's plan was aimed directly at Steuben's program, for Lee had hardly arrived in the American camp when he succeeded in having Steuben's powers as inspector general curtailed.[49]

Lee, however, could arouse little interest in his own plan. Both in Congress and among the senior officers of the army, he had gained a following among those men who disliked Washington or doubted his ability. But their preference for Lee was a matter of personalities rather than military theories. If any of them fully understood Lee's military arguments, they probably were puzzled or dubious. Although they preferred Lee, they lacked his radical perceptions, and they must have been attracted more by the promise of an army composed at last of *real* soldiers, able to fight redcoats and Germans in the open field. During his year in New York, the war seemed to have moved beyond Charles Lee.

Washington received Lee warmly, but may not have been altogether happy to have him back. By this time Washington had

learned of the disloyal letters exchanged by Lee and Joseph
Reed. Because of illness and a desire to visit Congress, Lee did
not join the army until May 20. Sir Henry Clinton, who had
succeeded Howe, sat in Philadelphia with the bulk of the British forces. The crucial questions for Washington were: when
and where would Clinton move, and what should the American
army do once the British began to march? Lee had been back
on duty less than a month when, on June 18, Clinton evacuated
Philadelphia, crossed the Delaware, and began marching across
New Jersey toward New York City. Within a few hours, the
American vanguard under Lee's command had begun to move
from Valley Forge on a parallel course.

The events of the next ten days were complicated and remain controversial.[50] Washington twice called a council of war,
on June 17 and 24, both of which revealed that he and his generals were torn between two desires: one was to fight; the
other, not to get hurt. Most wanted some "partial attack," but
all agreed that a "general action" was to be avoided. The key
issue was whether a "partial attack" would necessarily entail a
"general action." [51]

Lee advised caution, and, for the record, most of the council
went along with him. But Wayne, Lafayette, Greene, Knox,
and certainly the young aide, Alexander Hamilton, wanted to
strike a blow before Clinton reached New York. Hamilton described the council of war at Hopewell, New Jersey, on the
twenty-fourth, as doing "honor to the most honorab[le] body of
mid-wives and to them only." [52] No one was completely happy
with the compromise that was reached. When Washington decided to detach 1500 men from his 10,000 to harass the British
flank and rear, the detachment seemed either too large or too
small.

Lee, at first, declined the command of the force. But then
Washington decided to send another 1000 and to put Lafayette
in charge of all detached forces—over 4000 Continentals and

1000 New Jersey militia. At this point, Lee asserted his right as senior major general and asked for the command because it now included almost half the army. Washington agreed, and on June 27 Lee caught up with his troops around Englishtown.

Six miles east, at Freehold, lay the flank of the British column, stretching four miles along the road to Sandy Hook. The weather continued suffocatingly hot. Lee had argued against any action east of Princeton, down in the lowland where British cavalry superiority could prove decisive. Even Hamilton, so ardent for battle, suddenly feared that the main body, at Cranbury ten miles west of Englishtown, was not close enough to support the vanguard effectively. But now it was too late. On the twenty-seventh, Washington ordered Lee to attack the British rearguard over terrain that neither general had reconnoitered.

The approach to Freehold from Englishtown was along a road that ran on the high ground between two branches of swampy, westward-flowing Wemrock Brook.[53] In order to reach the British flank, Lee had to pass three ravines, created by the brook and its tributaries, that crossed the American axis of advance. The plan was to wait until the British column was on the march. But conflicting reports about British movements caused some confusion as Lee's command got under way from Englishtown early on the morning of the twenty-eighth. Soon after, the leading American units made contact with the British beyond the farthest, or eastern, ravine. Lee ordered Wayne to the front with reinforcements and told him to keep the enemy engaged. The action was on the left, with Freehold and the roads through it on the American right flank. The British were marching away toward the northeast. Lee meant to send most of his remaining troops behind and to the left of Wayne, thus cutting off and enveloping Clinton's rearguard, which Wayne had pinned down. But Clinton, to whom the attack was no surprise, anticipated the American maneuver. He held Wayne with minimum forces, halted the rearmost of the two British divisions, and sent it back down the road through Freehold against the American right.

The action took on a pinwheel pattern, with Clinton, able to use the road, outracing Lee, who had to cross rough, wooded and boggy ground. The American general, Charles Scott, who led the first element following Wayne, ran into Wayne in the woods instead of going behind and to Wayne's left. Neither Scott nor Wayne seemed to understand Lee's concept of the operation, and in the rapidly changing situation the system of mounted aides carrying messages merely added to the confusion. Lee was forced to order troops to Scott's right, toward Freehold, and placed Lafayette in charge of them. As Lafayette advanced and then fell back before the returning British division, Scott watched from across the 1000-yard gap that separated him from Lafayette. Afraid that he was going to be cut off when he saw the American troops moving rapidly back toward Freehold, Scott began moving his own men to the rear without orders and without informing Lee. Wayne soon followed.

Once the American half of the pinwheel had ceased to turn, a large part of Lee's command was in danger of being cut off. It might be trapped against one of the ravines and wiped out. With most of his force now marching instead of fighting, Lee had to move all of his units across the middle ravine and take up a defensible position. He gave the necessary orders, but in the noise and confusion he was unable to contact his scattered subordinates. At this point Washington arrived on the scene, and he and the hot and exhausted Lee exchanged some sharp words. The day ended better than the Americans deserved. They finally retreated to a strong position on the westernmost ravine and fought off repeated British attacks. Washington could claim victory, but it was a soldier's victory; none of the senior commanders—Scott, Wayne, Lafayette, Lee, or Washington—had performed with distinction. Clinton could smile at the American claim. From his point of view, the British had conducted a model rearguard action.[54]

Without doubt, Washington's sharp words precipitated Lee's ruin. Lee had reached the end of his patience: his advice on strategy had been rejected; his opinion in council was ignored; and while he was in the process of saving the army from a defeat he had foreseen, he was insulted. This was too much! Lee wrote to Washington, demanding an explanation of the treatment accorded him. He had not been dealt with fairly, he claimed. No doubt, he said, Washington's behavior had been "instigated by some of those dirty earwigs who will forever insinuate themselves near persons in high office." Washington replied that Lee would be given an opportunity to clear or hang himself. Lee fired back a letter referring to the "tinsel dignity" of Washington's office. In a third letter, Lee demanded a court-martial. His wish was soon granted.[55]

Lee was tried on three charges: disobedience of orders by not attacking; "making an unnecessary, disorderly, and shameful retreat"; and disrespect toward the commander in chief. No one who carefully reads the record of trial, examines the ground, and considers the British side of the battle would find Lee guilty of the first two charges. But no one who reads his letters to Washington will believe him innocent of the third. Under the circumstances an acquittal on the first two charges would have been a vote of no-confidence in Washington. Lee was convicted on all counts, with the wording of the second charge considerably softened. He was given the absurd sentence of suspension from command for one year.

The rest of the story is not pretty. Lee and his friends lobbied in Congress to disapprove the findings of the court-martial. A number of delegates must have squirmed, as did Gouverneur Morris when he wrote to Washington: "General Lee's Affair hangs by the Eye Lids. . . . Granting him guilty of all the Charges it is too light a Punishment. And if he is not guilty . . . there would be an Injustice in [delegates] not declaring

their Opinion." John Laurens expressed his fear to Alexander
Hamilton that "the *old faction,*" meaning Richard Henry Lee
and Sam Adams, might recruit a majority in Charles Lee's
favor. But Benjamin Rush was soon complaining that delegates
had begun to "talk of *state necessity* and of making justice yield
in some cases to policy." The sentence was confirmed, though
the vote was surprisingly close.[56]

Lee retired to his Virginia farm and vented his spleen for the
rest of his life. He was subsequently dismissed from the army
for a disrespectful letter to Congress and had to fight a duel
with John Laurens for his public attacks on Washington. To
Lee and his few remaining intimates, Alexander Hamilton was
"the son of a bitch" who had been out to ruin him and who had
perjured himself at the trial.[57]

Lee's few remaining years were pathetic. He lived in quarters
that were more like a barn than a house. There was no glass in
the windows, and the rooms were marked out by chalk lines on
the floor. In a pitiful letter to his sister, he recalled being asked
years ago when he would stop wandering, and reminded her of
his reply—". . . whenever I could find a Country where power
was in righteous hands." He felt further from his goal than
ever, and concluded, "I may be a pilgrim to all eternity." [58]
And so he was. Not long before his death in 1782, he was busily
drawing up Utopian plans for a military colony in the West.

The contribution of Charles Lee to the Revolution was sub-
stantial, though perhaps difficult to measure. His services
should not be minimized in the light of what finally happened
to his career. As the partisan Rush recalled, "He was useful in
the beginning of the war by inspiring our citizens with military
ideas and lessening in our soldiers their superstitious fear of
the valor and discipline of the British army." [59] At a glance, this
would seem to contradict the judgment of Alexander Graydon:
". . . if he committed a fault it was because he was too respect-
ful of the enemy; and that he was too scientific, too much of a
reasoner . . ." [60] But Graydon's statement contains the link be-

tween these two views of Lee: ". . . too much of a reasoner."
Intellectual that he was, Lee tried to see the Revolution as a
consistent whole, with every aspect in rational harmony with
every other. It was a fight by free men for their natural rights.
Neither the fighters nor the goals were suited to the military
techniques of despotism—the linear tactics, the rigid discipline,
the long enlistments, the strict separation of the army from
civic life that marked Frederick's Prussia. Lee envisioned a popular war of mass resistance, a war based on military service as
an obligation of citizenship. He sought a war that would use the
new light-infantry tactics already in vogue among the military
avant-garde of Europe, the same tactics the free men at Lexington and Concord had instinctively employed.[61] Such men
could not be successfully hammered into goose-stepping au-
tomatons and made to fire by platoons, but properly trained
and employed, they could not be defeated. Here lay the solution to any apparent contradiction in his opinion of American
soldiers as against British regulars.

Nathanael Greene's campaign in the South, and, on a far
larger scale, the early campaigns of the French Revolutionary
War, were to confirm Lee's prophetic insight.[62] But to Washington—a practical man not given to theorizing—this was all
madness. He never seriously considered resorting to a war of
guerrilla bands drawn from the militia. He would have recoiled
with horror from such an idea.[63] A strategy of that kind would
change the war for independence into a genuine civil war with
all its grisly attendants—ambush, reprisal, counter-reprisal. It
would tear the fabric of American life to pieces. It might even
undermine the political process, and throw power to a junta—
a committee of public safety with a Lee, not a Washington, as
its military member.

Historians have often noted that the American Revolution
was a "conservative" revolution, with surprising stability of institutions and continuity of leadership. But few have noticed
that it was also militarily conservative, and that its conventional

strategy served as a buffer for American society and politics. If Washington's strategy had failed, as it almost did in 1776, then the Revolution would have collapsed or turned sharply left-ward. Charles Lee was one who, by his alienation from the world to which other men were adjusted, could dimly see the full range of possibilities. He might then have had a chance to translate his vision into reality. Probably the true blessing of his unhappy career is that he never got the chance.

CHAPTER SEVEN

Hearts and Minds
in the American Revolution:
The Case of "Long Bill" Scott
and Peterborough, New Hampshire

The following essay grew out of teaching. Seeking some effective way to direct classroom discussion of an assigned text in the American history survey course, I stumbled across the passage in Peter Oliver's history of the American "rebellion," which led me to the anecdote about "Long Bill" Scott, which is the core of the essay. In addition, it led me to Jonathan Smith's history of Peterborough in the Revolution, an antiquarian work so carefully wrought that it invites systematic analysis. The question, on the motivation behind the armed struggle, which Oliver, Scott, Smith, and Peterborough helped me to answer, was suggested by an invitation from the University of Minnesota to take part in a Bicentennial conference, held in the spring of 1973, and the essay is a revised version of the paper read at that conference.

Armed force, and nothing else, decided the outcome of the American Revolution. Without armed force mobilized on a decisive scale, there would be today no subject for discussion. Deprived even of its name, the "Revolution" would shrink to a mere rebellion—an interesting episode, but like dozens of others in the modern history of Western societies. Crude, obvious, and unappealing as this truism may be, it is still true; without war to sustain it, the Declaration of Independence would be a forgotten, abortive manifesto. Writing about an earlier revolutionary war, Thomas Hobbes rammed home the point when he said that "covenants without swords are but words."

But the cynicism of Hobbes can too easily mask a second, equally important truism, perhaps best expressed a century later by David Hume. "As force is always on the side of the governed," Hume wrote, "the governors have nothing to support them but opinion." For all their peculiar aggressiveness, even human beings do not kill and risk death for no reason. Beneath the raw irrationality of violence lies motive—some psychic web spun from logic, belief, perception, and emotion that draws people to commit terrible acts and to hazard everything they possess. Perhaps Hume's view—that persuasion, not force itself, must ultimately govern, because no ruling minority can control a truly aroused majority—has lost some of its validity in our own time, when technology vastly multiplies the amount of force that a few people can wield, but it certainly held good for the eighteenth century, when even the best weapons were still relatively primitive and widely available. If Hobbes—like all his fellow cynics down through history—is right in believing that public opinion is a fairly fragile flower which can seldom survive the hot wind of violence, Hume reminds us that no one, not even a soldier, uses force without somehow being moved to do so.

John Adams put his finger on this matter of motivation when he said that the real American Revolution, the revolution that

estranged American hearts from old British loyalties and read-
ied American minds to use (and to withstand) massive violence,
was over before the war began. But Adams also opined that a
third of the American people supported the Revolutionary
cause, another third remained more or less loyal to Britain, and
that the rest were neutral or apathetic.[1] Clearly, Adams conceded that not all hearts and minds had been permanently affected in the same way. Many British observers thought that
the real American Revolutionaries were the religious Dissenters, Congregationalists and Presbyterians who had always
been secretly disloyal to the Crown because they rejected the
whole Anglican Establishment, whose head was the king; and
that these Revolutionaries persuaded poor Irishmen, who
poured into the American colonies in great numbers during
the middle third of the eighteenth century, to do most of the
dirty business of actual fighting. American Whigs, on the other
hand, generally assumed that all decent, sane people supported
the Revolution, and that those who did not could be cat-
egorized as timid, vicious, corrupt, or deluded. Each of these
opinions contains a measure of truth, but they seem to contradict one another, and they do not carry us very far toward understanding.

Like these stock opinions, we have two standard images of
the popular response to the Revolutionary War. One is of
whole towns springing to arms as Paul Revere carried his warning to them in the spring of 1775. The other is of a tiny, frozen, naked band of men at Valley Forge, all that are left when
everyone else went home in the winter of 1778. Which is the
true picture? Both, evidently. But that answer is of no use at all
when we ask whether the Revolution succeeded only by the
persistence of a very small group of people, the intervention of
France, and great good luck; or whether the Revolution
was—or became—unbeatable because the mass of the population simply would not give up the struggle, and the British
simply could not muster the force and the resolution to kill

them all or break their will or sit on all or even any large proportion of them. This problem posed by the motivation for violence breaks down into more specific questions: Who actually took up arms and why? How strong was the motivation to serve, and to keep serving in spite of defeat and other adversities? What was the intricate interplay and feedback between attitude and behavior, events and attitude? Did people get war weary and discouraged, or did they become adamant toward British efforts to coerce them? If we could answer these questions with confidence, not only would we know why the rebels won and the government lost, but we would also know important things about the American society that emerged from seven years of armed conflict. Differing answers to these questions lay at the root of what had divided Charles Lee and George Washington.

The essential difficulty in answering these questions lies less in the lack of evidence than in the nature of the subject. Violence, with all its ramifications, remains a great mystery for students of human life, while the deeper motivational sources of human behavior— particularly collective behavior under conditions of stress—are almost equally mysterious. When these two mysteries come together, as they do in wars and revolutions, then the historian faces a problem full of traps and snares for the unwary, a problem that challenges his ability to know *anything* about the past. A certain humility is obviously in order. If any of us are tempted not to be humble, we might recall how recently intelligent, well-informed American leaders spoke glibly about winning the "hearts and minds" of another few million people caught up by war and revolution. That, then, is the subject: the hearts and minds of Americans whose willingness to engage in violence, two centuries ago, fundamentally changed the course of history.

A suitably humble approach to these difficult questions lies at hand in a book written by Peter Oliver, who watched the Revolution explode in Boston. Oliver descended from some of the oldest families of Massachusetts Bay, he was a distinguished merchant and public official, and he became a bitter Tory. His book, *The Origin and Progress of the American Rebellion,* recently published in paperback, is a fascinatingly unsympathetic version of the Revolution, and in it Oliver makes an attempt to answer some of our questions. Using the device, more fully developed by S. L. A. Marshall during the Second World War, of the after-action interview, Oliver asked a wounded American lieutenant, who had been captured at Bunker Hill, how he had come to be a rebel. The American officer allegedly replied as follows:

> The case was this Sir! I lived in a Country Town; I was a Shoemaker, & got my Living by my Labor. When this Rebellion came on, I saw some of my Neighbors get into Commission, who were no better than myself. I was very ambitious, & did not like to see those Men above me. I was asked to enlist, as a private Soldier. My Ambition was too great for so low a Rank; I offered to enlist upon having a Lieutenants Commission; which was granted. I imagined my self now in a way of Promotion: if I was killed in Battle, there would an end of me, but if my Captain was killed, I should rise in Rank, & should still have a Chance to rise higher. These Sir! were the only Motives of my entering into the Service; for as to the Dispute between great Britain & the Colonies, I know nothing of it; neither am I capable of judging whether it is right or wrong.[2]

Those who have read U.S. Government publications of the 1960's will find this POW interrogation familiar; during the Vietnam War, the State and Defense Departments published many like it, and more than one Vietcong or North Vietnamese prisoner is said to have spoken in the accents of the wounded American lieutenant so long ago.

Now the lieutenant was not a figment of Oliver's embittered imagination. His name is given by Oliver as Scott, and American records show that Lieutenant William Scott, of Colonel Paul Sargent's regiment, was indeed wounded and captured at Bunker Hill.[3] Scott turns out, upon investigation, to have been an interesting character. Perhaps the first thing to be said about him is that nothing in the record of his life down to 1775 contradicts anything in Oliver's account of the interview. Scott came from Peterborough, New Hampshire, a town settled in the 1730's by Irish Presbyterians.[4] Scott's father had served in the famous Rogers' Rangers during the French and Indian War. At the news of the outbreak of fighting in 1775, a cousin who kept the store in Peterborough recruited a company of local men to fight the British. Apparently the cousin tried to enlist our William Scott—known to his neighbors as "Long Bill," thus distinguishing him from the cousin, "Short Bill." But "Long Bill"—our Bill—seems to have declined serving as a private, and insisted on being a lieutenant if cousin "Short Bill" was going to be a captain. "Short Bill" agreed. So far the stories as told by Oliver and as revealed in the New Hampshire records check perfectly. Nor is there any reason to think that "Long Bill" had a deeper understanding of the causes of the Revolution than appear in Oliver's version of the interview.

What Peter Oliver never knew was the subsequent life history of this battered yokel, whose view of the American rebellion seemed so pitifully naïve. When the British evacuated Boston, they took Scott and other American prisoners to Halifax, Nova Scotia. There, after more than a year in captivity, Scott somehow managed to escape, to find a boat, and to make his way back to the American army just in time for the fighting around New York City in 1776. Captured again in November, when Fort Washington and its garrison fell to a surprise British assault, Scott escaped almost immediately, this time by swimming the Hudson River at night—according to a newspaper account—with his sword tied around his neck and his watch pinned to his hat. He returned to New Hampshire during the winter of 1777 to recruit a company of his own; there, he enlisted his two eldest sons for three years or the duration of the war. Stationed in the Boston area, he marched against Burgoyne's invading army from Canada, and led a detachment that cut off the last retreat just before the surrender near Saratoga. Scott later took part in the fighting around Newport, Rhode Island. But when his light infantry company was ordered to Virginia under Lafayette in early 1781, to counter the raiding expedition led by Benedict Arnold, Scott's health broke down; long marches and hot weather would make the old Bunker Hill wounds ache, and he was permitted to resign from the army. After only a few months of recuperation, however, he seems to have grown restless, for we find him during the last year of the war serving as a volunteer on a navy frigate.

What would Scott have said if Oliver had been able to interview him again, after the war? We can only guess. Probably he would have told Oliver that his oldest son had died in the army, not gloriously, but of camp fever, after six years of service. Scott might have said that in 1777 he had sold his Peterborough farm in order to meet expenses, but that the note which he took in exchange turned into a scrap of paper when the dollar of 1777 became worth less than two cents by 1780. He might also have said that another farm, in Groton, Massachusetts, slipped away from him, along with a down payment that he had made on it, when his military pay depreciated rapidly to a fraction of its nominal value. He might not have been willing to admit that when his wife died he simply turned their younger children over to his surviving elder son, and then set off to beg a pension or a job from the government. Almost certainly he would not have told Oliver that when the son—himself sick, his corn crop killed by a late frost, and saddled with three little brothers and sisters—begged his father for help, our hero told him, should all else fail, to hand the children over to the selectmen of Peterborough—in short, to put them on welfare.

In 1792, "Long Bill" Scott once more made the newspapers: he rescued eight people from drowning when their small boat capsized in New York harbor. But heroism did not pay very well. At last, in 1794, Secretary of War Henry Knox made Scott deputy storekeeper at West Point; and a year later General Benjamin Lincoln took Scott with him to the Ohio country, where they were to negotiate with the Indians and survey the land opened up by Anthony Wayne's victory at Fallen Timbers. At last he had a respectable job, and even a small pension for his nine wounds; but Lincoln's group caught something called "lake fever" while surveying on the Black River, near Sandusky. Scott, ill himself, guided part of the group back to Fort Stanwix, New York, then returned for the others. It was his last heroic act. A few days after his second trip, he died, on September 16, 1796.

Anecdotes, even good ones like the touching saga of "Long Bill" Scott, do not make history. But neither can a subject like ours be treated in terms of what Jesse Lemisch has referred to as the lives of Great White Men—Washington, Adams, Jefferson, Hamilton, and the handful like them. Scott's life, in itself, may tell us little about how armed force and public opinion were mobilized in the Revolution; yet the story of his life leads us directly—and at the level of ordinary people—toward crucial features of the process.

Peterborough, New Hampshire, in 1775 had a population of 549.[5] Town, state, and federal records show that about 170 men were credited to Peterborough as performing some military service during the Revolution. In other words, almost every adult male, at one time or another, carried a gun in the war. But of these 170 participants, less than a third performed extensive service; that is, service ranging from over a year up to the whole eight years of the war. And only a fraction of these— less than two dozen—served as long as Bill Scott. In Scott we are not seeing a typical participant, but one of a small "hard core" of revolutionary fighters—the men who stayed in the army for more than a few months or a single campaign. As we look down the list of long-service soldiers from Peterborough, they seem indeed to be untypical people. A few, like Scott and his cousin "Short Bill" and James Taggart and Josiah Munroe, became officers or at least sergeants, and thereby acquired status and perhaps some personal satisfaction from their prolonged military service. But most of the hard core remained privates, and they were an unusually poor, obscure group of men, even by the rustic standards of Peterborough. Many—like John Alexander, Robert Cunningham, William Ducannon, Joseph Henderson, Richard Richardson, John Wallace, and Thomas Williamson—were recruited from outside the town, from among men who never really lived in Peterborough. Whether they lived *anywhere*—in the strict legal sense—is a question. Two men—Zaccheus Brooks and John Miller—are simply noted as "transients." At least two—James Hackley and Randall McAllister—were deserters from the British army. At least two others—Samuel Weir and Titus Wilson—were black men, Wilson dying as a prisoner of war. A few, like Michael Silk, simply appear, join the army, then vanish without a documentary trace. Many more reveal themselves as near the bottom of the socioeconomic ladder: Hackley, Benjamin Allds, Isaac Mitchell, Ebenezer Perkins, Amos Spofford, Jonathan Wheelock, and Charles White were legal paupers after the Revolution, Joseph Henderson was a landless day-laborer, Samuel Spear was jailed for debt, and John Miller was mentally deranged.

We can look at the whole Peterborough contingent in another way, in terms of those in it who were, or later became, prominent or at least solid citizens of the town. With a few exceptions, like "Short Bill" Scott and "Long Bill" 's son John, who survived frost-killed corn and a parcel of unwanted siblings to become a selectman and a leader of the town, these prominent men and solid citizens had served in the war for only short periods—a few months in 1775, a month or two in the Burgoyne emergency of 1777, maybe a month in Rhode Island or a month late in the war to bolster the key garrison of West Point. The pattern is clear, and it is a pattern that reappears wherever the surviving evidence has permitted a similar kind of inquiry. Lynn, Massachusetts; Berks County, Pennsylvania; Colonel Smallwood's recruits from Maryland in 1782; several regiments of the Massachusetts Line; a sampling of pension applicants from Virginia—all show that the hard core of Continental soldiers, the Bill Scotts who could not wangle commissions, the soldiers at Valley Forge, the men who shouldered the heaviest military burden, were something *less* than average colonial Americans.[6] As a group, they were poorer, more marginal, less well anchored in the society. Perhaps we should not be surprised; it is easy to imagine men like these actually being attracted by the relative affluence, comfort, security, prestige, and even the chance for satisfying human relationships offered by the Continental army. Revolutionary America may have been a middle-class society, happier and more prosperous than any other in its time, but it contained a large and growing number of fairly poor people, and many of them did much of the actual fighting and suffering between 1775 and 1783: A very old story.[7]

The large proportion of men, from Peterborough and other communities, who served only briefly might thus seem far less important to our subject than the disadvantaged minority who did such a large part of the heavy work of revolution. This militarily less active majority were of course the militiamen. One could compile a large volume of pithy observations, beginning with a few dozen from Washington himself, in which the military value of the militia was called into question. The nub of the critique was that these part-time soldiers were untrained, undisciplined, undependable, and very expensive, consuming pay, rations, clothing, and weapons at a great rate in return for short periods of active service. By the end of the war, the tendency of many Continental officers, like Colonel Alexander Hamilton, to disparage openly the military performance of the militia was exacerbating already strained relations between State and Continental authorities. And indeed there were a number of cases in which the failure of militia to arrive in time, to stand under fire, or to remain when they were needed, either contributed to American difficulties or prevented the exploitation of American success. But the Revolutionary role of the men from Peterborough and elsewhere who did *not* serve as did Bill Scott, but whose active military service was rather a sometime thing, is easily misunderstood and underestimated if we look at it only in terms of traditional military strategy and set-piece battles.

To understand the Revolutionary militia and its role, we must go back to the year before the outbreak of fighting at Lexington and Concord. Each colony, except Pennsylvania, had traditionally required every free white adult male, with a few minor occupational exceptions, to be inscribed in a militia unit, and to take part in training several times a year. These militia units seldom achieved any degree of military proficiency, nor were they expected to serve as actual fighting formations. Their real function might be described as a hybrid of draft board and modern reserve unit—a modicum of military training combined with a mechanism to find and enlist individuals when they were needed. But the colonial militia did not simply slide smoothly into the Revolution. Militia officers, even where they were elected, held royal commissions, and a significant number of them were not enthusiastic about rebellion. Purging and restructuring the militia was an important step toward revolution, one that deserves more attention than it has had.

When the news reached America that Parliament would take a very hard line in response to the Boston Tea Party, and in particular had passed a law that could destroy, economically and politically, the town of Boston, the reaction in the colonies was stronger and more nearly unanimous than at any time since the Stamp Act. No one could defend the Boston Port Act; it was an unprecedented, draconian law, the possible consequences of which seemed staggering. Radicals, like Samuel Adams, demanded an immediate and complete break in commercial relations with the rest of the Empire. Boycotts had worked effectively in the past, and they were an obvious response to the British hard line. More moderate leaders, however, dreaded a hasty confrontation that might quickly escalate beyond their control, and they used democratic theory to argue that nothing ought to be done without a full and proper consultation of the popular will.[8] Like the boycott, the consultative congress had a respectable pedigree, and the moderates won the argument. When Congress met in September 1774 there were general expectations in both Britain and America that it would cool and seek to compromise the situation.

Exactly what happened to disappoint those expectations is even now not wholly clear; our own sense that Congress was heading straight toward revolution and independence distorts a complex moment in history, when uncertainty about both ends and means deeply troubled the minds of most decision-makers. Congress had hardly convened when it heard that the British had bombarded Boston. For a few days men from different colonies, normally suspicious of one another, were swept together by a wave of common fear and apprehension. Though the report was quickly proved false, these hours of mutual panic seem to have altered the emotional economy of the Congress.[9] Soon afterward it passed without any serious dissent a resolution in favor of the long-advocated boycott, to be known as the Association. Local committees were to gather signatures for the Association, and were to take necessary steps to enforce its provisions. The Association was the vital link in transforming the colonial militia into a revolutionary organization.

For more than a year, a tenuous line of authority ran directly from the Continental Congress to the grass roots of American society. The traditional, intermediate levels of government, if they did not cooperate fully, were by-passed. Committees formed everywhere to enforce the Association, and sympathetic men volunteered to assist in its enforcement. In some places, like Peterborough, the same men who were enrolled in the militia became the strong right arm of the local committee; reluctant militia officers were ignored because, after all, not the militia as such but a voluntary association of militia members was taking the action. In other places, like parts of the Hudson valley and Long Island, reluctance was so widespread that men opposed to the Association actually tried to take over the committee system in order to kill it; when meetings were called to form the new armed organization of Associators, loyal militiamen packed the meetings and re-elected the old, royally commissioned lieutenants and captains.[10] But even where the Association encountered heavy opposition, it effectively dissolved the old military structure and created a new one based on consent, and whose chief purpose was to engineer consent, by force if necessary. The new Revolutionary militia might look very much like the old colonial militia, but it was, in its origins, less a draft board and a reserve training unit than a police force and an instrument of political surveillance. Although the boycott could be defended to moderate men as a constitutional, non-violent technique, its implementation had radical consequences. Adoption by Congress gave it a legitimacy and a unity that it could have gained in no other way. Ordinary men were forced to make public choices, and thus to identify themselves with one side or the other. Not until the Declaration of Independence clarified the hazy status of the traditional levels of government did the local committees, acting through the new militia, relinquish some of their truly revolutionary power.

It is difficult to overestimate the importance of what happened in 1775 to engage mass participation on the side of the Revolution. The new militia, which repeatedly denied that it was in rebellion and proclaimed its loyalty to the Crown, enforced a boycott intended to make Britain back down; Britain did not back down, but the attempt drew virtually everyone into the realm of politics. Enlistment, training, and occasional emergencies were the means whereby dissenters were identified, isolated, and dealt with. Where the new militia had trouble getting organized, there Revolutionary activists could see that forceful intervention from outside might be needed. Connecticut units moved into the New York City area; Virginia troops moved into the Delmarva peninsula; in Pennsylvania, men from Reading and Lancaster marched into Bucks County. Once established, the militia became the infrastructure of revolutionary government. It controlled its community, whether through indoctrination or intimidation; it provided on short notice large numbers of armed men for brief periods of emergency service; and it found and persuaded, drafted or bribed, the smaller number of men needed each year to keep the Continental army alive. After the first months of the war, popular enthusiasm and spontaneity could not have sustained the struggle; only a pervasive armed organization, in which almost everyone took some part, kept people constantly, year after year, at the hard task of revolution. While Scott and his sons, the indigent, the blacks, and the otherwise socially expendable men fought the British, James and Samuel Cunningham, Henry Ferguson, John Gray, William McNee, Benjamin Mitchell, Robert Morison, Alexander and William Robbe, Robert Swan, Robert Wilson, and four or five men named Smith—all militiamen, but whose combined active service hardly equalled that of "Long Bill" Scott alone—ran Peterborough, expelling a few Tories, scraping up enough recruits for the Continental army to meet the town's quota every spring, taking time out to help John Stark destroy the Germans at the battle of Bennington.

The mention of Tories brings us, briefly, to the last aspect of our subject about which more will be said in the next chapter. Peterborough had little trouble with Tories; the most sensational case occurred when the Presbyterian minister, the Rev. John Morrison, who had been having difficulties with his congregation, deserted his post as chaplain to the Peterborough troops and entered British lines at Boston in June 1775. But an informed estimate is that a half million Americans can be

counted as loyal to Britain.[11] Looking at the absence of serious
Loyalism in Peterborough, we might conclude that Scotch-Irish
Presbyterians almost never were Tories. That, however, would
be an error of fact, and we are impelled to seek further for an
explanation. What appears as we look at places like Peterborough, where Tories are hardly visible, and at other places
where Toryism was rampant, is a pattern—not so much an ethnic, religious, or ideological pattern, but a pattern of raw
power. Wherever the British and their allies were strong
enough to penetrate in force—along the seacoast, in the Hudson, Mohawk, and lower Delaware valleys, in Georgia, the
Carolinas, and the transappalachian West—there Toryism
flourished. But geographically less exposed areas, if population
density made self-defense feasible—most of New England, the
Pennsylvania hinterland, and piedmont Virginia—where the
enemy hardly appeared or not at all, there Tories either ran
away, kept quiet, even serving in the rebel armies, or occasionally took a brave but hopeless stand against Revolutionary committees and their gunmen.[12] After the war, of
course, men remembered their parts in the successful Revolution in ways that make it difficult for the historian to reconstruct accurately the relationship between what they thought
and what they did.

The view here presented of how armed force and public
opinion were mobilized may seem a bit cynical—a reversion to
Thomas Hobbes. True, it gives little weight to ideology, to perceptions and principles, to grievances and aspirations, to the
more admirable side of the emergent American character. Perhaps that is a weakness; perhaps I have failed to grasp what really drove Bill Scott. But what strikes me most forcibly in studying this part of the Revolution is how much in essential
agreement almost all Americans were in 1774, both in their
views of British measures and in their feelings about them.
What then is puzzling, and thus needs explaining, is why so
many of these people behaved in anomalous and in different

ways. Why did so many, who did not intend a civil war or political independence, get so inextricably involved in the organization and use of armed force? Why did relatively few do most of the actual fighting? Why was a dissenting fifth of the population so politically and militarily impotent, so little able to affect the outcome of the struggle? Answers to these questions cannot be found in the life of one obscure man, or in the history of one backwoods town. But microscopic study does emphasize certain features of the American Revolution: the political structuring of resistance to Britain, the play of social and economic factors in carrying on that resistance by armed force, and the brutally direct effects on behavior, if not on opinions, of military power.

CHAPTER EIGHT

Armed Loyalism:
The Case of the Lower Hudson Valley

An invitation from Professor Robert A. East, director of the Program for Loyalist Studies and Publications, to speak at a conference on Loyalism sponsored by the Sleepy Hollow Restoration was the origin of this essay. Perhaps in reaction to the "consensus" school of historical writing on the Revolution, so influential during the 1950's, which tends to treat the Revolution as a more or less unanimous act of the American people (which it most certainly was not), a number of historians have recently found in the study of Loyalists, those "losers" in the Revolution, a fresh approach to what it was that divided Americans from one another. But only a few historians have given any serious attention to the most extreme form of Toryism, those actually in arms for the king, and this essay is my own modest contribution to that neglected side of Loyalism in the American Revolution. A slightly different version of this essay appeared in The Loyalist Americans: A Focus on Greater New York, *edited by Robert East and Jacob Judd (Sleepy Hollow, 1975).*

The American Revolution was a civil war. In proportion to population, almost as many Americans were engaged in fighting other Americans during the Revolution as did so during the Civil War. But not until the twentieth century did historians, with a very few notable exceptions, find that fact interesting, and only in the last decade or so have historians begun to find it very interesting. We now think that at least a fifth of the white population—a half-million people—behaved in ways that enable us to identify them as Loyalist, and it is reasonable to wonder what such a large, actively dissenting minority means for our understanding of the nature of the Revolution.[1]

Certain specific questions keep coming to the surface as we ponder the significance of Loyalism. One concerns apparent British inability to tap effectively this large reservoir of political sentiment and military potential.[2] Could the British government and high command, given an earlier, clearer sense of the kind of war they were involved in, have used militant Loyalism to build a basis for ultimate pacification of a weary, bankrupt rebel movement? A second question, less frequently raised but always lurking beneath the surface of every comparative discussion of the American Revolution, concerns violence: the American Revolution somehow avoided the extremes of murderous behavior that so disfigured and poisoned other great revolutions. Or did it? Hannah Arendt has brilliantly contrasted the limited, almost benign, and therefore successful quality of the American Revolution, with the untidy, horrific failure of the French Revolution to achieve a just and stable society.[3] But Robert Palmer, in an undeveloped few paragraphs in his *Age of the Democratic Revolution,* suggests that, measured by the relative numbers of refugees from revolution, the American may have been as violently intolerant as the French; and in a short article Gordon Wood, drawing on the most recent studies of European mobs in the eighteenth century, also concludes that the alleged differences between Europe and America in the amount and quality of violence may be less important than the similarities.[4] With thousands of armed Loyalists in the field, the tentative thoughts of Palmer and Wood indeed seem plausible.

A third question grows directly out of the second: if Palmer and Wood are right, and the civil, internecine violence of the American Revolution was not so very different from what the histories of other civil wars and revolutions would lead us to expect, then how do we explain the relatively quick subsidence of the Tory issue after the war? Palmer suggests that, unlike France, the American counterrevolutionary refugees never returned, creating an illusion of tranquility and unity in the postwar Republic. But only a fraction of the half-million Loyalists was ever able or perhaps willing to emigrate, and my own impression is that more returned than Palmer thinks. Most Loyalists appear to have been reintegrated, speedily and painlessly, into American society, and Hannah Arendt's conclusion, if not her explanation, seems supported by that fact—if it is a fact.[5] There was no Red Terror of 1783, not even in Bergen and Westchester counties, or in Ninety-Six District of South Carolina, to match the Terrors, both Red and White, described for France so graphically by Richard Cobb.[6] In the preceding essay, microscopic analysis was applied to the difficult question of the "hearts and minds" of American Revolutionaries. Something similar will be done in this essay to these equally troublesome questions about Loyalism and its role in the military struggle.

In the latter half of 1776, British forces occupied Staten Island and drove the rebels out of western Long Island and off Manhattan. For the next six years the military situation changed very little. Based solidly on the three great islands that form New York harbor, the British made their military presence felt throughout Long Island, west and north into New Jersey as far as the Watchung and Ramapo mountains, into Westchester County to the Croton River, and even into the western part of Fairfield County, Connecticut. Never, of course, could the British control or dominate this vast arc of territory, but they did create conditions under which rebellion did not flourish. Unlike those in the hinterlands of New England, Pennsylvania, and Virginia, armed American rebels around New York City were unable to intimidate their recalcitrant or apathetic neighbors. Instead, repeated British forays broke up rebel committees, killed, captured, and dispersed their leaders, and encouraged the reluctant and the timid to stand up for their king.

Within a year after the seizure of New York, British strategy began to undergo a reappraisal that was truly agonizing. A small field army under Burgoyne had just been lost at Saratoga, the French were moving toward open intervention, and little had been accomplished by the Howe brothers' elaborate invasion of Pennsylvania. Rebellion was still intact, and thus far the costly efforts made to put it down seemed futile. A new approach was needed. The new approach which emerged during 1778 emphasized the role of loyal Americans. It was at last admitted that, ultimately, restored British authority would have to depend on Americans themselves, and that even the strongest army and navy could do no more than create favorable conditions for the Americanization of the war. Moreover, facing a global war against France, the British government and high command found it convenient to draw more heavily upon American military manpower, and to justify a long, expensive war to an unhappy public on the ground that the king had a solemn commitment to defend his numerous American supporters against a rebel bloodbath. Thus, during 1778, Loyalists moved from the periphery toward the center of the war, and as they did so the lower Hudson valley became especially important as the place where first-hand British impressions of American Loyalism were most readily and influentially formed.[7]

Months before the British army and navy arrived in 1776, the whole area had become notorious for its political apathy and open opposition to the Revolution. The Westchester committee formed to enforce the boycott of trade with Britain had

had to call on the New York Provincial Congress for an armed guard to protect its meetings against Tory assault.[8] In Bergen County, across the Hudson, an open election had returned a distinctly counterrevolutionary delegation to the New Jersey Provincial Congress.[9] Orange County south of the Highlands (modern Rockland County) had much the same kind of experience. Further up the river, in Dutchess County, almost as many men had refused to sign the "Association" of 1775 as had agreed to support it. Many local explanations have been advanced for the strength of Loyalism in the lower Hudson valley—Anglo-Dutch antagonism, splits within the Dutch Reformed Church, hatred of the great landlords—but none that can account for the entire region. In any case, the British in 1776 moved their main base into an unusually favorable political environment. Oliver Delancey and Beverley Robinson in New York, Cortlandt Skinner in New Jersey, and several other leading Loyalists recruited thousands of American soldiers to fight for the king in provincial battalions. Well before the agonizing reappraisal of strategy in 1778, British commanders were seeing a good deal of Loyalism in action.

What, actually, did they see? They saw, it seems, what they wanted to see. Two very different views of the significance of Loyalism were emerging by 1778. For some, like the young Earl of Carlisle, who headed the peace commission sent to America by the North government, no hopes should be placed in widespread American loyalty:

> The leaders . . . are too powerful; the common people hate us in their hearts, notwithstanding all that is said of their secret attachment to the mother country. . . . Formerly, when things were better for us, there was an appearance of friendship by their coming in for pardons, that might have deceived even those who have been most acquainted with them. But no sooner our situation was the least altered for the worse, but these friends were the first to fire upon us. . . . In our present condition the only friends we have, or are likely to have, are those who are absolutely ruined for us. . . .[10]

By "those who are ruined for us," Carlisle referred to those Tory refugees who had actually joined the army, either in anger or in desperation, and had thereby burned their bridges. Carlisle and his fellow peace commissioners favored a strategy of destruction—"a war of expedition" as it was called—laying waste American towns, forcing every colonial to choose one side or the other. If terrorism became the new strategy, no one was readier to carry it out than armed Loyalists. Major Patrick Ferguson, who would die two years later at King's Mountain (North Carolina) at the head of armed Loyalists, agreed with Carlisle: "It is surely become necessary," he wrote to General Clinton, "to exert a degree of severity, which would not have been justifiable at the beginning . . . if necessary lay waste the Country." Ferguson wanted to promise every Loyalist recruit a farm, which would "at once detach from the Rebels, the common Irish and other Europeans who make the Strength of their armys." [11]

For others, equally able to observe, the evidence of American Loyalism conveyed a different message. Peter DuBois, an active New Jersey Loyalist, a spy for the British, and later a police magistrate in occupied New York City, argued that visible Loyalism was only the tip of an iceberg. "General discontent prevails," he wrote to Clinton, "amongst the most disloyal and disaffected." In Bergen County not more than two hundred people supported the rebellion, and even those were scattered—at Closter near the Hudson, at Paramus in the center of the county and westward around Preakness, and "some pestilent fellows" up in the hills around Ringwood.[12] A flow of intelligence reports into Clinton's headquarters told the same story, of rebel weakness and demoralization; these reports were confirmed by a stream of deserters from the Continental army, and even by the behavior of some captured rebel officers, who appear to have turned completely against the Revolution. Captain Moore Fauntleroy of Moylan's 4th Continental Dragoons, captured at Germantown and a member of one of the First

Families of Virginia, told the British commissary of prisoners that "our affairs are as dark as they can be; & I really believe the game is up." He promised to send back intelligence reports while on parole, and he did. After going home to Virginia and returning to New York, Captain Fauntleroy said that "the whole continent is starving. . . . The Continental money is not worth a curse . . . everybody is tired; & those red-hot Virginians who were so violent are all crying out for Peace; & I don't wonder at it, for by God that Province at least will be starved." [13] Other reports supported Fauntleroy: "There is a Number of persons in this Neighbourhood," said one from Bedford in Westchester, "who have been the first Leading Men that are almost ripe to join you"; and in fact James Holmes of Bedford, who had commanded a rebel battalion of Westchester militia until 1777, was just then changing sides, and would end the war leading a force of Westchester Loyalist Refugees.[14]

The picture of Loyalism in the area around New York, then, was not altogether clear. Still less clear was what to do about it. Those who perceived a vast body of incipient or covert Loyalists wanted to encourage them, and in general opposed the deliberate use of terrorism. They argued that the great middle ground between active rebellion and active Loyalism should be broadened and strengthened, not cut away, as Lord Carlisle and Major Ferguson would have done. And at the heart of the developing debate over a new British strategy lay the question of the armed Loyalists: what part should they be assigned? Carlisle and Ferguson wanted them unleashed against rebellion; others, who favored a conciliatory approach to Americans in the middle ground, argued for a strictly limited, tightly controlled use of armed Loyalists. The debate never became perfectly straight-forward, in part because the proponents of conciliation had to be cautious in speaking of their American allies. But certain groups of armed Loyalists were notorious for engaging in the ugliest kinds of violence, and inevitably that reputation, however justified it may have been, colored the issue.

Andrew Elliott, a royal official and later lieutenant governor of British-controlled New York, warned that a "destructive war" would be counterproductive, and would simply fill British prisons with victims of what he called "private revenge." [15] Some experienced regular officers, including General Clinton himself, agreed, although they were circumspect in expressing their views.

The war being fought out, day by day and night by night, in dozens of nasty little raids, ambushes, and encounters all over Bergen and Westchester counties, was complex and confusing; it is almost impossible to state with certainty what actually happened in many controversial episodes—how many atrocities? committed by whom? and why? But it is beyond doubt that the armed Loyalists had a problem, both with their image and with their troops. Again and again, the very orders given by Loyalist officers to their men reveal the seriousness, perhaps the hopelessness, of the problem. "Seize Kill or Apprehend the Rebel Guards," reads one directive for a Tory raid on Closter, New Jersey,

> in that or *any other part of the Country you may March through also every other disaffected person that is known to be aiding or assisting the Rebellion.*

This license to kill every "disaffected person" was tempered by a caveat: "You are not on any Pretence whatever to Hurt or injure any of the well disposed loyal Inhabitants," implying that without explicit orders some of the Loyal inhabitants might have been fair game. How seriously the Tory raiders took this warning is suggested by the final sentence of the order, directing that all rebel property seized be divided into equal shares. [16]

Not only did the British commander in chief and many of his more knowledgeable subordinates know that the dirty little war going on around New York was murderous, they also knew that in other ways it was deeply corrupt. One example can serve. In June 1780 John André, British adjutant general, received a letter from Captain Samuel Hayden of the King's American Rangers, a Loyalist unit. Hayden wrote that his brothers, who had been spying for the king in and around Woodbridge, New Jersey, had been caught by the rebels and were on trial for their lives. On hearing the news, Hayden had led a small detachment of volunteers to Woodbridge and seized the only six men whose testimony could convict his brothers. Now, Hayden wrote, someone was proposing that one of these prisoners and potential witnesses, Thomas Edgar, be exchanged for a Loyalist militia officer in rebel hands. The release of Edgar, Hayden argued, would endanger his brothers; moreover, Edgar and his fellow prisoners had lost any claim to humane dealing because their Whig friends had executed four of the Tory volunteers captured during the expedition to Woodbridge.

Without other evidence a historian might well accept Hayden's letter at face value. It conveys a picture of bitter civil war, in which Americans by 1780 had committed themselves to one side or the other, and dealt ruthlessly with their enemies: American brothers spying for the king, caught by a half-dozen Whig neighbors, the neighbors in turn kidnapped by a Tory captain and brother of the spies, Whigs then killing four prisoners in fury at the Tory coup.

But a second letter to André, written a week later by Cortlandt Skinner, chief of the Loyalist New Jersey Volunteers, throws the whole affair into a very different light. Whether the Hayden brothers were employed by the Crown to gather intelligence, Skinner wrote, he had no way of knowing. But he did know, because Captain Hayden had told him, that the brothers were arrested by the rebels for *counterfeiting*. Captain Hayden had been authorized to seize only one man, Barns Burns, also a counterfeiter and the only strong witness against the Hayden brothers. Why Hayden also took six other prisoners, and then let Burns escape, was mysterious, but Skinner thought that Burns's former partnership with the Hayden brothers must somehow be involved, and that the other six men were carried off because the Loyalist soldiers had plundered their property. And the four Tory volunteers captured and hanged by the Whigs, in the first place, were not even authorized to be on the expedition, and, in the second place, had been executed for murder; they had been caught with their pockets full of the money being printed by yet another counterfeiter, whose body had been found by the Whigs. Thomas Edgar, the prisoner whose exchange Captain Hayden opposed, was not a notorious rebel, wrote Skinner, but a man who had accepted royal pardon and signed an oath of allegiance when the British occupied New Jersey in late 1776, and since then had remained quietly at home in Woodbridge, carefully staying out of the war and its politics.

What in one document looks like a clear case of civil war between Whig and Tory, becomes in another a messy affair in which political commitment and revolutionary emotion are less in evidence than personal prudence and blatant criminality. Eventually an inquiry upheld Skinner's version of the event; but to expect the British actually to punish an enthusiastic American supporter of royal authority like Captain Hayden is to expect too much.[17]

The British debate over the specific role of armed Loyalists in the new strategy of pacification after 1778 was never wholly resolved. It was confused by the fact that both sides of the question sought to exploit the potential of American Loyalism, but each would have exploited a different sector of that potential. The tension and dilemma imbedded in the debate, so visible around New York, remained to plague operations in the Carolinas in 1780 and 1781. Clinton refused to unleash the Tory dogs of war; he sometimes resisted, sometimes evaded pressure to turn the war into one of counter-insurgent terrorism. No doubt his reluctance owed something to a sense of honor, of what a gentleman could—and could not—stoop to in his capacity as a military officer. But certainly his refusal to un-

dertake a full-scale campaign of terrorism stemmed also from a
well-documented sense that the chief instrument of terrorism,
the armed Loyalist, would poison the American political atmosphere beyond recovery, at best turning the colonies into a
larger, more remote, less manageable version of Ireland, where
British authority maintained itself by a mixture of corruption,
armed force, and a brutal readiness to resort to either on the
slightest provocation.

Surely the puzzling question of why the American Revolution never suffered quite the extremes of violence, nor much of
its enduring, destructive social effects, finds some answer in the
way the British chose to wage the war, which choice in turn
emerged from the way that British leaders saw at close range
Loyalism operating in the lower Hudson valley.

CHAPTER NINE

British Strategy for Pacifying the
Southern Colonies, 1778–1781

Appropriately, North Carolina in 1775 sponsored a Bicentennial symposium to reassess the neglected role of the South in the American Revolution. My own contribution, which appeared originally in The Southern Experience in the American Revolution, *edited by Jeffrey J. Crow and Larry E. Tise (Chapel Hill, 1978), is here reprinted. It develops in detail the rationale and results of the fascinating shift in British strategy that is briefly sketched in chapters 5 and 8 of this volume.*

When news of the surrender of General John Burgoyne and his army at Saratoga in October 1777 had spread through North America and across the Atlantic, it became clear to all informed persons that the war raging in the mainland British colonies had entered a new, perhaps decisive, phase. After several years of little success on the battlefield, the American rebels not only had won a remarkable military victory, but their success surely would alter the international context within which the Revolutionary War was being fought. France, previously no more than a covert supporter of the rebellion, probably would enter the war directly, encouraged by the success of her American clients, to seize this moment to reverse the defeat Britain had inflicted on France in the last war. So unfavorable did the situation seem to many Englishmen and their allies that they frankly advocated ending the American war in order to meet the far more dangerous threat from France. Major General Friedrich Wilhelm von Lossberg, for example, commanding German troops in Rhode Island, exuded pessimism over the prospects for ever pacifying the rebellious colonies: "We are far from an anticipated peace," Lossberg wrote, "because the bitterness of the rebels is too widespread, and in regions where we are masters the rebellious spirit is still in them. The land is too large, and there are too many people. The more land we win, the weaker our army gets in the field. It would be best," Lossberg concluded, "to come to an agreement with them."[1] Informed sources believed that Lord North himself, head of the government, was for peace "at any rate," and Lord Howe, commanding the navy in American waters, was said to be "decided in his opinion that America must be abandoned."[2]

But Britain did not make peace in 1778, nor was the American war abandoned; instead, King George III and his more determined ministers decided to continue it on "a different plan" from that hitherto followed. The key element in the "different plan" of 1778 was the scheme to pacify the American

South. This scheme, its implementation and its results, is the subject of this essay.[3] Professor Ira Gruber of Rice University has carefully described British strategy and the motives behind it in the southern colonies, from the earliest effort of 1775–76 to support the armed rising of Scottish Highlanders in North Carolina, down to the ultimate failure of that strategy at Yorktown in late 1781.[4] His argument may be summarized here as the baseline from which the present inquiry begins.

In the beginning, Gruber says, munitions and some troops had been diverted to the South in order to exploit strong Loyalist support reported to exist in Virginia and the Carolinas. British strategy in 1775–76 centered on New England and the North, but the king and his ministers hoped to gain major successes in the South in return for a fairly modest military investment. This secondary effort, plagued by haziness of conception and shortness of time, failed badly in the defeat of the Loyalist Highlanders at Moore's Creek Bridge in February and the repulse of a British amphibious attack on Charleston in June 1776. Not until two years later would the British government and high command again think seriously about the strategic role of the South.

After the disaster at Saratoga in late 1777 and open French intervention early in 1778, the British gave the South a central role in strategy. Since previous campaigns had failed to break the back of rebellion in New England and the New York–Pennsylvania area, the South seemed to offer a last chance to win the war. Reports of extensive and militant southern Loyalism were attractive to a government nearly frantic for new sources of military manpower and equally desperate to justify an increasingly unpopular war. Because French intervention brought new demands on British forces in North America, the first move south was weak—only three thousand men—and late—not until the end of 1778. But it was a spectacular success, seeming to justify all optimistic predictions: rebel resistance in

Georgia collapsed quickly, and soon Charleston was being threatened.

The year 1779, as Gruber makes clear but does not especially emphasize, is a curious one for those seeking some coherence in British strategy; rather than quickly exploiting the initial success in Georgia, Sir Henry Clinton, the British commander in chief, spent months trying once more to bring Washington's main army to a decisive battle in New Jersey or New York. A small British raid in May on tidewater Virginia had seemed to give added proof of the strength of Loyalism in the South, but not until more than a year after the first invasion of Georgia did the additional forces needed to capitalize on the victories of the previous winter actually arrive. Why the government and high command wavered in its original, clearly expressed plan to push the war in the South is a question better left for later discussion. In any event, delay did not appear to have done serious harm to British chances, for within weeks after the arrival of reinforcements in Georgia, Charleston was laid under seige, and rebel resistance had begun to crumble in South Carolina. Even before learning of its army's most recent successes, the London government reiterated to Clinton its desire to make the main war-winning effort in the South. Charleston fell in May 1780, with the biggest bag of rebel prisoners taken during the entire war, and in August, at Camden, the main rebel army in the South was literally destroyed. But in this summer of success basic weaknesses in British southern strategy became apparent, and inability to deal effectively with those weaknesses would pave the road to defeat at Yorktown in the following year.

Gruber points out that, as late as October 1780, twice as many troops remained in and around New York as were deployed in the South. Only after a second expedition went to the Chesapeake, followed by a third and a fourth during the winter and spring of 1781, each intended to support its predecessor against a strong rebel reaction, were a majority of British forces operating in what ostensibly had been for some time the main theater. By midsummer 1781, British troops in the Carolinas, under Cornwallis, had joined the combined Chesapeake forces, making Virginia, for the first time, the seat of war. The rest of the story is well known: the sudden arrival of a superior French navy off the Chesapeake and a rapid movement of a French and rebel army from the North closed a trap on the British forces in Virginia. The political earthquake in Britain set off by the surrender at Yorktown, more than any purely strategic effect, ended the war.

Gruber, in his meticulous account and judicious summing up, suggests that incoherence within the British high command, an incoherence compounded of Cornwallis's impulsiveness, of Clinton's apparent hesitation—in 1779, 1780, and 1781—about fully committing himself to the southern strategy, and of the reciprocal failure of their minds to meet on what they were trying to do, lay behind British failure. Though recognizing that British efforts to pacify the South had "foundered at last on determined opposition in a difficult country," Gruber also concludes that the "British had never really given their strategy a full trial."

What, exactly, was that strategy? Basic to it were a number of ideas. First was the belief, repeated frequently by those British officials and supporters with most direct knowledge of the South, that Georgia, the Carolinas, and even the Chesapeake were hotbeds of Loyalism, ready to support royal authority whenever it appeared with sufficient force.[5] Second was a desire to cut off the principal channels of overseas trade through which foreign aid for the rebellion was being purchased; tobacco shipments from the Chesapeake and export of rice and indigo from the Carolinas were believed to be those channels. Third was the view that strategic and social geography—the proximity of the South to the West Indies where the major French threat soon would manifest itself, the strong pro-British Indian tribes along the southern frontier, the even more explosive potential of black slaves concentrated in the southern tidewater, and the extent of territory (which had made Lossberg despair) more thinly settled and loosely organized than in the North—favored a new, aggressive campaign to conquer and control the South. Deprived of southern resources, the reasoning went, the rebellion would become weak and demoralized in the middle provinces and eventually could be isolated and dealt with in New England, where it had begun. Crucial to the whole concept of winning the war in the South, however, was what strategic theorists call "economy of force." No longer would British troops try to occupy and hold directly every square foot of territory; instead, the war was to be "Americanized"—territory once liberated would be turned over as quickly as possible to loyal Americans for police and defense, freeing redcoats to move on to the liberation of other areas. With care and patience, Americanization meant that a relatively small British force could conquer the whole South and thus win the war.

Understanding the concept of Americanization—a term, of course, not used at the time—enables us to grasp why adoption of a southern strategy did not necessarily entail an immediate, wholesale redeployment of British troops. Recognizing the military unorthodoxy of the concept provides a clue to why neither Clinton nor Cornwallis pursued it as consistently as they might have—never giving it "a full trial" in Gruber's words, setbacks and other distractions seeming to create doubts in their minds from early on as to whether the new plan actually could be made to work.[6]

Before 1778, British leaders had not thought very carefully about exactly how military operations were to be translated into political stability. Various feeble overtures had been made to the Continental Congress, but clearly these were less important than an unspoken assumption that military victories would produce, more or less automatically, either serious political negotiations with rebel leaders or a complete collapse of rebellion. By 1778, however, experience had all but discredited this assumption, for an impressive list of military victories had left a political settlement further away than ever. Although a new peace commission was sent out in 1778, Britain's war leader, Secretary of State Lord George Germain, put his hopes in "Americanization" as the best—perhaps only—way to win the war.

The idea was attractively simple. A small British army would liberate those thousands of southern Americans who, openly or secretly, sincerely or from fear, longed for a return of royal authority. These loyal Americans were to be armed, organized, and trained; hard-core rebels would be punished and removed and suspicious persons kept under watch. When the armed Loyalists were strong enough both to defend and to police their communities and districts, the British army would move on. Step by step, from Georgia to the Chesapeake, the South would be pacified. Previously, Loyalists, if not neglected altogether, had been recruited to join the king's forces, abandoning their homes and sometimes their families, or turning themselves into refugees living under the protection of British guns. All that, in Germain's plan, was going to be changed, and he spelled it out in a long letter to Clinton in March 1778: royal authority in America ultimately would grow from the barrels of guns held, not by redcoats and Hessians, but by Americans themselves.[7] And the process would begin in the South.

The new plan contained a few problems immediately apparent. One was the chronic uncertainty created by movements of the French navy in the North Atlantic; no military plan could be implemented without reckoning the chance that a French fleet, perhaps carrying an expeditionary force, suddenly might disrupt it. Second, any opportunity to lure Washington's army out of the hills and into a decisive battle must not be missed, for destroying the Continental army might do in a day what would take a year or more to do in a methodical southern campaign of Americanization and pacification. Third, a small dilemma lurked in the letter in which Germain laid out the new plan. Assuming that operations in the South were best conducted in the cool weather between October and May, he urged Clinton to use available land and naval forces to raid the coast of New England, destroying rebel supplies and shipping, hitting the bases from which privateers preyed on British commerce, and bringing the war home to wavering Americans. The dilemma lurked not only in the optimistic idea of a seasonal shuttling of forces between North and South, but still more in the decision to strike terror into American hearts by amphibious raiding at the same time British soldiers were being asked to win American hearts and minds back to the royal cause. There was a certain fuzziness about how British armed forces were supposed to operate on American popular attitudes, whether they were to spread fear and demoralization or to induce a sense of security and self-reliance.

Despite these problems, whose significance is obvious in retrospect, there is little doubt that both Germain and Clinton, and later Cornwallis, who would be directly responsible for implementing the plan, accepted its basic premises: that Loyalism was an unexploited source of British strength, that British forces alone were inadequate to end the war and restore political stability, that the South was vulnerable to British operations, and that the exploitation of southern Loyalism as a war-winning strategy would require careful management. One man who did not accept much of this thinking was the outgoing commander in America, the luckless Sir William Howe. In one of his last official dispatches, he dismissed the idea of southern Loyalists being able to hold territory won by British troops. At best, Howe thought, the so-called Loyalists would behave with "an equivocal neutrality. Experience," he concluded, "has proved this to be the case, in every province."[8]

But Howe had been demonstrably a less thoughtful strategist than Germain, Clinton, or Cornwallis, and his status as an unsuccessful commander gave his views on the war little weight.

As Gruber reminds us, the new plan at first seemed brilliantly successful in Georgia and Virginia in 1779 and in South Carolina in 1780. What happened, then, to make the visceral Sir Billy Howe a better strategic prophet than his more cerebral, and apparently more optimistic, colleagues? Most obviously, the French intervened. In the same ship that brought the "new plan" to Clinton arrived a second letter, written two weeks later, in which Germain warned Clinton that the French were coming, ordered him to send large reinforcements to the West Indies, and effectively suspended the plan for southern pacification.[9] Not until early August 1778 did Germain return to his original idea. "The recovery of South Carolina . . . is an object of much importance in the present State of things," he wrote, and told Clinton to put as much of the March plan into effect as he thought could be done successfully.[10] But just as Germain was regaining his confidence, Clinton was close to losing his nerve: frightened by French naval movements, he was seriously thinking of evacuating both Rhode Island and New York and withdrawing his army to Halifax.[11]

By September the French fleet itself had withdrawn, discouraging and angering the rebels by its failure to carry through a combined attack on Rhode Island, and Clinton was free to send troops to the West Indies and again turn his attention southward.[12] But at this moment he raised a point that would trouble British strategic coordination for the next three years. Once troops were sent southward, he insisted, barely enough would remain to hold New York and Rhode Island, and he would have to remain "on a most strict defensive next year," freeing Washington from the pressure that had kept the Continental army pinned to the protective highlands of New York and New Jersey.[13] Clinton continued to accept the importance of the South and of the need to exploit Loyalism there, but he never ceased to assign at least equal priority to the confrontation with Washington in the lower Hudson River Valley.

Germain, on the other hand, tended to shift priorities, almost from one month's letter to the next, even from paragraph to paragraph. Nothing was more important than the West Indies, he wrote, but he also thought the war might be ended if attacks on the American coastline cut off rebel trade. The evacuation of New York was unthinkable, of course, and no chance should be missed to destroy Washington; holding major seaports was a key to British strategy, Germain thought, yet the Loyalists were another key, and Clinton should send expeditions out to encourage them. And, finally, there was the South, which more than once, when he felt that Clinton was too concerned with luring Washington into battle or reinforcing Canada, Germain would describe as an object of "vast" importance, *vast* being one of his favorite words.[14] Clinton, for his part, saw strategy as hard choices between competing objectives, and in reaction to Germain's chronic optimism emphasized, perhaps more than his situation actually warranted, the need to do one thing or the other. The new plan of March 1778, so forcefully stated, in time became blurred by this exchange of orders, complaints, charges, and clarifications that passed between the two men.

The early success of the expedition to Georgia, so weak and late in getting under way, would prove illusory, Clinton feared, if British forces could not hold firmly what they had occupied. As concerned with exploiting Loyalism as was his chief, Clinton saw the main danger to lie in abandoning to rebel vengeance people who had taken risks to support the crown, and thus losing their goodwill and the credibility of British promises, perhaps forever.[15] Not only did Germain seem to overlook this danger in his reiterated desire to move as rapidly as possible to and through the South, but Clinton

found it difficult to keep his more energetic but less experienced subordinates alert to the problem. Lamely explaining
his advance to Augusta, Georgia, and subsequent withdrawal,
Colonel Augustine Prevost told Clinton in March 1779 that he
had been "bringing to the test the professions of loyalty of the
back settlers, and by this appearance of support in their neighbourhood to countenance their rising, and give them an opportunity to do it successfully." When "no considerable numbers [of armed Loyalists] appeared," Prevost pulled out.
Clinton was not pleased.[16]

When, two months later, Commodore George Collier and
Major General Edward Mathew, in charge of the small expedition to the Chesapeake intended to tie down Virginia troops
and to destroy shipping, waxed enthusiastic about the rampant Loyalism they had seen in Virgina, Clinton was dubious.
It was no surprise, he informed Mathew, to find the people
around Norfolk Loyalist in sentiment. But, he continued, "if
they have declared openly for you, it is an urgent reason for
remaining to protect them; But I wish, that until we had determined to establish ourselves amongst them, the inhabitants
had not been invited to join least our circumstances should
oblige us to abandon them to the insult and oppression of the
rebel faction. In a political light I fear the attachment of
these...counties would not be very important, either as an
example, influence, or internal strength."[17] A few days later,
exasperated by his subordinate's eagerness to be reinforced
and to continue operations in Virginia, Clinton was blunter.
He sent Mathew a copy of a letter of his own, written to Howe
in 1776, outlining the Loyalist situation in the Chesapeake
which Mathew was just now discovering with wide-eyed enthusiasm, and he explained to Mathew what staying in Virginia would entail: arming all the inhabitants around Norfolk,
because any fewer than two thousand Loyalists well organized
and armed would be defeated and pillaged as soon as the British withdrew; building galleys to scout and raid the Chesa-

peake shore, keeping the rebels off balance and at arm's length; and immediately stopping the recruitment of blacks as soldiers for fear of antagonizing the loyal whites.[18] Mathew, in the end, got back on Collier's ships and came home to New York, as ordered.

Clinton's performance in 1779 needs both rational and psychological explanation. Waiting for reinforcements from Europe and for the return of at least part of the force he had sent to the West Indies in 1778, sure that a French fleet would reappear on the American coast in 1779, and above all afraid that his small victorious army in Georgia would be overwhelmed or forced to withdraw from liberated territory by rebel reinforcements, Clinton decided to use all his resources to pressure Washington in the Hudson Valley and prevent any detachment from the Continental army from moving southward. His estimate of the situation may have been too cautious, but it certainly was not unreasonable. There is, however, evidence that Clinton's powers of perception and decision were being sapped by something like nervous exhaustion. In a remarkable private letter to Germain, he complained bitterly of the weakness of his army and of being tied down by Germain's endless stream of orders and insisted—in obvious reference to plans for the exploitation of Loyalism—that the secretary of state stop listening to "the ill digested, or interested suggestions of people who cannot be competent judges.... For God's sake my Lord," he concluded in an incredible demand, "if you wish that I should do anything leave me to myself."[19] Reading Germain's letters, one can sympathize with Clinton's exasperation, while also recognizing that his outburst was irresponsible and disturbing.

Entry of Spain into the war in mid-1779 set off a new wave of panic in London and New York. Not until late October did the three thousand reinforcements, regarded by Clinton as the vital increment needed for any active operations, arrive, and by then a French fleet and American troops were attacking

Savannah. Once again, panic set Germain and Clinton on two almost diametrically opposed tracks. While Germain conveyed bad news from the West Indies (the loss of St. Vincent and Grenada in the Windward Islands) by calling for redoubled efforts everywhere else, Clinton prepared to evacuate Rhode Island in order to find the troops needed to expand operations from Georgia into South Carolina.[20] Yet the two men could agree on the importance of the South: when Germain learned that Rhode Island had been evacuated, he accepted it as necessary to the conquest and pacification of the southern provinces, "upon the success of which all our hopes of a happy termination of the American war in a great measure depend."[21] With the repulse of the Franco-American attack on Savannah in late 1779, the last act of the war may be said to have begun.

Clinton, together with Cornwallis who recently had returned from England, took the large reinforcement to South Carolina, landing just above Charleston in early 1780. Clinton understood better than anyone else what Germain's war-winning plan required. From his arrival, he laid great stress on encouraging, protecting, and organizing Loyalists, while being careful to do nothing that would discourage Americans who might be inclined to support royal authority.[22] Germain had harped constantly on reported American eagerness "to take up arms" at the first sign of a British military presence and also was pressing for the earliest possible restoration of civil authority in Georgia, which would demonstrate British good intentions. Clinton knew these matters were not so simple. Not only were Loyalist attitudes highly susceptible to even momentary setbacks and extremely difficult to measure accurately, but the connection between Loyalist *attitudes* and Loyalist *behavior* was equally tenuous and obscure. Caution was Clinton's watchword. During this successful advance through South Carolina and the siege of Charleston, he declined to call for Loyalist support in the province because he feared that the appearance of a French fleet and a consequent concentration of British troops, temporarily withdrawing from outlying areas, might expose some Loyalists to the enemy and thus undermine British credibility everywhere.[23]

Immediately after the fall of Charleston in May 1780, Clinton sent James Simpson, former attorney general of South Carolina and perhaps the most influential of the southern "experts" who had been advising Germain, to sound opinion in the province. Simpson's first report, made at a crucial moment and promptly forwarded to Germain, deserves careful attention. Simpson had talked only to the leading men because he thought that the more numerous lower classes of people would follow their leaders. The leaders, he said, fell into four groups: those loyal by principle; those who were demoralized by revolutionary and military upheaval and ready to embrace royal authority as the best available form of government; those who still would defend the revolutionary experiment but saw no option except reluctant accommodation to royal authority; and those defiant ones who meant to continue the struggle. Although he found fewer Loyalists by principle than he had expected, Simpson reported that the first two groups—the sincere and the demoralized—far outnumbered the last group— the defiant. But in closing he pointed to yet another category, those Loyalists who had fled Charleston *before* the arrival of British forces and had taken refuge from their persecutors in the back-country. These men were numerous and, having been driven from their homes, they had no intention of letting peace return to the province until the guilty had been punished. Under the circumstances, Simpson concluded that it was going to take "time and address" to restore royal government in South Carolina.[24]

Yet another issue British strategists never quite resolved is raised by the last part of Simpson's report. Clinton felt constantly pressured by what he considered the ill-informed optimism of Germain, old Admiral Marriot Arbuthnot, and a few

others who saw virtually all Americans as being Loyalists in
their hearts, misled and coerced by a group of wicked leaders,
but ready to support their king if given the chance to do so.[25]
But he also felt increasingly pressured by another larger,
better-informed group that advocated the use of fire and sword
to defeat American rebellion. Hotheaded young officers like
Banastre Tarleton and Patrick Ferguson were part of this
group, and so were men like the Earl of Carlisle (head of the
1778 peace commission), Thomas Hutchinson (exiled former
governor of Massachusetts), Admiral George Rodney (commanding naval forces in the West Indies), and William Tryon
(former governor of North Carolina and New York and serving actively as a major general with the army).[26] Clinton, Germain, and Cornwallis, for all their differences, never accepted
the principle of a war of all-out terror, though each of them
toyed with it at certain times for certain places; a strategy of
terror flatly contradicted the belief that most Americans were
basically loyal, but the use of terror did fit more easily with
what Simpson had reported about diehard Loyalist refugees in
the Carolina backcountry—men who never would rest until
they had taken vengeance for their sufferings.

Clinton knew about the propensity of Loyalist refugees for
terrorism long before he sailed to Georgia, and in a carefully
worded letter to Germain he had tried to explain the problem
they posed for any strategy based on Loyalism. They were, he
wrote,

> a class of . . . men of a more ardent and enterprizing disposition,
> whose zeal and courage I have not yet been able to bend to the
> useful purposes they are by many thought equal to. Their former
> stations in life were above the level of the private soldier, and their
> spirits are not such as will permit them to submit totally to mili-
> tary control. Stung with resentment at the ignominious treatment
> they have received, and urged by indigence to venture their lives
> for the supply of their wants, their wish was to gratify their double
> impulse, and to ravish from their oppressors the property which

had often in fact been their own. Such dispositions, as far as they induced the capture of obnoxious persons, of militia, and other soldiers, of forage wood, cattle and property of persons in rebellion, I was willing to encourage . . . . But fearing indiscriminate depredations, and having some cause to suspect that a spirit of licentiosness was the chief motive with many adventurers of this class, I endeavoured to restrain their irregularities . . . . These efforts have not as yet had the wished for effect.[27]

In plain words, Clinton knew that the most militant Loyalists were essentially uncontrollable and if left free to fight their own war were little better than bandits who would sabotage every effort to restore peace, law, and order in South Carolina or any other rebellious province.

Caught between the enthusiasts for Loyalism like Germain and Arbuthnot and the advocates of terrorism like Tarleton and Rodney, Clinton tried to combine his habitual caution with a bold stroke that would preempt the possibility of terrorism. By proclamation he released prisoners of war from parole and restored them to full citizenship, but also required them to take the oath of allegiance and to support efforts to restore peace to South Carolina. The proclamation was a mistake. Too lenient for the diehard Loyalists to accept, it pushed former rebels, most of whom sought only to withdraw quietly from the struggle, to choose between a pretense of Loyalism or a return to rebellion. Cornwallis, moving up the country, trying to organize a reliable loyal militia, complained that the proclamation was forcing dangerous men into the heart of his new organization, and soon he was modifying or ignoring the proclamation.[28]

Clinton did not wait to see the effects of his bold stroke. He reported to Germain that his rosiest predictions seemed to have come true ("there are few men in South Carolina who are not either our prisoners or in arms with us"), turned the war in the South over to Cornwallis, and sailed back to New York.[29] Less than three months later Clinton was singing a very different song. In a letter whose curious phraseology thinly masks his exasperation and fury, Clinton told Germain what he had always known in his more pessimistic moods and no doubt should have told him two years sooner: "The revolutions fondly to be looked for by means of friends to the British government, I must represent as visionary. These [friends] I well know are numerous, but they are fettered. An inroad is no countenance, and to possess territory demands garrisons. The accession of friends, without we occupy the country they inhabit, is but the addition of unhappy exiles to the list of pensioned refugees."[30] He must have known then, more than a year before Yorktown, that the southern strategy was not going to work.

Events of the summer of 1780 explain Clinton's renewed pessimism, now expressed in such blunt terms. A French expeditionary force had landed at Rhode Island, and the threat to New York was greater than it had ever been. Early reports from the Carolinas confirmed his worst fears about what could go wrong with a strategy that was heavily dependent on Loyalists. Cornwallis had won smashing victories at Camden and elsewhere. But the Loyalists of Tryon County, North Carolina, had risen prematurely and been defeated. Beyond the zone of British control, to the east, west, and north, rebel guerrillas began to disrupt the neat process of Americanizing the war. And while Cornwallis at first expressed satisfaction with the numbers and attitude of the loyal militia, he doubted that they ever would acquire the discipline and confidence needed to dispense with regular troops, "until," he concluded, "North Carolina is reduced."[31]

Cornwallis seemed ready enough to carry out the plan of pacification through Americanization, but from July 1780 he believed that its success depended on driving rebel forces far away from those areas where armed Loyalists were trying to breathe life back into royal authority. He would invade North Carolina to protect South Carolina, arguing that no more reg-

ular troops were needed to hold both provinces than one because a North Carolina garrisoned by regulars would protect
those Americans who were protecting South Carolina. And
when North Carolina proved a geographical and political
mare's nest, Cornwallis would argue that only the conquest of
Virginia by British regulars would give Loyalism a chance to
flourish in North Carolina. Cornwallis clung pathetically to
Germain's strategy for Americanization while undergoing a
more bitterly disillusioning experience with Loyalism than
Clinton had ever had. Whole Loyalist units defected to the
rebels. Calls for Loyalist support, even for information, went
unanswered. As he advanced northward, supposedly pacified
areas in his rear crumbled back into rebellion. Rebel terrorism
was met with Loyalist retaliation, and on, and on. Even Governor James Wright in Savannah and Governor William Bull
in Charleston were appalled by the brutal spectacle of civil
war, the very opposite of what Americanization was supposed
to bring.[32]

By the spring of 1781 the gap between strategic concept and
operational realities was so wide that none of the three British
leaders any longer knew what he was doing. Clinton sent successive diversionary expeditions to the Chesapeake, but otherwise seemed to withdraw into his familiar and soothing
obsession with New York. Cornwallis may have believed his
own rationalizations for what he was doing as he roamed
through the Carolinas and, eventually, into Virginia, but
there is a marked deterioration in the lucidity and logic of his
letters.[33] Germain's optimism reached the pitch of hysteria as
he seized on every scrap of favorable information and lectured
Clinton on the same points that Clinton himself had been
stressing a year and more before.[34]

In the end, American guerrillas did not defeat Cornwallis,
nor would they ever have been able to defeat him decisively.
Only a brilliant and lucky concentration of regular land and
sea forces around the Yorktown peninsula defeated Cornwallis

and ended the war. But to understand the bizarre chain of ideas and circumstances that brought Cornwallis to such an unlikely spot, so helpless to help himself, and cut off from the massive forces in New York, the West Indies, and Britain that might have supported him, we must understand how the British had planned to win the war by pacifying the American South.

CHAPTER TEN

The Military Conflict
Considered as a Revolutionary War

This essay, like the last one in the volume, is a product of the Vietnam War. In 1965 I was invited to take a small part in a contract-research project for the Pentagon on "Isolating the Guerrilla" from his civilian supporters. Skeptical of the project as a whole, I justified taking its modest stipend by thinking that the American Revolutionary War had a few lessons for our own time. Whether it does or not, I worked out the three-phase picture of British (the "incumbent" in project lingo) strategy while preparing my project case study, which I now suspect was never read by anyone of influence, perhaps not even by those who prepared a slim volume of conclusions and recommendations allegedly based on the historical case studies written by the rest of us. However ineffectual my minuscule effort to influence American foreign policy in the twentieth century may have been, it sharpened my own understanding of what was happening in the eighteenth century, which after all is the historian's proper business.

Stephen Kurtz, then director of the Institute of Early American History and Culture at Williamsburg, by organizing what may have been the first Bicentennial conference, in 1971, gave me the incentive to write the other half of the essay, looking at the same things from what the Pentagon project called the "insurgent" side. The result was first published in Essays on the American Revolution, *edited by Kurtz and James Hutson (Chapel Hill, 1973).*

To ask whether the military conflict of the American Revolution was in any sense a "revolutionary war" is to bring together two distinct and troubled lines of historical inquiry. One is the line followed by military historians, who from the time of Charles Stedman have tried to explain the outcome of the war and especially to answer the question of how one of the greatest military powers in the world could have been defeated by a few million scattered, inadequately armed, and badly trained colonials. The question itself, when posed in this way, has half suggested to some military historians an answer that would necessarily go beyond conventional forms of military explanation and would emphasize revolutionary methods of fighting and revolutionary sources of military strength. But perhaps a majority of the military historians of the American Revolution have rejected any such interpretation; they explain British defeat in terms of British mistakes, without resorting to American marksmanship, Indian fighting tactics, or massive popular resistance as major factors. Between these two schools of thought, a narrowly cast, poorly focused debate has gone on for almost two centuries over whether the war demands a "revolutionary" interpretation.[1]

The other line of inquiry has concerned a greater number of historians, though for a shorter period of time. It became truly prominent less than fifty years ago when J. Franklin Jameson gave his famous lectures on the social effects of the Revolution. Since then, no question has aroused more interest and drawn more scholarly energy than the one posed by Jameson: did the Revolution change American society?[2] Although wars are notoriously effective agents of change, the war of the American Revolution has received little attention from those historians who have tried to answer Jameson's question. Perhaps most of the difficulty lies in Jameson's categories, which were not directly related to the war and its effects. Moreover, the debate among historians over the question of revolutionary change has largely been an argument with Jameson and other historians of the Progressive school, who combined their faith that revolutionary change had indeed occurred with a deep distaste for all things military: neither they nor their critics have been much disposed to consider the possibly revolutionary effects of the war itself.[3]

It is in this dual sense, then, that we can ask about the military conflict—revolutionary in structure? revolutionary in effects? And, of course, it is likely that the answers to these two questions are related to each other.

Some risk is run by asking questions in this way. Jameson and other Progressive historians projected the social and political concerns of industrial America onto an eighteenth-century screen, thereby confusing their and our understanding of what actually happened in the Revolution.[4] Likewise, much writing on the military history of the Revolution is contaminated with the preoccupations of military theory, especially with the application and illustration of so-called principles of war, which lie near the center of what has passed for military science in the nineteenth and twentieth centuries.[5] Both lines of inquiry have thus been stunted by unhistorical thinking, and the warning to us is plain. When we ask in the 1970s about "revolutionary war" in the eighteenth century, we should admit that our own nightmares, as much as any desire to push back the frontier of historical knowledge, give rise to the question. By being candid about the reasons why "revolutionary war" seems especially interesting at this time, we may be able to avoid some of the pitfalls that our predecessors unwittingly dug for themselves. We dare not argue that the American Revolutionary War was basically like modern revolutionary wars in Indochina and elsewhere; rather, we ask only whether the doctrines, the studies, and the general experience of "revolutionary warfare" in the twentieth century provide some insight into the American Revolutionary War. The answer, with due caution and qualification, is yes.[6]

The social history and the military history of the Revolution have seldom come together in the past because military historians tend to regard the war as an instrument managed on each side with more or less skill, while social historians treat military operations, if at all, as incidental to the study of politics and public finance. But if the war is restored to the central position that it had for the Revolutionary generation, and if it is seen not merely as an instrument but as a process, which entangled large numbers of people for a long period of time in experiences of remarkable intensity, then it may be possible to bring the study of the war and the study of the Revolution more closely together, to the benefit of both.

It is easy to direct attention to the neglected question of the war's impact on society; it is more difficult to discover effective means for answering the question. Tangible effects—death, destruction, the disruption of life and property—seem the obvious and most interesting way to begin. Considering the enormous energy expended on the study of the American Revolution, one is surprised to find information so scarce on the raw quantities of revolutionary violence and upheaval. Except for the laborious military chronicles compiled mainly in the later nineteenth century and some rather tenuous estimates of the magnitude of Loyalism, historians have done little to answer the questions of how many? how much? how often? when and where? Though we are told that there were 231,950 separate enlistments in the Continental army, that the logistical requirements of that army generated about $4,000,000 worth of so-called military certificates, and further that the distribution of both enlistments and certificates throughout the society was quite uneven, we have not begun to grasp the historical meaning of those numbers.[7] Several recent studies in social history are at least suggestive in this connection, because from them a hypothesis emerges that one measurable effect of war might have been to widen the gap between richer and poorer

Americans.[8] The straightforward if lengthy task of extracting from local histories and records a complete list of all the petty alarms, raids, and skirmishes, the instances when daily routine was disrupted, people harmed, property lost or destroyed, and perhaps atrocities perpetrated, would be a useful exercise.[9] If the list were placed in the context of the then existing patterns of settlement and economic activity, it would restore a part of the Revolution that has become encrusted by neglect, both by historians interested only in military operations on a large scale and by historians not interested in military operations at all. At least such a compilation would correct the illusion that the American Revolution, including its war, somehow took place outside the dynamics of violence that have afflicted revolutionary struggles elsewhere.

Yet this kind of list making and quantification has its limitations; quantities must be translated into qualities. When no testable proposition is put to the evidence, there is the danger of simply piling up data to demonstrate a prior conclusion. How much violence or destruction is consequential? how little, negligible? Moreover, if research of this kind is motivated by the strong impression that a large slice of revolutionary life is being overlooked, it is only fair to take account of another impression, conveyed most readily by travel accounts of the 1780's, that recovery from the direct physical effects of the war was rapid. The second impression does not negate the first, but it does warn us against confusing the compilation of evidence with its analysis. Though the possible revolutionary effects of the war may seem the more accessible and more broadly interesting half of our dual question, we lack any clear conception of "impact" or any satisfactory framework in which to set this raw evidence of wartime destruction and disruption. It may be that the other half of the question, concerning the structure of the war, can lead to a more satisfactory result.

The structural feature of modern revolutionary wars that has most impressed intelligent observers is not the use of guerrilla tactics but the triangularity of the struggle.[10] Two armed forces contend less with each other than for the support and the control of the civilian population. Invariably, the government and its forces are reluctant to perceive this essential triangularity, while the rebels use whatever strength they can muster to break the links between governor and governed. Revolutionary violence is less an instrument of physical destruction than one kind of persuasion; the aim is to destroy responsiveness to the state, at first within the general population, ultimately among those who man the military and administrative arms of the state. Ideally, government ceases to function because no one any longer obeys; old authority is displaced by revolutionary organization without the massive confrontations of conventional warfare or the *force majeure* of the *coup d état*. To organize revolution means going beneath the normal level of governmental operation, reaching the smallest social groups and even individuals, indoctrinating everyone so recruited, and of course using those forms of violence, particularly threats, terrorism, and irregular or guerrilla warfare, that are at once most difficult to stop and most likely to change docile, obedient subjects into unhappy, suggestible people. The keys, if there are any, to modern revolutionary warfare are time and survival: hope remains as long as revolutionary organization survives, and the very passage of time can convince the most skeptical subject and sap the will of the most determined government.

This model of modern revolutionary warfare is not altogether congruent with the structure of the American Revolutionary War, but the fit at some points is close enough to be worth exploring. The most important points of dissimilarity are the relative ease with which local instruments of government fell into the hands of American rebels, the relative dependence of the rebels on conventional forms of military action, and their relative innocence of any explicit doctrine of revolutionary warfare, like that developed in our own time by Mao Tse-tung and his admirers. The latter two dissimilarities, on the forms and doctrine of military action in the American Revolution, deserve further elaboration.

In the first place, the prevalent image of the American Revolutionary War distorts the role of what, then and now, may be designated irregular warfare. Because part-time soldiers involved in small-scale, hit-and-run action were peripheral to the contest between main armies, they have had peripheral attention. Only on the few occasions when there was no rebel main army, as around Boston in the spring of 1775 and in South Carolina during the autumn of 1780, or when militia forces took part (almost always with unhappy results) in a regular military confrontation, have these part-time soldiers come into historical focus. In fact, even the correspondence of Washington, who disliked and mistrusted militiamen because they were not regular soldiers, reveals the neglected importance and frequency of what in the twentieth century is labeled unconventional warfare, and what was called in the eighteenth century *la petite guerre* or "war of posts." [11] This said, there is still no denying that Washington, the Congress, supporters of rebellion, and foreign observers regarded the survival and the success of the Continental army, engaged for the most part in a classical war of maneuver, siege, and battle, as the chief military factor on which the Revolution depended. The *petite guerre* of the rebel militia had important social consequences, about which more will be said later, but almost certainly these consequences were not of the quality and magnitude that modern doctrines of revolutionary warfare consciously set out to achieve. Instead, the willingness of both British and rebel leaders to accept, if not always enforce, the fairly humane conventions of eighteenth-century warfare served to mitigate some of the radical effects that civil wars often have on society.

The doctrinal divergence between our time and the eighteenth century is the other point of difference to be examined. American strategy from 1775 to 1783 was indeed keyed to con-

ventional operations, not simply to spare women, children, the
aged, and property from the horrors of guerrilla warfare, but
because a central army visibly helped to meet two acute needs:
the need for internal unity, and the need for external support.
By being militarily conventional, American Revolutionaries
created at least the illusion of unified purpose, military
strength, and political respectability, both at home and abroad.
Whether they might have done better to be less conventional is
an unanswerable, perhaps idle, question, but it is not an anachronistic one, because it was raised at the time. Charles Lee,
the eccentric former British officer who stood second only to
Washington in the first years of the war and who was admired
by some of the more radical members of Congress, like John
Adams and Benjamin Rush, offered an alternative strategic
conception.[12] Lee thought that a conventional approach, which
he ridiculed as Prussian, played to British strength and from
American weakness, and he offered his own Swiss model for
revolutionary war. He would have based American strategy on
the militia and used regular forces primarily as a means to protect the militia from attack while it was being organized and
trained. He would not have faced large British forces in
pitched battles, except under the most favorable conditions like
those at Bunker Hill or at the attack on Charleston in 1776, but
would have given way to strength while nibbling it to death. He
said little about the likely social consequences of his Swiss strategy, though presumably—political radical that he was—he was
ready to accept them. His thinking was never consciously implemented or even fully developed before his downfall in 1778,
but both its existence and its rejection are a measure of the extent to which the American Revolution was *not* a modern revolutionary war.

    Far more important than the differences between the Ameri-
can Revolutionary War and modern revolutionary warfare are
the structural similarities. But rather than becoming mired in

the old historical arguments, like those over whether the Continental army or the militia, formal tactics or guerrilla action, French aid or American patriotism, really won the war, we need to detach ourselves from the polemics of American folklore and to view the war as a whole, from outside. There is no better way to do that than by exploiting recent scholarship which makes it possible to see the war in British perspective.[13] In the preceding chapter we applied that perspective to the problem of Loyalism; here we will apply it to the war, and the Revolution, as a whole.

British understanding of the war was often cloudy and sometimes completely wrong, but the record of British experience provides a uniquely valuable way of looking at the war; like most modern historians, British leaders were less interested in allocating praise or blame among the Americans than in grasping the nature of the phenomenon with which they had to deal. Like other leaders in more recent, comparable situations, they were slow to learn, almost blind to certain key elements of their problem, badly confused beneath a veneer of confidence and expertise, and repeatedly caught in military and political traps of their own creation. But they were not stupid, and their persistent efforts to understand in order to act effectively give us the chance to consider the Revolutionary War apart from the parochial concerns and commitments that have paralyzed so many efforts to analyze it from the inside. Moreover, our own painful experience with revolutionary war may give us an empathetic understanding, a special sensitivity needed for the extraction of meaning from the record of British frustration.

British efforts to interpret and put down rebellion in the American colonies divide into three distinct stages. For almost a decade of agitation before the war, successive British governments had defined their American problem as one of law enforcement and the maintenance of order; in general, legal measures were bound by the belief that, once legitimate grievances were redressed, trouble and resistance was the fault of a few recalcitrant individuals. Policy based on this belief failed, most obviously because these individuals seemed to command widespread local sympathy, an attitude that crippled judicial machinery. In early 1774, after the destruction of tea at Boston, the British government adopted a new interpretation of its American problem, which was that insurgency had a center—Boston—and that this center could and ought to be isolated and punished. The new policy assumed that other colonies, and even rural Massachusetts, were disturbed by the extremity of the latest acts of Boston insurgents and could be intimidated by the example made of the Boston community. The policy was thus seen to depend upon the application of overwhelming force, within the framework of civil law, to achieve clear-cut success at a single geographical point.[14]

Of course, the assumption proved completely wrong. Coercive laws and the manifest intention to enforce them with troops gave insurgent leaders greater leverage than ever before outside Boston itself.[15] Despite their misgivings, inhabitants of rural Massachusetts and other colonies concluded that they had no choice but to support Boston, since the new policy of community isolation and punishment seemed to threaten the political and legal integrity of every other community and colony. From this support, Boston acquired sufficient force to make the first military encounters—at Lexington, Concord, and Bunker Hill—inconclusive and thus susceptible to interpretation as moral victories for the insurgents. Nothing did more to expand and consolidate rebel support throughout America.

Some aspects of the British performance in this first stage are worth noting. The outbreak of open fighting came in an attempt to break up what may be described as an insurgent base area whose existence cast doubt on the basic assumption. British intelligence of the target was good, but it failed in two other critical respects. It could not prevent the transmission of every British order and movement throughout the civilian population, and it grossly underestimated the rebel will and capability

for large-scale combat: "These people show a spirit and conduct against us that they never showed against the French, and
everybody has judged them from their former appearance and
behavior, which has led many into great mistakes," General
Gage reported after the battles of Lexington and Concord.[16]
Related to this failure was the psychology of the British command. The long period of relative inaction before the outbreak
and Gage's increasingly pessimistic estimates of the situation
during that period finally put him in the position of having to
take some action in order to redeem himself in the eyes of his
own government. The first setback at Lexington in April prepared the way for the second at Bunker Hill in June, since an
even more sensational success was required to redeem the initial failure. General Burgoyne explained why a tactically
reckless assault was made at Bunker Hill when he wrote that
"the respect and control and subordination of government depends in a great measure upon the idea that trained troops are
invincible against any numbers or any position of untrained
rabble; and this idea was a little in suspense since the 19th of
April." [17]

With the outbreak of actual fighting, the concept of the problem as essentially a police action, however massive and extraordinary that action might be, quickly faded away and was replaced by the belief that the government faced a fairly
conventional war that could be conducted along classical lines.
The American rebels were hastily organizing an army on the
European model, and the game now seemed to be one of maneuvering in order to bring the rebel army to decisive battle or,
better still, to destroy it without costly fighting. Accordingly,
the British shifted their base from Boston, a dead end in terms
of classical strategy, to New York, which was a superior port
with access to the best lines of communication into the American interior. An incidental consideration, but no more than
that, was the greater friendliness of the civilian population in

the Middle Atlantic theater of operations as compared with New England.[18]

The underlying policy assumption of this second stage, not very closely examined at the time, was that success in conventional operations against the main rebel army would more or less automatically bring a restoration of political control in the wake of military victory. The assumption proved to be not wholly wrong. A series of tactical successes through the summer and fall of 1776 not only secured the New York port area but produced a striking collapse of resistance in New Jersey as well. Without any special effort by the British command, local rebel leaders fled or went into hiding as the main rebel army withdrew. The local rebel militia, which had firmly controlled the communities of New Jersey, tended to disintegrate and to be replaced by an improvised Loyal militia. It is clear that almost every civilian in New Jersey believed that the rebellion would collapse completely and that it was not too soon to reach an accommodation with the royal authorities. The government granted free pardon to all civilians who would take an oath of allegiance, and almost three thousand Americans accepted the offer in a few weeks, including one signer of the Declaration of Independence.[19]

The failure of the British campaign in New Jersey, after such a promising start, had two major causes, one external, the other internal. The internal cause is summarized in the remarks of two British observers: one noted that the lenient policy toward the civilian population "violently offends all those who have suffered for their attachment to government"; the other noted "the licentiousness of the troops, who committed every species of rapine and plunder." [20] There is ample evidence from both sides to confirm these observations. British regulars and especially their non-English-speaking German auxiliaries—products of the hard school of European warfare—tended to regard all civilians as possible rebels and hence fair game. Even if civilians avoided the regular foragers, they were not permitted to relapse into passive loyalty if they had ever shown the slightest sympathy for the rebel cause. Loyal bands of native militia regarded retribution as their principal function and were determined that no rebel should escape, pardon or no pardon. In many cases, former neutrals or luke-warm rebels found no advantage in submission to government and came to see flight, destruction, or resistance as the only available alternatives.[21]

The other, external cause of failure stemmed from the Brit-ish attempt to control and live off the central part of the state: brigade garrisons were deployed among towns, mainly for ad-ministrative convenience. Not surprisingly, the rebel main army, weak as it was, managed to achieve local superiority and exploit its excellent tactical intelligence to pick off two of these garrisons, at Trenton in late December and at Princeton in early January. The tactical effects of these small battles were modest, but the strategic and psychological effects were enor-mous. British forces withdrew from all exposed locations and henceforth concentrated in the area from Perth Amboy to New Brunswick. The morale of rebels, already sensitized by harsh treatment, soared; while the morale of Loyal civilians, now out of range of British regular support, dropped sharply. Almost all New Jersey quickly came under insurgent control. The in-ternational repercussions of Trenton and Princeton were like-wise serious.[22]

One noteworthy point: in the only intensive study made of a single community during this period (Bergen County, New Jer-sey), it is apparent that the local and bloody battles between rebel and Loyal militia were related to prewar animosities be-tween ethnic groups, political rivals, churches, and even neigh-bors.[23]

The campaign of 1777 was essentially a continuation of the strategy of 1776; its object was to destroy, disperse, or demoral-ize the rebel main army and to quarantine New England insurgency by gaining control of the Hudson valley. But the assessment of civilian attitudes became more important than it had been in 1776 and affected planning in two ways: because the unexpected continuation of the war for another year strained British military manpower, one British force would move to Philadelphia, not only luring the main rebel army to defend its capital but also permitting the recruitment of badly needed provincial troops from the supposedly friendly population. Another British force would move down the Champlain-Mohawk-Hudson corridor on the assumption that the scattered population of the area was Loyal or at least not actively hostile and that Indian auxiliaries could intimidate those who might lean toward rebellion.[24] The campaign was a disaster, in large part because the intelligence estimates, gleaned mainly from exile sources, were much too optimistic. The Canadian force simply drowned at Saratoga in a hostile sea, which its Indian allies had done something to roil and its commander had not foreseen and done little to calm. The army at Philadelphia, whose commander had assumed that the northern army could take care of itself, found that the march of his men through the countryside from Chesapeake Bay had created new rebels and that Pennsylvania "friendliness" did not go beyond selling what was needed to feed the troops penned up in the city.[25] Other factors contributed to the disaster of 1777, especially a three-way failure to agree on the basic idea of the whole operation, which was attributable only in part to the slowness of transatlantic communications. But primary was the miscalculation of objectives and of time-space factors through an erroneous conception of the civilian environment within which military operations were to be conducted.[26]

Throughout this second stage of the war, the British military and naval commanders, the brothers Howe, were empowered to negotiate with rebel leaders. These negotiations came to nothing because the rebel military situation was never truly desperate except briefly at the end of 1776 and because rebel

unity so patently depended on adherence to political demands
that the British government was not yet willing to concede. It
has sometimes been argued that the British attempt to unify
politics and warfare inhibited military operations, because the
Howe brothers allegedly withheld the full force of the military
stick in order to dangle the political carrot more enticingly.
Little contemporary evidence supports the criticism, though
the Howes were bitterly attacked once their failure was apparent. The effects that a ruthless naval blockade and the pursuit
of armed rebels to utter destruction might have had on any
real pacification of the troubled areas were unpredictably
double-edged. The Howes knew this, and so did everyone else;
awareness did not depend on having formal powers to negotiate. Only after their strategy had failed, and especially after the
fiasco of 1777, did their critics become retrospectively wise
about the campaign of 1776. In fact, the Howes conducted
operations in that first year with great skill and smoothness;
understanding between army and navy was never better. Washington's army had been shattered at minimal cost; to have expected relentless exploitation of success was to ignore the basic
character of eighteenth-century armies, technology, and military doctrine. Battles were murderous, desertion rates soared
whenever an army became dispersed and control relaxed, tactical fortunes often turned abruptly at just the moment when
one side tried to push an advantage beyond the limits of a powerful but rigid system of fighting, and trained replacements
were pure gold. All these characteristics of eighteenth-century
warfare were more acute when operations occurred in a large
and distant country, against a semi-skilled but numerous and
enthusiastic enemy; but they were by no means peculiar to
American conditions. If anything, the lessons learned from the
American campaigns of the Seven Years' War, not to mention
Lexington, Concord, and Bunker Hill, pointed to the need for
more, not less, than the usual amount of tactical caution. The

most serious criticism of the Howes' campaign in 1776 is simply that it failed to end the rebellion.[27]

The outline of the third and last stage of British strategy took a year to emerge from the confusion that followed the defeat at Saratoga. The French fished more openly and aggressively for advantage in North America, and the British response was to escalate by declaring war against France. The West Indies, where both powers had large economic and military stakes, pulled the strategic center of gravity southward and seaward. During 1778, the British army on the continent remained on the defensive, cut its commitments by evacuating Philadelphia, and used bases at New York and Rhode Island to carry out a campaign of coastal harassment, while Indian allies put pressure on the rebel frontiers. Meanwhile, a general reevaluation of British strategy was taking place.[28]

For the first time, the civilian population came to be the major factor in planning. As never before, it was seen that Loyal and neutral civilians had to be organized and protected before any lasting results could be achieved and that the great pool of civilian manpower largely accounted for the surprising resilience of the rebel main armies. Because civilian response had so far been disappointing in New England and the Middle Atlantic states, because West Indian and mainland operations now had to be coordinated, and because earlier, small-scale operations had produced an unexpectedly favorable response from civilians in the southern colonies, it was decided to begin the new campaign in the South. Some British officials had always seen the South as the soft underbelly of the rebellion, with its scattered population, its fear of slave uprisings, strong Indian tribes at its back, and a split between tidewater and upcountry societies in the Carolinas that approached a state of civil war. A heavy stream of information from Loyal Americans supported this kind of thinking. At last it was understood that the recruitment of Loyal provincial troops merely for use in conventional operations often had deprived an area of the very people who might control it; high priority would now be given to the formation of local self-defense forces. The basic concept was to regain military control of some one major colony, restore full civil government, and then expand both control and government in a step-by-step operation conducted behind a slowly advancing screen of British regulars. From a police operation, and then a classical military confrontation, British strategy had finally become a comprehensive plan of pacification directed against a revolutionary war.[29]

The new strategy was linked to the political situation in Britain itself: increasingly, the government had justified a costly and controversial war to members of the House of Commons on the ground that Britain had an unbreakable commitment to defend Loyal Americans against rebel vengeance. The government thus staked its political life on the success of pacification in the South. The decision, however, was not seen as a gamble so much as the pursuit of a logical course, because the government, especially the king and his principal strategic planner, Lord George Germain, had always believed that most Americans, given a chance to choose freely, would support the Crown. When Lord North, nominally prime minister, but in a weak position within his own government, expressed an opinion that the war was no longer worth its cost, the king rebuked him by saying that "this is only weighing such events in the scale of a tradesman behind his counter" and that American independence would surely lead to the loss, piece by piece, of the rest of the British Empire, including Ireland. It might be said, without exaggeration, that North's cost-benefit analysis of the situation lost out to the king's domino theory.[30]

The new campaign began well. Amphibious attack captured Savannah at the end of 1778 and led to a collapse of rebel resistance in the more densely populated part of Georgia. Twenty Loyal militia companies were organized, and 1400 Georgians swore allegiance to the king. Yet certain problems appeared that would never be solved. In attempting to clear rebel remnants away from pacified areas, British regulars pushed detachments to Augusta and toward Charleston, beyond the limit where they could be permanently maintained at that time. Subsequent withdrawal of these detachments led to the deterioration of Loyal militia units left behind in the outlying areas and to an adverse effect on the future behavior of their Loyal and neutral residents. Furthermore, regular commanders revealed themselves as unduly optimistic in deciding that any particular area had been pacified and could safely be left to defend itself. Finally, the troops, and even some of their commanders, simply could not be made to treat civilians—except those actually in arms for the Crown—as anything but suspected rebels despite explicit directives from London and headquarters to the contrary.[31]

Large reinforcements in 1780 brought about the capture of Charleston and its large rebel garrison in May; a small rebel army that entered the Carolinas in August was quickly destroyed at Camden. Now British mounted forces successfully employed irregular tactics and achieved tactical mobility equal or superior to that of the rebels themselves. Upcountry, the Loyal militia was organized district by district; men over forty were assigned to local defense, while those younger served as territorial auxiliaries. Every effort was made to meet the rebel threat by effective countermeasures at the local level. Moreover, the orders from General Clinton to the inspector of militia show the spirit in which these measures were undertaken: "You will pay particular attention to restrain the [Loyal] militia from offering violence to innocent and inoffensive people, and by all means in your power protect the aged, the infirm, the women and children from insult and outrage." [32]

In the end, the policy failed; the question is why? Small groups of rebel irregulars could not be eliminated altogether. They hid in some of the least accessible swamps and mountains or operated from unpacified pro-rebel locations on the periphery—in upper Georgia or southern North Carolina. These irregular bands made complete physical security unattainable for many pacified areas. Rebel guerrillas and militia could achieve local superiority against any particular body of Loyal self-defense militia and sometimes even against mobile detachments. In an action reminiscent of both Trenton and Saratoga, a group of rebels quickly built up strength in October to wipe out an overextended Loyal force of a thousand men at King's Mountain, North Carolina. Thus, neither side had the capability of fully protecting its supporters among the civilian population, and a ferocious guerrilla war spread throughout South Carolina and into Georgia and North Carolina. Areas thought to have been pacified quickly slipped out of control, sometimes because Loyal forces fought their own little wars of counter-terror against rebels, rebel sympathizers, suspects, and anyone else they disliked.

Almost every British action appears to have exacerbated this situation. The chronic rough treatment of civilians by regulars simply could not be curbed to any significant extent. Moreover, the British force under Tarleton that had successfully employed irregular tactics soon acquired in the course of its operations a reputation for inhumanity that drove apathetic civilians toward the rebels for protection. A proclamation offering full rights of citizenship and pardon to all who would take the oath of allegiance, but declaring all others as rebels, drove many paroled rebel prisoners out of the neutral position that they had assumed and back into active rebellion. At the same time, the conciliatory aspect of this policy infuriated Loyal auxiliaries, militia, and irregulars, who increasingly ignored official policy and orders and took matters into their own hands. A Loyalist observer, who had defected some time before from the rebel side, described South Carolina as "a piece of patch work, the inhabitants of every settlement, when united in sentiment, being in arms for the side they liked best, and making continual inroads into one another's settlements." [33] During this civil war, there was little difference between Loyalists and rebels in terms of organization, tactics, or the use of terror. Pacification had failed well before a new rebel army was organized under General Nathanael Greene in central North Carolina.

The failure of pacification, and the appearance of this large rebel force to the northward, led General Cornwallis to return, almost with a sigh of relief, to more conventional operations. Priorities were shifted, mobile forces were concentrated, and the principal objective became the destruction of the rebel army through maneuver, battle, and pursuit.[34] This reversion to the strategy of 1776–77 ended in the disaster at Yorktown in October 1781, when the British navy momentarily lost control of sea lines of communication with its southern army. From that time on, all serious attempts to pacify the American interior were given up, and only New York and Charleston were kept as impregnable enclaves until the declaration of peace in early 1783.[35]

Certain aspects of the failure of this third stage of British strategy require emphasis. One is that neither British nor rebel leaders regarded the bloody civil war in the South as "favorable" to their side; both tried to curb it in order to gain political control and to prevent large-scale alienation of potentially friendly civilians. But it *was* beneficial to the rebels inasmuch as they could choose to operate in pro-rebel areas while the British were constrained to operate everywhere. Furthermore, the relative proximity of a large British regular army had a surprisingly unfavorable effect on civilian attitudes. Civilians tended to over-react to the army. Depending on the particular circumstances, civilians were intimidated by it and so behaved "Loyally," for which they later suffered; or they were disillusioned by its predatory conduct and lack of sympathy for the precarious position of the civilian; or they felt secure in its presence and committed violent acts under its aegis, which ultimately created pro-rebel sympathy; or they saw it as an alternative, a place of flight and refuge; or they were demoralized when it moved away and refused to protect them, their homes, and families.

This last point is most important to our subject: every major British troop movement in the American Revolution created shock waves of civilian behavior in the surrounding area. Only the scale of British operations in the South, where the British were more aware of the problem and tried to control it, makes those shock waves especially visible in the latter stages of the conflict. But repeatedly, throughout the war, Loyal and neutral civilians had responded excessively, prematurely, and unwisely, at least in terms of their own personal security, to the appearance of British troops, only to see those troops withdraw or move elsewhere. British leaders throughout the war had assumed that civilian attitudes and behavior were more or less constant factors that could be measured by civilian actions; American behavior on any one occasion was taken not only to indicate attitudes but also to predict behavior on the next occasion. In fact, each of these occasions brought about a permanent change in the attitude and behavior of those civilians who were involved in, or even aware of, what happened; over time, these occasions had a major, cumulative effect. By 1780–81, earlier in some places, most Americans, however weary, unhappy, or apathetic toward the rebellion they might be, were fairly sure of one thing: the British government no longer could or would maintain its presence, and sooner or later the rebels would return. Under these circumstances, civilian attitudes could no longer be manipulated by British policies or actions.[36]

British strategy may seem but distantly related to the war's impact on American society; in fact, analysis of the first illuminates the second, leading us directly back to the question of effects posed by Jameson. Reflected in the foregoing account of British operations and their difficulties is a changing pattern of American behavior. More direct kinds of evidence, generated by the American war effort itself, distort the picture by concentrating either on a committed but small minority or, in the tones of Jeremiah, on the failure of others to do all that they could or should have to support the Revolution. What the British record on the other hand reveals is something rather different: the response of the whole population to the multifarious stimuli of war. British estimates of American attitudes were frequently in error, but seldom were they completely mistaken. They were prone to exaggerate the intensity of Loyalism, they usually blurred the relationship between attitude and likely behavior, and they often mistook Loyal behavior as a sign of unshakable loyalty. But these estimates, when placed in the context of the British experience and when tested against evidence from the other side, give us a way of understanding the effect of the war on American society.

In the first place, two standard versions of the war are called into question, if not discredited altogether, by a British perspective. One is the interpretation that turns the fact of British military failure into a hymn to the American spirit, recounting how Revolutionary courage, belief, and solidarity frustrated every British design. The other interpretation would reverse the emphasis; according to it, nothing but luck, timely French aid, and a tiny group of dedicated men stood between American liberties and British repression. The British version of the war indicates that the Revolution was neither as irresistible nor as fragile, respectively, as these other versions suggest.

What emerges from the British record, especially when an effort is made to distinguish between the earlier wishful fantasies and the cold insights wrung from later disillusionment, is a picture of the great middle group of Americans.[37] Almost certainly a majority of the population, these were the people who were dubious, afraid, uncertain, indecisive, many of whom felt that there was nothing at stake that could justify involving themselves and their families in extreme hazard and suffering. These are the people lost from sight in the Revolutionary record or dismissed as "the timid." With not even poverty to redeem them, they are also passed over by historians who believe that the inert mass of people in any epoch deserve nothing better than obscurity. These people, however, did count, because they made up a large proportion of a revolutionary republic whose very existence depended on counting.

From a British perspective, it appears that a great many of these people were changed by the war. Beginning as uneasy but suggestible, manipulable, potentially loyal subjects of the Crown, they ended as knowing, skeptical, wary citizens of the United States. In this sense, the war was a political education conducted by military means, and no one learned more than the apathetic majority as they scurried to restore some measure of order and security in their disrupted lives. The British army was, of course, one of the chief political teachers; in its erratic progress from North to South over the course of seven years, the army directly touched hundreds of thousands of individuals, eliciting behavior that would identify each in political terms while teaching him something about politics. Nothing shows better the success of its instructional effort than its ever-greater difficulty in predicting and controlling the behavior of the presumably apathetic majority. And as we examine the British record for more specific clues to the impact of the war, a second institution, which also played the role of political teacher, comes into clearer focus. That institution is the militia. Earlier essays in this volume have discussed, from several viewpoints, the political and military importance of a population legally required to own and bear arms. Here that discussion can be summarized, amplified, and set in the broadest context of the Revolution.

The British and their allies were fascinated by the rebel militia.[38] Poorly trained and badly led, often without bayonets, seldom comprised of the deadly marksmen dear to American legend, the Revolutionary militia was much more than a military joke, and perhaps the British came to understand that better than did many Americans themselves. The militia enforced law and maintained order wherever the British army did not, and its presence made the movement of smaller British formations dangerous. Washington never ceased complaining about his militia—about their undependability, their indiscipline, their cowardice under fire—but from the British viewpoint, rebel militia was one of the most troublesome and predictable elements in a confusing war. The militia nullified every British attempt to impose royal authority short of using massive armed force. The militia regularly made British light infantry, German Jäger, and Tory raiders pay a price, whatever the cost to the militia itself, for their constant probing, foraging, and marauding. The militia never failed in a real emergency to provide reinforcements and even reluctant draftees for the State and Continental regular forces. From the British viewpoint, the militia was the virtually inexhaustible reservoir of rebel military manpower, and it was also the sand in the gears of the pacification machine.[39]

When we look more closely at the rebel militia, an interesting if obvious fact confronts us: the prudent, politically apathetic majority of white American males was not eager to serve actively in the militia, but many of them did nonetheless. Their wives were perhaps even less enthusiastic; in an agrarian society with a chronic labor shortage, manpower was too important to the welfare, even the survival, of the family. But the sheer busyness of British strategy in the early years of the war—from Boston to New York to Philadelphia, into Long Island and Rhode Island, across New Jersey and Delaware, along the Carolina and Connecticut coasts, up Lakes Champlain and George and down the Mohawk River—made it difficult to know how to be prudent. In the later years of the war, growing British sophistication about the nature of the war made prudence increasingly dangerous, especially from Virginia southward and in a great arc around New York City. Under the circumstances, enrollment in the militia could be a test of loyalty

to one side or the other, and it could be a kind of insurance—
the readiest form of personal security in a precarious world.
But the militia was also a coercive instrument: it was the ultimate sanction of political authority in its own district, and in
the mysterious way of all large organizations it kept its own
grumbling membership in line. Of course, whole districts might
go Tory, just as whole militia units crumbled under pressure,
but rarely were nearby rebel forces unable to intervene, salvage, and restore these situations. A reservoir, sand in the
gears, the militia also looked like a great spongy mass that
could be pushed aside or maimed temporarily but that had no
vital center and could not be destroyed.

Take a concrete example: in December 1776 the new State of
Connecticut passed a law, not very different from old laws in
Connecticut and elsewhere, establishing a military organization.
It reiterated the obligation of all males between sixteen and
sixty to serve in the militia, excepting only congressmen, certain members of State government, ministers of the gospel,
Yale tutors and students, and Negroes, Indians, and mulattoes.
Officers were to be elected, and no one over fifty could be
forced to march out of the State. As in the past, it was legally
possible to provide a substitute or pay a £5 fine, but only if
drafted for active service.[40]

Five months after the passage of the new militia law, a committee of the Connecticut Assembly reported on the case of
Nathaniel Jones and seventeen other men from Farmington.[41]
Jones and his associates, imprisoned "on suspicion of their
being inimical to America," had petitioned for pardon and release and swore that they were now "ready and willing to join
with their country and to do their utmost for its defence." They
found themselves in jail because, a month before, they had
failed to join their militia unit in opposing Governor Tryon's
destructive raid on Danbury; their negative act had identified
them as suspected persons, if not outright Tories. In order to
clear themselves, they were forced to undergo individual grill-

ing by the legislative committee, which finally reported favorably on the men from Farmington in the following terms: ". . . They were indeed grossly ignorant of the true grounds of the present war with Great Britain. . . . They appeared to be penitent of their former conduct, professed themselves convinced since the Danbury alarm that there was no such thing as remaining neuters. . . . The destruction made there by the Tories was matter of conviction to them."

It is a simple story, repeated hundreds of times in the course of the Revolutionary War, and it makes a simple but very important point. While military historians have generally clucked over the failure of the Connecticut militia to trap and destroy Tryon's raiders, the real significance of this episode is that Nathaniel Jones and many other apathetic, apolitical men, who simply did not want to become perilously involved in a civil war, learned that trying to "remain neuter" was also perilous. In late April 1777 they had tried to evade a political choice, but in the end they had to beg, in the old language of religious conversion that spoke of "matter of conviction," for a second chance to choose. The mechanism of their political conversion was the militia. Unlike other tests of allegiance, which either applied to only a few of the most prominent or notorious, or else, like the oath, lacked both the urgency and the administrative machinery needed to make it effective, the military obligation sooner or later thrust itself directly into the lives of even the most apathetic. Mere enrollment and occasional drilling were not all that the militia demanded, because eventually almost every colonial county had its equivalent of the Danbury raid, when men actually had either to take arms in an emergency or to do something that would visibly label them as suspicious or "disloyal" persons. Popular military service was as old as the colonies, but never before had its performance or avoidance defined political categories.

Evidence from both sides records how time and again, in place after place, the movement of British forces combined

with the American obligation of universal military service to
politicize communities and individuals. John Davies of Charlestown, South Carolina, was able to evade the rebel oath until
1779, when he was obliged to take up arms; having refused, he
spent four months on a prison ship. The same thing happened
to John Pearness, Thomas Mackaness, David Lorimer, and Colonel John Philips and his two sons, who learned that refusal to
serve in the militia meant trial by court-martial. Alex Chesney,
on the other hand, gave in and served actively in the American
forces on three separate occasions. In England after the war,
Colonel Philips testified in Chesney's behalf: "He does not
think the worse of him because he served in the Rebel Army,"
said Colonel Philips, "many good men were obliged to do it." [42]
While these good men and others were suffering for their reluctance to serve in the South Carolina militia, George Grant
was being hauled before the Commissioners for Detecting and
Defeating Conspiracies in Albany County, New York, "as a Person of suspicious Character"; he was given the choice of jail or
"enrolling himself in some Militia Company." [43] To the Albany
commissioners, the militia was as much a political as a military
organization; when they learned that some of the people who
lived on the frontier and enrolled in Major Ezekiel Taylor's
militia regiment were rumored to be "disaffected," they asked
the major for a regimental roll with the "Political Character of
Each Man" noted so that the "disaffected" might be "removed"
from this sensitive part of the state.[44] A similar crunch had
come for many Pennsylvanians in late 1776; it did not come for
most Virginians until the spring of 1779.[45] But virtually everywhere, in time, it came.

   The pattern of wartime politicization may be seen in dozens
of minor military actions; one last example will suffice. When
the British established a small post on the Penobscot River in
June 1779, Brigadier General Francis McLean, an exceptionally able officer, found the local settlers terrified by their belief

"that His Majesty's troops were accustom'd to plunder and treat the Country where their operations led them with the greatest inhumanity." McLean set out to correct this mistaken idea. Through promises and humane treatment, he persuaded some five hundred people to come in and take the oath to the king; "yet numbers of the young men of the country have gone westward," he reported, "and attempts have been made to raise the people tho' hitherto without success." He was sure that most of the settlers between Boston and the Penobscot were Loyal, but he also saw that "the impossibility in our present circumstances of affording them protection from the threats of the opposite party obliges them to act with caution. . . ." For three weeks in July and August, McLean's force was under attack and siege by an amphibious expedition sent from Boston. The siege failed and the American fleet was driven off, but McLean had to report that "most of the inhabitants . . . notwithstanding their oath of allegiance, and fidelity to His Majesty were compelled to join the enemy. . . ." He still had hopes and worked to recapture the popular support enjoyed by the British in June. Tories from Boston swore that a strong force of Loyal militia could be organized around the Penobscot garrison. But by October, McLean had all but given up; in spite of his gentle policy and their oaths of allegiance, he did not believe that the king could count on more than ten of the inhabitants along the whole river. Things looked a little brighter in November, but only because refugees from the rebels had begun to stream into the area around the British post. Eighteen months later, McLean's successor begged to evacuate the Penobscot post because he could not stop the local settlers from enticing his redcoats to desert.[46] As in New Jersey earlier and the Carolinas later, the dynamics of British intrusion and American reaction produced first a change, then a hardening of the local political situation. A tough or desperate few fled to the British for protection, while the rest gave at least the appearance of zeal for the American cause. But whether sham or not, their new Revolutionary commitment could rarely be reversed again, either by the tact of a McLean or the terrorism of a Tarleton.

It has always seemed slightly implausible that the American Republic was born out of a congeries of squabbling, unstable colonies, and that labor was induced by nothing more than a few routine grievances expressed in abstract if elegant prose. The Revolutionary War, considered as a political education for the masses, helps to fill the explanatory gap, provided we are willing to extrapolate a little from the evidence.

The broad popular basis of military organization forced thousands of more or less unwilling people to associate themselves openly and actively with the cause. In an age when single-shot muzzleloaders were the standard instrument of coercion, sheer numbers were most important, and naked majoritarianism could grow from the barrels of muskets. The absolute need to organize and hold a majority of gunmen had still wider implications: it required some kind of consensus, at least among the armed majority, in order to ward off incipient mutiny and dissolution. In the last years of the war, consensus probably operated to ease some of the pressure within the militia itself; derelictions of duty, once minimal loyalty to the Revolution could be taken for granted, were no longer treated as political crimes, but rather were punished as minor offenses. Likewise, the readiness shown soon after the war of the whole society to stop persecuting those Loyalists who had not actually emigrated, despite the desire of many to purge the Republic of Toryism, may be a measure of the curiously moderating effect of mass military participation.

Another effect of the war was the rapid erosion of deferential political behavior, which had characterized above all the apolitical majority; once they had seen and even taken part in hounding, humiliating, perhaps killing men known to them as social superiors, they could not easily reacquire the unthinking respect for wealth and status that underpinned the old order. And in a time of notorious duplicity and corruption, evident by 1779 in contemporary accounts from every hand, it was equally difficult to defer to new leaders, though many of them had been part of the old elite.

American laments for the decline of public virtue in the later years of the war may be read simply as so many jeremiads, but British evidence points to the sordid reality beneath the rhetoric. The British interpreted what they saw as war-weariness; what they actually were seeing was the extent to which rebellion had successfully recruited the apathetic.[47] The continuing obsession with "virtue," so central to political discourse during the postwar years, derived as much from the depressing spectacle of the compromises forced by the irresistible demands of revolutionary warfare as it did from the logic of classical republican theory.[48] In the end, of course, military and diplomatic success colored memory. Reluctance and resentment were readily forgotten, and the bare record of participation was all that mattered. After the fortunes and pressures of war had destroyed his other alternatives, each member of a large majority could claim his tiny but concrete share in the creation of the United States.

Beyond this hothouse nationalism, whose strengths and weaknesses would baffle observers for decades, there was at least one more visible effect that the war, working through the agency of the militia, had on American politics: the sharpening of the struggle between central and local authority. The many bitter words of Washington about the militia, the public outburst between Aedanus Burke and Alexander Hamilton over the respective roles of militia and regular forces in the southern campaign, prefigure the constituencies who fought over the Constitution and later organized as political parties.[49] If the Revolutionary militia is considered in its political role, then the relative apathy of the more numerous Antifederalists in 1787–88 is less puzzling.

That a long, straggling, often disruptive and sometimes atrocious war had lasting effects on a society of three million people is not surprising. The difficulty has always been in discerning and describing those effects and in explaining them, without resort to some mystical notion of American character. The correctness in detail of my own oblique attack on this problem through the medium of British strategy and American response is less important than the concept of the Revolutionary War, not as an instrument of policy or a sequence of military operations, but as a social process of political education that can be explored, and should be analyzed.

CHAPTER ELEVEN

The Legacy of the
American Revolutionary War

A telephone call in 1975 from Utah started the process that produced this essay. Far from the site of the eighteenth-century revolutionary struggle, Utah rightly directed Bicentennial attention to the enduring consequences of that struggle. My own contribution, improved by attentive and responsive audiences in Ogden, Provo, and Salt Lake City, as well as in Eugene, Oregon, first appeared in Legacies of the American Revolution, *edited by Larry R. Gerlach, James A. Dolph, and Michael L. Nicholls (Logan, Utah, 1978).*

In January 1838, a young Illinois lawyer and politician gave a lecture to the Springfield Lyceum, a group like so many others of its time dedicated to self-improvement through the exchange of information and ideas. In his lecture, the speaker pointed to a phenomenon familiar to his audience. In their midst, he said, lived a handful of old men, one or two of whom died every year, all of whom would soon be gone. This handful of old men, some of them sick, others senile, was all that remained in any tangible sense of the American Revolutionary War. These were the veterans, the men who had served in the Continental army and the Revolutionary militia. Even in 1838, memories were dim and distorted, and the events of sixty years ago were as remote for Abraham Lincoln and his audience as the sinking of the *Lusitania* and General John J. Pershing leading the A.E.F. to France are for us—perhaps more remote, because the people of Sangamon County, Illinois, had no photography, no television, no mass media to bombard them with sense impressions of what Lexington and Valley Forge and Yorktown must have been like. Lacking the technology which keeps our own memories vivid if not always clear, Lincoln in his lecture used these old men and their memories to speak about our subject, the legacy of the American Revolutionary War.[1]

What *was* its legacy? Did, in the long run, the war—except for its obviously crucial outcome— make any real difference? Or did its effects fade quickly after the fighting had stopped in 1783? Historians are better at telling stories accurately than at answering questions, particularly broad and hazy questions like this one. Dozens of historians have told the story of the war without seriously trying to assess its lasting effects. By doing so, they have suggested two contradictory conclusions: one is that the important effects of the war are too obvious to need discussion; and the other is that the war itself (as contrasted with its outcome) was actually not very important— birth replaced death, damage was soon repaired, and life

quickly returned to normal. To observers like ourselves, creatures of the twentieth century, during which the hammer
blows of war have bent or even broken the lives of almost
everyone born during the last hundred years, neither conclusions sounds right. At best, each seems too simple or merely
half true; the question, however difficult it may be to answer,
deserves better than silence.

Begin by imagining what would have happened had there
been no war, or a very short war. General Thomas Gage,
commander of British forces in North America, wanted to
withdraw his troops from Boston in 1774 and suspend the "Coercive Acts" until Britain was ready for a massive military
effort or until the American leaders were ready to negotiate.[2]
At the same time, both the British Secretary at War and the
Adjutant General, Lord Barrington and General Edward
Harvey, argued against trying to fight a land war in North
America.[3] None of the three actually opposed a war to enforce
Parliamentary sovereignty in the Continental colonies, but
their advice might ultimately have meant no war like the one
that took place between 1775 and 1783. After the outbreak of
fighting in 1775 had led to British failure at Boston and an
imminent American declaration of independence, which
would foreclose a negotiated reconstruction of the old Empire,
others in Britain, like Dr. Richard Price, argued that the best
interests of all parties dictated a cessation of hostilities and a
recognition of the new political realities. Had Britain done in
1776 what it eventually did in 1783 (as Price argued it should in
a pamphlet which sold thousands of copies in a few days), the
war would have been brief and left American society relatively
unscathed.[4] Stopping the war early, or even before it started,
was thus at least imaginable, and by imagining this possibility
we can bring what did happen to America during almost eight
years of war into sharper focus.

A long war meant that more that 150,000 and perhaps as
many as 200,000 American men served actively in the armies

of the Revolution.[5] In a population of less than three million, an estimated half million of whom became Loyalists and opposed the Revolution, and another half million of whom were black (almost all enslaved and legally barred from bearing arms), military service approached one in ten of the available population. Colonial governors had usually reckoned that one person in five, allowing for women, children, and old and unfit men, were eligible for enrollment in the militia, which was virtually a universal military obligation. Even allowing for some 5000 black men who, in spite of legal obstacles, served as soldiers or sailors of the Revolution, and for an indeterminate few thousand men who bore arms for the Revolution only to change their loyalties before 1783, we can say that a very large proportion of the adult white male population of the new United States had served six months or a year or more in the Revolutionary armies.[6] Without a long, hard war, most of these men would never have left their homes, many having seen parts of the continent they would never have seen otherwise.

A long war killed, in one way or another, perhaps a tenth of the men who served. About 8000 died in battle, at least as many more died of disease on active service, and an estimated 8000 died as prisoners of war. The approximate total of 25,000 service-related deaths many not seem a large number for a war that lasted almost eight years.[7] But it is the per capita equivalent of about two million deaths in the present United States, and it is almost ten times the number of service-related deaths suffered in the 1973 war by Israel, with a population roughly the size of that of the United States in 1780.[8] The effect of the 1973 casualty list on Israel was traumatic; though the tenfold-larger casualty list of the American Revolution was compiled over a much longer period of time, its size in comparison both to modern American equivalents and to recent Israeli experience suggests that 25,000 is a large number.

Death was only the most severe kind of impact felt in the

Revolutionary War. The few thousand veterans who are known to have received disability pensions—men who had lost an arm, a leg, or an eye, or whose health was permanently damaged—between the end of the war and the first comprehensive pension act of 1818 can be no more than the visible remnant of a much larger group, most of who had died before their cases could come up as individual claims or before they could apply under one of the pre-1818 laws, or whose records were lost in the fires of 1800 and 1814 that destroyed War Department files.[9] It is difficult to estimate the total, but evidence from other wars, before the advent of modern medical knowledge, suggests that for each wartime service-related death there is at least one survivor crippled by battle or disease, yielding us a round guess of 50,000 serious American "casualties"—soldiers dead and badly hurt—for the Revolutionary War.[10]

Disrupted lives and communities were also casualties of war. Not even a reasonable guess is possible for the number of civilians killed or hurt by the war but missed in the military recording of casualties. At least 60,000 white persons, loyal to their king or at least not loyal to the Revolution, felt compelled to leave their homes for Nova Scotia, New Brunswick, Canada, the West Indies, or England, most never to return.[11] Slave owners claimed, after the war, that thousands of black people had "disappeared"—seized by British raiding parties, or run away in the midst of wartime weakening of the slave system. Some slaves "disappeared" into freedom, in which case the only sufferers were their owners; but others were simply shipped as slaves to the West Indies, others must have died without leaving a trace for the historian, and still others, who had earned their freedom by joining the British, found life in Canada so unrewarding that they were re-emigrating to West Africa in the 1790's and even returning to a virulently racist United States by the early nineteenth century.[12]

Less ambiguously among the casualties of the Revolution

were Indians. The destruction of the great Iroquois Confederation of upstate New York, part of it fleeing to Canada while the remnant came under U.S. domination, was only the most dramatic case of general tragedy for the Indian tribes of eastern North America, most of whom when forced to choose sides had supported the Crown, which in the past had offered some protection against the rapacity of white traders, speculators, and frontiersmen. It is not possible to reckon the total number of Indians killed, maimed, and displaced by the war, but it is certain that the Revolutionary War shattered beyond repair the power of these Indians to resist white pressure on their lands and their way of life.[13]

Another kind of wartime statistic was created by the army itself, divided like all armies into the mysterious hierarchy of officers and soldiers. Somewhere between 15,000 and 20,000 Americans became officers in the Revolutionary armies.[14] Before the Revolution, no other institution had made it possible for so many people—approaching one in every hundred of the white population—to achieve a position of equivalent status. Washington and others, including European observers, noted that American officers often were not "gentlemen"; such observations confirm our own hunch that, for many, military service in the Revolution deflected life not only outward but upward. More will be said about this aspect of the war later.

In a society bereft of centralized institutions aside from the remote presence of an imperial government based in London, and an improvised "Congress" comprised of something like ambassadors from the various states, fighting a long war with a centrally directed army imposed an enormous and unprecedented strain. After the first flush of enthusiasm had faded in 1775, and especially after the disastrous campaign of 1776 had made it clear that military service would mean something more dangerous than a day or two of sniping at British soldiers from behind trees and stone walls, recruiting men for the Continental army became a critical problem. The colonial tra-

dition had been one of recruiting "volunteers" for active service. Even in rare instances when men had been "drafted"
from the colonial militia for active service, only those who
could not buy their way out were required to serve; personal
service by the draftee, taken for granted in the twentieth century, was rarely required in the eighteenth.[15] Volunteering
and conscription thus tended to boil down to the same thing:
economic inducements that attracted those least able to resist
them. But money was always in short supply during the Revolution, and by 1776 Congress as well as the states were exploiting the one resource of which America had a vast supply—
land. The promise of land seems to have been an effective
appeal to enlist men for the duration of the war, particularly
those who by the later eighteenth century could not have expected to acquire land by any other means. In the postwar era
almost ten million acres, or roughly fifty acres per soldier,
were patented from land warrants issued by the federal government alone for service in the Revolutionary War. Even
though a large part was patented by speculators, who bought
up warrants from soldiers at a fraction of their true value, the
very act of distributing such an enormous segment of the nation's wealth is one significant effect of the war.[16]

Supplying the Continental soldiers recruited by promises of
land was an even greater strain on the improvised, decentralized confederation. At first these men were paid and supplied
in the traditional colonial way, by the issuance of paper
money—governmental promises to pay (eventually) those who
received them, and themselves payable (usually) against taxes.
Wars in the past had been financed in this manner, with the
additional advantage of pumping badly needed circulating
currency into colonial economies chronically short of money.
Inflation and governmental recklessness, as in the case of
Rhode Island, had sometimes been a problem, but in general
the colonial assemblies had kept their wartime issues of paper
money under reasonable control. But the American Revolu-

tion, in its duration and in the size of its demands, was breaking down the old system by the third year of the war. Once the economy had absorbed about 25 million dollars of paper currency, additional issues began to drive prices up at an accelerating rate. Plans for taxation were administratively difficult under wartime conditions, politically even more difficult in a loose confederation whose members inevitably suffered unequally from the burden of war, and wherever they were tried could never catch up with the heavy and unremitting demands of military operations. By 1778 chaos and bankruptcy loomed; by 1780 they had arrived; a Continental dollar at the end of 1780 was worth one cent in hard money.[17]

The American states were populous and rich enough to sustain war indefinitely; ideally, no one should have had to serve for long in order to field an army larger than anything the British could muster, nor should that army ever had been in need of food or clothing. Bankruptcy, in theory, looks avoidable. The actual problem, however, was a predictable product of two factors: weak central direction, both politically and administratively, of a highly centralized military strategy; and the economic and technological difficulties of an unprecedented redistribution of plentiful resources.

Every historian has dwelt on the weakness of central authority during the war, but badly neglected is the story of procuring and transporting supplies.[18] Not until we see the delays, frustrations, and misunderstandings endemic in the task of getting, on some regular basis, cattle from eastern Connecticut and flour from western Pennsylvania and northern Virginia to 15,000 men in New Jersey and New York, where they had eaten the land bare, with the British navy denying use of the cheap and fast water routes and the British army menacing the more direct and better kept roads, can we begin to appreciate why the Revolutionary War brought runaway inflation and, finally, bankruptcy. Simply to find wagons, teams, and drivers on the required scale and frequency was extremely difficult, sometimes impossible; the prewar market economy had developed in conditions of internal peace and free use of waterways, and was not geared to distribute its products over-land at such distance. Competition between government agents and contractors for a hopelessly inadequate supply of transportation drove these costs to fantastic levels, dragging all other prices up with them, widening the gap between public revenue and expenditure, and sowing the seeds of civil war as some people profited and others faced ruin. Even the need to keep experienced, long-service soldiers in the field rather than distribute the burden of military service more equitably, ex-acerbated the situation. State and local governments were less interested in taking care of long-service soldiers recruited by them at great expense from among the socially expendable segment of the population—in other words, the typical Conti-nental soldier by 1777—than in supplying their own militia—that is, voters and taxpayers who would soon come home after a few months in the field. By 1779 the Continental forces were often taking what they needed, when they could find it, even plundering supply trains destined for other parts of the Con-tinental army.[19] Under the circumstances, central control, ra-tional planning, good temper, and the spirit of cooperation virtually disappeared. More specifically, two effects of this de-teriorating situation, caused solely by the need to support a Continental army, were particularly marked and exceptionally important. One was the loss of authority and prestige by the Continental Congress as it failed to cope with the impossible problem of wartime finance and supply, and the consequent slide of power, from 1778 onwards, down to the state govern-ments.[20] The other was the widespread loss of faith—perhaps a naïve faith but nonetheless held by almost everyone commit-ted to the Revolution—in the special ability of Americans, with their absence of poverty and their security and equality arising from widespread ownership of land, to meet the chal-lenge of war without behaving badly. American Revolutionaries had pinned both their hopes on what they called the "virtue" of the people, and that "virtue" most decidedly and spectacularly broke down on the anvil of war. In the words of David Ramsay, who lived through the war as an unswerving Whig and wrote his history of it soon after the peace treaty: "The iniquity of the laws [which vainly tried to regulate the wartime economy] estranged the mind of many of the citizens from the habits and love of justice." [21] More will be said later about the widely ramifying effects of congressional decline and the loss of "virtue" under the impact of war.

Looking far beyond the end of the war, we can specify its impact in yet one more way. As Revolutionary veterans turned gray and arthritic, and their numbers dwindled, the Federal government attempted to solve an embarrassing problem of surplus revenue by doing something for their old age. In 1818 Congress passed a law giving a modest pension to anyone who had served nine months in Continental pay and who stood in need of public assistance. Expecting at most a few thousand applicants, in hardly more than a year Congress found almost 20,000 veterans drawing pensions for Revolutionary War services, spurred no doubt by the economic "Panic" of 1819. A new act in 1820 tightened the loose language of the 1818 law, requiring a certified inventory of property; even so, after thousands of names were struck from the pension rolls, about 12,000 remained. Again, in the 1830's when a politically disturbing Treasury surplus and economic depression coincided, new pension laws extended Federal largesse to those who had served six months in the active militia, and eventually to widows and orphans of veterans. Successively broadened through the 1850's, Federal pension files for the Revolutionary War today contain data, much of it rich and fascinating, on about 70,000 veterans and their families.[22] These people, already old when the promise of a pension impelled them to tell their stories, were beneficiaries of the first, little-known Federal program of massive public welfare. The

Census of 1840 made a special project of counting these people, and found about 20,000 of them still alive. When Lincoln spoke to the Lyceum at Springfield in 1838, certainly he knew and probably was thinking of Phillip Crowder, Joel Maxcy, and John Lockridge, Revolutionary War veterans in their seventies, living and collecting their pensions in Sangamon County.[23]

Facts and figures do not interpret themselves. Perhaps 200,000 veterans, maybe 50,000 casualties, as many as 100,000 emigrés (counting Loyalists, slaves, and Indians), almost 20,000 officers, ten million acres of Federal land, about 70,000 pensioners, hundredfold inflation, and ultimate bankruptcy— these facts acquire meaning only when we explore and even, where evidence fails, speculate on their consequences. One possible consequence may be disposed of quickly: the demographic effects of the war were slight. Historically, war is much less efficient than disease and starvation in altering the structure of a population, and with its rapid rate of growth the population of Revolutionary America easily absorbed its losses. The deaths of 25,000 young men, plus the loss of other lives through emigration and the delay of births because of military service, hardly dented the long-term upward trend. At most, the abrupt removal of these people, mainly younger males, from the society may have eased some of the pressure against land and opportunity in the more settled areas, which in a relative sense were becoming noticeably "crowded" by the mid-eighteenth century.[24]

But other speculative thoughts on the impact of the war seem more persuasive and of greater lasting importance. Robert R. Palmer has compared the per capita incidence of emigration for Revolutionary America and Revolutionary France, and found it significantly higher for the American Revolution; considering the fact that many French emigrés returned in the early nineteenth century to constitute an intransigent Right wing in French politics thereafter, Palmer suggests that the apparently "mild" character of the American Revolution, and the stability of its postwar institutions, were a result of permanently expelling those very people who otherwise might have been the missing party in the politics of the New Republic—the counterrevolutionary conservatives and reactionaries.[25]

A more tenuous, but equally intriguing, thought has been put forth concerning slavery. Where slavery was a minor aspect of society, and where large numbers of blacks served in the Revolutionary armies, the principles of the Declaration of Independence were applied strictly, and slavery was abolished soon after the war. But where slavery was an important social and economic institution, from Maryland southward, where the British had recruited numbers of blacks to fight for the king and induced thousands of slaves to run away from their owners, and where plans to recruit black soldiers for the Revolution met bitter resistance, the Revolution and its protracted war seems to have made slavery a tighter, more rigorous system than it had been in the last decades of the old Empire. By 1783, Southern slave owners, previously content to run a system more flexible and less harsh in practice than it appeared in the statute books, realized as never before how fragile and vulnerable the system actually was, and how little they could depend on the cowardice, ignorance, and gratitude of their slaves. Troubled by the agitation, even within themselves, created against slavery by the rhetorical justification of the Revolution, slaveowners set about giving legal and institutional expression to a new level of anxiety about the system. New rules governing slavery and a new articulation of racist attitudes may have been one of the most important, enduring, and paradoxical legacies of the Revolutionary War.[26]

The question for the society as a whole may be put in terms of movement, or, as sociologists might prefer, mobility: how much displacement of life was there that would not have happened without a long war? No answer that ignores the variety and particularity of individual human lives can be satisfying; but using our basic facts about the war, fragments of research done so far on the question, and some imagination, we can briefly sketch an answer. First, people began to move across the face of the land—more numerously, more frequently, and for greater distances than ever before. Geographical mobility soon after the war may have approached twice its rate today, when the United States seems to be a society in perpetual motion.[27] The so-called Indian barrier was now breached and crumbling, and the prewar migratory trends simply accelerated. Land grants, land speculation, postwar depression with its uncertainties and frustrations for returning veterans, all drew these men and their families into Vermont, upper New York, and the great Ohio Valley. Uprooted once by the war, veterans were ready to move again when conditions at home disappointed them.

Not only did they begin to pour into the vast territorial openness of trans-Appalachian North America, but the war had created other kinds of "space" into which veterans could move. The flight of emigrés, many of them holders of property and position, created one kind of space, and mobilization had created another. Without a long, bitter war, Loyalists would not have been forced to flee by the thousands. Without a long, bitter war, a myriad of public offices, major and minor, civilian and military, would not have been needed to represent, to persuade, to guide, to coerce, and to keep watch on three million unruly, scattered, and relatively ungoverned people. We know about the thousands of new military officers, many of whom reappeared later in political roles; and we also know about the wartime creation of a new tier of government at the national level, and about the wartime doubling or tripling in size of state legislatures, both of which often made the reappearance of Continental officers possible. But we are just beginning to learn about the veritable wartime explosion of local government, when a handful of surnames who had run a town or a county were quickly joined and sometimes even displaced by dozens of new names filling up the spaces on those local committees needed to run the war and watch the Tories.[28] Parkinson's law tells us how emergency expansion never wholly contracts once the emergency is passed, and local government in the postwar Republic followed the law; it remained permanently larger than before the war, and so men who chose not to move out could the more easily move up.

But people hit by the war also moved down. There had been a perceptible prewar trend toward a widening gap between rich and poor, rich getting richer and poor getting relatively poorer and more numerous; this trend must have been affected by wartime inflation, bankruptcy, and general economic dislocation.[29] It is possible to recite case after case, at least one for every case of a man moving upward, of men and their families ruined economically by the war. But in our present state of knowledge it is impossible to say with any confidence whether we are seeing a further social splitting caused by the war of the fortunate few at the top from the unlucky group near the bottom, or its opposite—a general socioeconomic scrambling whose net result may have been to make American society more equal than it had been before the Revolution. Statistical research done so far is inconclusive, but tends to support the former view, that the overall economic impact of the war was to make America less, not more, democratic.[30] Without a solid basis for judgment, however, we can turn again to the informed opinion of the contemporary historian David Ramsay. Ramsay saw inflation, coupled with laws to fix prices and to force the acceptance of paper money, as having ruined widows, orphans, old and retired persons, those with savings and inheritances or who were owed money. "On the other hand," Ramsay continued, paper money was the occasion

> of good to many; it was at all times the poor man's friend; while it was current, all kinds of labor very readily found their reward.

In the first years of the war, none were idle from want of employment, and none were employed without having it in their power
to obtain ready payment for their services. To that class of people,
whose daily labour was their support, the depreciation was no
disadvantage; expending money as fast as they received it, they
always got its full value. The reverse was the case with the rich,
or those who were disposed to hoarding. No agrarian law ever had
a more extensive operation, than continental money. That for
which the Gracchi lost their lives in Rome, was peaceably effected
by the United States, by the legal tender of these depreciating
bills. The poor became rich, and the rich became poor.[31]

Whether Ramsay was right in his socioeconomic arithmetic
must remain an open question, but his concluding sentences
drive home a less arguable point—that the wartime economic
troubles had made a powerful impression on the lives, including the minds and memories, of those who survived it. He
believed that ''The experience of this time inculcated on youth
two salutary lessons; the impolicy of depending on paternal
acquisitions, and the necessity of their own exertions.'' But if
the wartime economy had stimulated American youth to new
heights of initiative and self-reliance in the postwar world,
Ramsay, as mentioned earlier, also thought it had been a
deeply corrosive experience:

Truth, honour and justice were swept away by the overflowing
deluge of legal iniquity, nor have they yet assumed their ancient
and accustomed seats. Time and industry have already, in a great
degree, repaired the losses of property, which the citizens sustained during the war, but both have hitherto failed in effacing the
taint which was then communicated to their principles, nor can its
total ablution be expected till a new generation arises, unpracticed
in the iniquities of their fathers.[32]

Ramsay's speculations lead us to a final question about the
legacy of the Revolutionary War, concerning its psychological
effects, especially insofar as those effects can be seen in the
political institutions and character of the postwar nation.
Historians generally agree that a marked feature of pre-
Revolutionary America was ''deferential'' political behavior.

Although a large proportion of adult white males had the right to vote, they regularly chose their political leaders from a few families of high social and economic position; that is, the mass of voters seemed to "defer" instinctively to a "natural" elite or aristocracy, and the pattern was as plain in New England as it was in Virginia and South Carolina.[33] Though not destroyed by the war, the deferential pattern of political behavior was definitely undermined by it. Nearly every observer, American and foreign, had noted that the weakest point in the Revolutionary army was its officer corps—lieutenants and captains who claimed all the pay and perquisites of military leadership without either displaying the competence or commanding the respect that would have justified their elevated positions. Washington had complained about the problem from his first glimpse of the Yankee regiments at Boston in 1775, and until the end of the war one encounters similar observations.[34] These officers, to a surprising degree for a revolution ostensibly democratic in its premises and goals, came from the same families that had supplied magistrates, selectmen, and representatives to colonial government. More important, perhaps, was the prevailing image of the military officer as "a gentleman"—an extension of the natural political, economic, and social aristocracy. Whether an officer in fact came from the natural aristocracy or not, his commission gave him some claim to be so regarded, and his performance was judged accordingly. The military performance of the typical American officer in the Revolutionary War was not good; after all, very few had been schooled to lead men into eighteenth-century battle, or even to keep them clean, clothed, fed, sheltered, and sober under field conditions. Discipline was poor, and the junior officers were obviously to blame. So after eight years in which about 200,000 of the masses watched perhaps 20,000 of the so-called elite perform more or less incompetently, the postwar voter had lost much of his habitual deference to men allegedly "better" than he was. The rhetoric of the Revolution articulated these new social theories and political attitudes, but the experience of war gave a compelling concreteness to what otherwise might have been merely words.[35]

While the unprecedented experience of a long war weakened the position of the aristocracy, it also created a new basis for social prestige and political power. American Revolutionaries let their fears of militarism and standing armies carry them to extremes that now seem almost ludicrous, but at the same time they were deeply impressed by the martial virtues. Before 1775, only Benjamin Franklin had enjoyed the kind of American "fame" that the war, chiefly through military service, would make possible for dozens of men, heroes of the Revolution. Washington's God-like reputation gave a luster to his whole corps of general officers, and at the local level colonels, majors, and even common soldiers, back from the war, often commanded a measure of respect that heretofore only a few clergymen and other local worthies had enjoyed. There is no contradiction between this point and the one preceding: the old colonial elite was tested by the war and found wanting, but the war rewarded all those who had met its test. Revolutionary Army officers, as a group, may not have been highly regarded by their men, but individual officers, as well as soldiers, often emerged from the war as "famous" persons in the eyes of their fellow citizens. America is not a militaristic society, so runs one cliché about its history, but historians have often remarked on how readily, ever since the Revolution, military "fame" has found its natural expression in postwar politics.[36]

Lincoln, in preparing his Lyceum lecture, surely was thinking of those old men, drawing their pensions and telling their stories, too ancient to wield power or stand for office, but, with all the others who had been dying off through the years, a constant reminder of the Revolutionary past. Lincoln's message, specifically, was a plea for law and order and for an end to runaway violence. By linking the American propensity for violence with the struggle against Britain and with the Revolutionary generation, he tactfully suggested that violence was once an acceptable, even admirable, form of behavior, but in the new generation, his own, violence was obsolete, even dangerous, and that only respect for law and the rights of others would keep American society intact. Lincoln went further than we dare go, suggesting that part of the legacy of the Revolutionary War was to encourage the violent side of the American character. But it is an intriguing thought, as are some other conjectural connections between the Revolutionary War and the later course of American history. How far, for example, did the long military struggle implant an ineradicable national pride that hardly existed before 1775? Or did that sickening slide of power under wartime pressure, out of the hands of Congress, down to the states, who were then unable to bring it to bear on the key problems of Revolutionary strategy, induce the strange ambivalence built into the federal system? Or did massive participation in the war convince Americans, once it had been won, that sheer numbers and raw courage, not professional diplomacy or professional armies, gave the nation guaranteed security from any foreign threat, and so permitted Americans to grow up without thinking much about the rest of the world? Like our original question, these are more easily asked than answered. But, however difficult to define precisely and to prove beyond doubt, the legacy of the American Revolutionary War was real, and it shaped American life unto Lincoln's day and beyond.

CHAPTER TWELVE

The American Military Experience:
History and Learning

A delightful sabbatical year in London, courtesy of Princeton University and the American Council of Learned Societies, ended in 1967 with scenes on BBC television of Newark and Detroit burning, and an awful feeling that the hopeless war in Vietnam was wrecking my country. Suddenly, as never before, I felt irrelevant, busily accumulating data for a comparative study of the military profession in the eighteenth and the early nineteenth centuries. And so I started in the few weeks left to write a book on the American experience with war, carrying the story down to the present, in order to explain at least to myself the terrible troubles of 1967. That book is still unfinished, but the intense effort was therapeutic, and the following essay extracted from the draft chapters what struck me as the most important single theme. The recasting of that theme within the framework of "learning theory" occurred more slowly, in conversation with friends and students more knowledgeable in the social and behavioral sciences than I, and in response to the interest expressed in the essay by the editors of the then new Journal of Interdisciplinary History, *where it was published in February 1971.*

An old, yet compelling idea states that international behavior may be best understood in terms of national peculiarities. In other words, a nation's behavior toward the rest of the world cannot be adequately explained as a function of the universal factors of power and interest when its behavior is irrelevant or even detrimental to those factors. And, as the debate over American international behavior has grown increasingly bitter, this idea has moved toward the center of a controversy among those who can agree only in their unhappiness with American foreign and military policy.

Within the current welter of criticism and conflicting interpretations of American international behavior, one can discern at least three basic types of explanation. The *accidental* type of explanation is proffered by those who insist that what they dislike is essentially a product of bad leadership: misinformation, lack of understanding, and poor control of the pressures of time and high office have caused mistakes that might have been avoided.[1] Radically opposed to the accidental explanation are various *structural* explanations: a "military-industrial complex," or something similar, is viewed as having debased the process of rational thought and choice, and to be dictating decisions and policies which are harmful to the true interests of the society as a whole. The structural explanation implies conflict, because it assumes that there are intelligent, responsible people who have been overcome by others whose self-interest and political strength are produced by a level of annual military expenditure far exceeding the gross national product of all but a few other nations.[2] A more sophisticated version of the structural explanation emphasizes less the machinations of a coalition of selfish, willful magnates than their more diffused way of seeing the outside world. "The military metaphysic" was C. Wright Mills's term for this world view, which never fails to find a foreign danger that will justify subordinating all other considerations to an ever inadequate, ever more costly, and ever bolder system of "national security."[3] Marxist and neo-

Marxist analysis provides the chief but by no means the only form of structural explanation—witness Eisenhower's Farewell Address. Superficially similar to the concept of a military meta-physic is the *cultural* form of explanation, which attributes unfortunate international behavior to some characteristic of American culture: racisim, or endemic violence, or aggressive and materialist ethnocentrism.[4] The difference between structural and cultural modes of explanation is clear: one points to powerful interest groups within the society, while the other points to the whole society. Yet both agree in asserting the importance of characteristically American patterns of behavior, as against those explanations that see no more than avoidable error and the accidents of personal choice.

None of these explanations are especially new or American. The behavior of Russia, and, before that, Germany, has been debated in much the same categories. The aberrant personalities of Hitler and Stalin, Prussian militarism or Nazi ideology and Communist conflict doctrine, German megalomania and Russian paranoia—each is respectively a crude version of accidental, structural, and cultural explanation. The disasters of the twentieth century have given a special potency to the idea that there are national patterns of international behavior, an idea as attractive to some as it is repulsive to others, but one that seems to grip the imagination of everyone. In addition, both structural and cultural explanations of behavior have been maddeningly vague and one-sided. They are so obviously linked to moral judgment and political argument that one has little confidence in the use and selection of evidence. More serious is their habitual failure either to deal with alternative explanations or to set forth criteria for testing any explanation, which may be to say only that the entire question of national character is extremely complex and far from being satisfactorily answered.[5] And yet even after all of its deficiencies have been admitted, the idea that there are national patterns of international behavior retains an impressive degree of plausibility. The evidence seems too strong for serious doubt. Fuzzy as the idea may be, its intrinsic importance and the probability that it contains some measure of vital truth make it worth pursuing further.

This essay does not attempt to answer the question of national character, nor does it claim to remove any of the main weaknesses in that concept. It is open to the charge of trying to solve an undemonstrated problem, because it begins with the premise that American international behavior has been and is sufficiently unusual to require some unusual kind of explanation. It seeks to place that behavior in a historical context more satisfying than those offered by available modes of explanation which emphasize social structure or national culture. In particular, it is concerned with the military dimension of American behavior, with thought and action involving war and the threat or use of force.

We need at the outset to recognize that there is something peculiar about *all* military activity, and that its peculiarities demand attention. Military activity, compared to other forms of human activity, and considered historically along the dimension of time, is unique in two respects: it is violent, and it is episodic. Violence continues to be an area of great ignorance, even of mystery, and its primal quality, the way it touches the very root of our existence, ensures that the use or contemplation of violence will trigger the most powerful emotions. The episodic or intermittent character of warfare has less obvious effects, but they are no less important. Intense, usually quite brief, periods of military activity are separated by long, sometimes very long, periods in which the activity itself is replaced by anticipation of the military future, and by recollection of the military past. The key process is memory. Operating, as it must, in a climate of strong feeling and considerable ignorance induced by the violent nature of war, memory becomes a strange and selective thing; but the brevity, intensity, and relative infrequency of war drastically reduce the chance for mili-

tary memory to become more empirical, to learn from the
feedback of trial and error as men do in more continuous, less
exciting, and better understood forms of activity. Again and
again, we find military memory, under the pressures of war,
failing to adapt readily to the unanticipated or unprecedented
results of action, and, instead, trying to hammer facts into the
mold of preconceptions derived from the remembered military
past. Trench warfare in 1917, strategic bombing in 1943, and
search-and-destroy missions in 1967 are only the most notorious cases in point. Shattering defeat may indeed trau-
matically change thinking, but fear, ignorance, and belief seem
all but to strangle the capability for more gradual kinds of ad-
justment. We are speaking here not simply of military technicians or theorists, but of whole societies.

When we consider war in this way—not as a set of military
operations, an instrument of policy, or even as an agent of
social change, but as a recurrent activity, always intense, sometimes traumatic, which closely touches national identity—then
we may reasonably look for help to whatever theory deals with
the recurrent behavior of human beings. The very words
("learn," "memory") used to describe the subject suggest a relevant theory: the branch of psychology that deals with learning.

Elementary concepts of learning, which have a strong experi-
mental foundation, appear most immediately useful:

> That learning occurs more readily through repeated en-
> counters with what the learner perceives to be similar situations;
> That the learner tends to remember only those features of a
> recurrent situation that in some way dictate or control his "suc-
> cessful" response; and
> That the pattern of successful responses is best learned when
> it is "reinforced" by the experience of subsequent encounters.

Learning theory also teaches us that a certain lapse of time between encounters may actually strengthen learning in comparison with the results of a more nearly continuous set of encounters. Moreover, learning, in the sense of the tendency to repeat

a pattern of responses, is further strengthened by "partial reward" or "intermittent reinforcement," which means that if the
response is sometimes unsuccessful the learner will learn not to
be discouraged by an occasional setback, and so will tend all the
more to respond in the patterned way that he has previously
learned. A corollary of the concept of intermittent reinforcement would seem to be that the learner-actor is made less sensitive to the "irrelevant" features of each situation, even to anomalous features which might otherwise suggest to him that the
situation is essentially different from those about which he has
previously learned. Finally, there are two experimentally
derived hypotheses that appear useful for our purposes: One
states that *infrequent* situations tend to be perceived in terms of
a very small number of "preferred cues"; the other states that
complex situations tend to be studied by the technique called
"successive scanning." The two hypotheses converge when they
are applied to situations that are both infrequent *and* complex:
The use of "preferred cues" means reducing complexity to a
few "key" features, while "successive scanning" means selecting
information by a relatively clumsy method that leads to relatively simplistic conclusions; in terms of results, the one process
sounds very much like the other.[6]

The relevance, or at least the suggestiveness, of this body of
theoretical insight for the historical study of war should be obvious. Wars are recurrent, remembered, similar, separated by
intervals of time, various in form and outcome, relatively infrequent in the life of an individual or a generation, and highly
complex. That the behavior associated with war is often "traditional," insensitive to nuance, inflexible, compulsive, and simplistic hardly needs demonstration. One may object, however,
to the intrusion of theory by asking what historical insight it
offers that might not be attained as easily and more safely from
a direct study of historical data and a normal exercise of historical imagination. A preliminary answer to the question is that
the use of learning theory in the study of the military history of

American society reverses a frequently encountered, but rarely articulated, common-sense approach to the analysis of contemporary military affairs. This approach rests on the working assumption that the current significance of an event decreases directly with its distance in time from the present: the more remote, the less likely it is to be important. Thus, all events before 1945 or 1940 may be relegated to an introductory "background," and those before 1900 or 1890 may be ignored.[7] Learning theory invites us to challenge this common-sense approach by considering the possibility that the explanatory importance of events should be reckoned not by *proximity,* but by *priority* in historical time.

Learning theory, applied to the military history of a whole society, obviously entails assumptions and biases of its own. One is that a society and a person are not crucially dissimilar, and that individual and collective perception, memory, and behavior may be treated as comparable. Another is that time will be measured less in days or years than in decades and centuries, and action less in terms of the differences and conflicts that divide society than in terms of the shared attitudes that unite it. By thus measuring long-run continuity and broad consensus, rather than change or internal conflict, we are regarding American society as in some sense a living organism whose behavior reveals coherence and consistency, and which can be said to learn from and remember its military past. We are saying, in effect, that the emotional stress of combat, the enduring mysteries of violence, and the intermittent character of war create a situation not unlike that created by a psychologist in his laboratory when he examines perception and action, under conditions of ignorance and stress, by means of intermittent encounters. Using this conception of military history, we raise questions about the American military experience—about what patterns are evident in that experience, about how that experience has been perceived, and about how discrete episodes appear to be related in time. Instead of assuming that nothing that happened prior to the steam engine or the machine gun or the atomic bomb or America's rise to world power is relevant to what happened subsequently, we assume that a remembered past has always more or less constricted both action in the present and thinking about the future.

Let us begin by dividing almost four centuries of military experience into smaller units of time, according to major changes in the historical situation. The seventeenth and eighteenth centuries appear as the first natural unit: they represent not merely "colonial background" but a formative period of quite serious military troubles which gave rise to considerable anxiety and led to ways of thinking about war, and of acting in war, that set British North America clearly apart from Europe. To call these first centuries an age of survival may seem hyperbolic, but military "survival," at least in a political if not a physical sense, was an important question for American society even to the end of the War of 1812. The second natural period, a golden age, or "age of free security" as Vann Woodward has called it, was the nineteenth century.[8] There were of course wars and rumors of war in the nineteenth century, and it is possible to argue that the Civil War is the most important single episode in American history. But it is unreasonable to argue, as has recently been tried, that the nineteenth century was almost as full of real and perceived military perils and problems as is our own time.[9] The truth is that for about a century after 1815 American society enjoyed, and was conscious of enjoying, a remarkable freedom from external military threat.

Exactly when the age of free security ended is a complex question, and the answer depends very much on our perspective. Woodward selects 1945; other historians would point to 1898. But the emerging tendencies of the third age, our own age, are clear enough. To call the twentieth century an age of power and insecurity sounds like a textbook cliché, but such a label is an accurate and useful characterization. On the one hand, by the turn of the century there was a growing sense of insecurity, of new threats perceived although the specific dangers could not, and even now cannot, be clearly defined. On the other hand, as American society itself grew in numbers and wealth, there was a growing accumulation of potential military power, with no apparent economic or demographic limits on how much military power it might be possible to accumulate. The limits of American power were thus not seen to be intrinsic, as they were in France, for example, but rather were to be set by the political process, which presumably would establish them on the basis of some strategic calculation. But without clearly defined dangers, such calculations could not be made, at least not convincingly, and any politically established level of military power inevitably seemed arbitrary. These, then, are the principal features of American military experience since the end of the nineteenth century: military insecurity without a clear definition of danger, and military power without any apparent limits—the two constantly interacting to produce a kind of military indeterminacy, and giving a name to our own age of power and insecurity.

With the basic outline of American military experience established, we can now turn to the most important relationships and patterns within this general framework.

The first English colonies were planted in an extraordinarily violent and ideologically polarized period of Western history. It is an obvious point, but one that American historians for some reason have frequently ignored.[10] They have tended instead to treat colonization as a successful flight from European violence and insecurity, as indeed it was seen by many colonists themselves; but to view colonization in that way hardly reduces the historical significance of this particular aspect of the environment in which the colonies originated. The early history of any seventeenth-century colony, even as late as the settlement of Pennsylvania and South Carolina, reveals that these were dangerous times, with violent people and tough leaders who felt the dangers keenly and were ready to use

violence themselves.[11] The frightfulness of the Thirty Years'
War, which coincided with the settlement of Virginia and
Massachusetts, had been prefigured in late Elizabethan Ireland, and Irish pacification and early American colonization
were closely related in method, problems, and personnel. We
should remember, for example, that while Sir Humphrey Gilbert allegedly prayed aloud when his ship foundered on his
last voyage to the New World, he was much better known to
contemporaries for the way he had lined the path to his tent
with the severed heads of Irish peasants.[12] Gilbert and his numerous English successors knew very well that their ventures
in the Western Hemisphere were semi-military, semi-piratical
intrusions on the established empire of Spain and the antece-
dent colonial claims of France. The likelihood of violent consequences was never far from their minds.

The irony is that during most of the seventeenth century
these European threats failed to materialize. Instead, the chief
threat came from those on whom considerable hopes had been
centered. Conversion of Indians to Christianity stood higher
among the priorities of early English colonizers, even in
Virginia, than is usually recognized, and serious (though ultimately futile) efforts were devoted to that end.[13] But the normal pattern of Anglo-Indian relations became one not of Christian conversion and worship, but of uneasy truce, punctuated
by incredibly barbaric warfare, often followed by migration or
subjugation. From about 1650 to about 1750, when European
states were moving toward forms of military organization, techniques of fighting, goals of foreign policy, and a generally accepted code of military and diplomatic behavior that eliminated
or mitigated the worst effects of warfare on society, the English
colonists in North America found themselves re-enacting on a
small scale the horrors of Irish pacification and the Thirty
Years' War.[14]

There is no need to exaggerate either the frequency of Indian warfare or the vulnerability of colonial society to it, but

the difference between American and European military experience in this period is unmistakable and extremely important. The colonies did not have the means to create a hard military shell, composed of specialists, that could protect the soft center of society, composed of the great mass of people, nor would such a shell have been effective against Indian tactics.[15] The colonies, as they became more heavily and densely populated, soon acquired a high military potential, much greater than that of even the strongest Indian tribes, but they never had more than a fairly low capacity for effective self-defense. The distinction between potential strength and defensive capacity is crucial. Moreover, the fighting strength of the colonies was mobilized in wartime only at the price of considerable social disruption caused by the militia system—a general, unspecialized obligation for military service. With great strength but weak defenses, the colonies experienced warfare less in terms of protection, of somehow insulating society against external violence (as was increasingly true of European warfare), than in terms of retribution, of retaliating against violence already committed.

The consequences of this situation would surely have been much less severe if, at the time when hostile Indians were losing their own capacity to do really serious harm to the English settlements, a long period of war between England and France, usually joined by Spain, had not begun. Both sides used Indian auxiliaries against the other, but the English were far more numerous; as a result, the relative weakness of the thinly populated neighboring French and Spanish settlements, plus the costliness and inefficiency of regular troops transported to the Western Hemisphere, forced the French and Spanish to depend heavily on Indian allies, and thus on the forms of Indian warfare. The effect was to perpetuate, and in some areas of English settlement even to intensify, the quality of the seventeenth-century military experience.[16] This effect was further reinforced because these new dangers could be perceived in terms of anti-Catholicism, just at a time when religious antagonism was no longer a major factor in European diplomacy and warfare.

These European wars in America, like the purely Indian wars before them, puzzled and frustrated the English colonists. Invariably war originated in Europe, beyond their reach and even their understanding. Its causes had nothing to do with anything that had happened or been done in the colonies, or so it seemed, but every European war meant inevitable and often horrible death and suffering in the Western Hemisphere. Schemes of neutralization were tried but soon broke down. The delicate territorial adjustments of European diplomacy had no meaning in a wilderness where boundaries were seldom known (even when they could be established) and never respected, just as the elaborate defensive arrangements of forts and lines that suited the Low Countries or the Po Valley were almost completely ineffective where spaces were vast and armies ill-trained and numerically small.[17]

Strong but highly vulnerable, angered and frightened by repeated and ruthless attack, bewildered by the causes of war, disrupted by its effects, and powerless to prevent it, articulate English colonists by the end of the seventeenth century were making extreme proposals for the solution of their military problem. Nothing would do, they wrote, but the complete elimination of French and Spanish power from North America; anything less, it was claimed by those who purported to speak for America, was worse than useless, because it would create a false sense of security.[18] Of course these were fantastic demands by European standards; territorial exchanges and adjustments followed every eighteenth-century war, but the actual conquest and retention of large spaces was too costly militarily and too dangerous diplomatically. When the fortress of Bergen-op-Zoom—a place few colonists could have found on a map—fell to the French in 1747, it became necessary to give Cape Breton Island back to France after Massachusetts had seized it in 1745. These were the rules of the game, but the Americans wanted to change them. Even the Anglicized, judicious, and irenic Benjamin Franklin is found in 1760 reiterating what was by then the classic American demand for a definitive military solution. After recounting the atrocities of the French and Indian wars, he called for the "extirpation" of the French in Canada because of their manifold wickedness. He was writing for the public, to be sure, but there is no evidence to suggest that he did not sincerely believe every word that he wrote.[19]

Several things may be said about this typically American belief that nothing less than a complete solution was required to solve the problem of American military security: One is that it seems a not unreasonable response to difficult military circumstances; another is that it was grossly unrealistic in terms of normal eighteenth-century international relations; a third is that in three great wars, from 1760 to 1815, it was almost completely realized. Precisely how and why an understandable but unrealistic belief which gave rise to a set of fantastic demands was translated into concrete reality is an interesting story; but more important here is the fact of realization itself.

Considered together, from the American point of view, the Seven Years' War (1754–63), the Revolutionary War (1775–83), and the War of 1812 reveal a remarkable pattern. In each the very existence of American society was seen to be at stake; invasion and early defeats brought hopes in each of these wars to low ebb. But early setbacks were followed by military recovery, perseverance, and ultimate victory. And the magnitude of victory was the most remarkable and important similarity of all. In 1763, following British naval success so great as to be politically and diplomatically embarrassing, all French and Spanish power on the North American continent east of the Mississippi was actually "extirpated." The British government paid for these extraordinary military and diplomatic results when, twenty years later, isolated by its own success, it was forced by a hostile

France, an unfriendly Europe, and rebellious Americans to give the new United States most of what had been previously won. And thirty years later the United States, caught squarely between Napoleonic France and its strongest enemy, emerged from an unwanted war with a virtual (and within a few years obvious) guarantee that the threat of European military intervention in American affairs was finally at an end.

The American Revolutionary War thus became in the national memory and imagination paradigmatic of how America saved itself from being like, and part of, Europe and Europe's problems. The Revolutionary story of defeat (Bunker Hill), near collapse (Long Island and New Jersey), desperate hope (Trenton, Princeton, and Saratoga), endurance (Brandywine, Valley Forge, and the loss of the whole deep South), and ultimate, almost miraculous victory (Yorktown) has the same rhythmic structure apparent in both the Seven Years' War and the War of 1812. The Revolutionary War repeated and permanently implanted in national consciousness the patterned experience of the last and greatest colonial war, and the War of 1812 reinforced this collective, enduring perception of what a major armed struggle must—and ought to—look like. The great wars of the future, the Civil War and the Second World War, fit and intensified this early, formative image. First Bull Run (1861) and Pearl Harbor (1941), like Braddock's Field (1755), Fort William Henry (1757), Detroit (1812), and Bladensburg (1814) rehearsed the unforgettable story of Bunker Hill (1775) and Long Island (1776). Americans, never ready for war, often surprised by it but always boyishly confident about their knack for waging it, were repeatedly brought to their knees by the first battles and campaigns. At best gallant, at worst disorganized and demoralized, they came close to complete defeat again and again. Never, however, did they give up. And beyond the humiliation of Brooklyn and the Brandywine lay Saratoga and Yorktown—or Quebec, New Orleans, Gettysburg, Missionary Ridge, Omaha Beach, Leyte Gulf, and Inchon. The Revolutionary War told the story so that all could remember and later repeat it. The myth, like the event itself, was truly "revolutionary" in its effects. Seen together and in conjunction with the earlier colonial experience, the three wars of this "revolutionary generation" (1754–63, 1775–83, 1812–15) reiterated on a grander historical scale the internal rhythmic structure of each separate war: from the frequent little disasters and occasional despair of colonies that had been beset for a century by ruthless Indians and "implacable" Catholics, to the eventual recovery, total victory, and—by the second decade of the nineteenth century—unique security of a free, successful, and republican nation.

The military experience of these first two centuries was described earlier as formative, and that description seems to be true in a quite literal way. American society entered its age of free security with certain military attitudes which had already been implanted and powerfully reinforced: (1) a deep respect for the kind of military prowess that had become so closely bound up with the very definition of American nationhood, a respect tinged with contempt for military professionalism which was viewed as unnecessary, ineffectual, and thus somehow un-American;[20] (2) a concept of military security that was expressed not in relative but in absolute terms (the society knew both extremes: what had seemed to be total military insecurity, and what now looked like total military security— though opposite, the two were perceptually linked); and (3) an extraordinary optimism about what, when necessary, could be achieved by the exertion of American military force, as the three wars demonstrated beyond all doubt.

Little happened in the nineteenth century to call any of these attitudes into question, and much to reinforce them still further. In particular, the belief that military security was an absolute value, like chastity or grace, and that American society had been granted it, presumably deserved it, and ought to be able to keep it, was verified simply by the passage of time without the appearance of any perceptible threat. Foreign relations ceased to attract the popular and political attention that they had received for so long. American diplomacy became increasingly free-wheeling, even careless and bombastic, but the occasional confrontations with a European Power—with Spain over Florida after the War of 1812, with all the Powers over Latin American independence and recognition in the 1820's, with France over unpaid American claims in the 1830's, with Britain over Oregon in the 1840s, again with France over Mexico in the 1860's, with Germany over Samoa in the 1880's, with Britain and Germany over Venezuela at the end of the century—always ended in what looked very much like a Great Power back-down. And in fact no Great Power could find that its interests were served by pushing disagreement with the inept, unpredictable, but very numerous Americans to the point of war.[21]

The several wars actually fought by the United States during the nineteenth century can be divided into two categories: the Civil War, and all the others. The others—the Mexican War, the Spanish-American War, and the many small wars against various Indian tribes—make up a disparate group, but they have essential features in common. The causes of each could be traced back to atrocious behavior by the enemy: the usual murders and mutilation connected with every Indian war, the massacres of the Alamo and Goliad by the Mexicans, and the brutal pacification policies of the Spanish in Cuba. Enemy atrocities were by no means the only or even the main cause of these wars, and in all of them Americans themselves flagrantly broke the rules of civilized warfare—the Illinois militia in the Black Hawk War, Texans at San Jacinto, and the U.S. Army during the Philippine insurrection committed some major atrocities of their own.[22] But the main point is that it was very easy for Americans to explain and justify the outbreak of war in terms of the criminal conduct of an inhuman, perhaps degenerate, foe. And once Americans had been attacked and killed, whether they were a few Western farmers or fur traders, a detachment of soldiers on the Rio Grande, or sailors on a battleship in Havana harbor, other arguments about the causes and the objectives of war came to seem irrelevant.[23]

Each of these nineteenth-century wars also ended in a similar way, with an important extension of American territory and control. A defeated Indian tribe could mean the opening of a future State to American settlement; the Mexican War secured an enormous southwestern territory for the United States; and the war with Spain brought in its wake Hawaii, the Philippines, and new bases in the Pacific and Caribbean. These gains were not the avowed war aims of the United States, nor even the conscious objectives of most war leaders; rather, they seemed, under the circumstances, to be the natural rewards of superior virtue and military skill.

Perhaps the most important similarity of these wars is that in every one the enemy was very weak and easily beaten. There were, obviously, military difficulties: the old Duke of Wellington believed—with some reason—that Winfield Scott would be defeated before he could get his army to Mexico City; the Seminoles in Florida fought tenaciously, and, of course, the Sioux defeated General Custer in 1876; and Colonel Theodore Roosevelt thought that the American military situation was desperate during the siege of Santiago. But in the end the United States always managed to achieve an overwhelming victory at a fairly small cost. Nothing happened in any of these wars to shake American optimism about the ability of the society to use military force successfully, and a great deal happened to strengthen further that already well-established attitude.

The Civil War is obviously a quite different case. As the bloodiest war in American history, and as unmistakable evidence of failure in American society, we might expect the Civil War to have disrupted or rearranged the evident patterns of American military experience. The curious fact is that it did not have this effect, and the important question is, why not?

We have already noted that the key to understanding the deeper effects of the other wars of the nineteenth century is the weakness of the enemy. There is a comparable key to understanding the Civil War; that key is *symmetry*. Both sides were American, and both went to war with a characteristic American optimism about its outcome. Both had to start from scratch and improvise huge war machines, so neither had any immediate military advantage over the other in the beginning. Both sides had been schooled in the same ways of looking at war and both drew their military cadres from the same source, so there was little sense that a tradition was being tested by a new, external standard. Although the human damage done to American society by the Civil War was comparable to that done to European society by World War I, the fact that it was a civil war protected Americans against many of its potentially traumatic effects. A long, bloody stalemate might logically have shattered optimistic ideas about the use of armed force, but with Americans on both sides it was possible to regard the Civil War as a military anomaly—an exceptional case that proved nothing. The only mistake seen in retrospect was that of underestimating the fighting qualities of other Americans. The concept of "intermittent reinforcement," which explains how perversely the mind may read lessons into a single unhappy experience, helps us to understand why the Civil War may have even strengthened an older, seemingly inappropriate pattern of perception and response.

Because the South lost the war, some historians have argued that the experience of military defeat changed that region in fundamental ways, setting it apart from the rest of American society and producing much of its odd behavior over the next hundred years.[24] If their argument is sound, we would have to modify our own argument that the Civil War was a symmetrical experience in which the military resultant was close to zero. But those who stress the peculiar impact of defeat on the South may not have grasped the nature of Southern "defeat."

When the Confederacy gave up, its main armies had been destroyed, its people were tired, and its resources depleted. Continued military resistance, however, was possible and was seriously considered at the time. There were historical precedents for such resistance in the American Revolution and the Spanish opposition to Napoleon, and later it would become common for wars of national independence to be carried on with few resources and without conventional military means. The defeat of regular armies does not, in itself, explain capitulation when manpower, basic weapons, and the will to resist are still present as they were in 1865. The vast spaces, rural economy, and poor transportation system of the South were ideal factors for an effective large-scale resistance movement along guerrilla lines, and it seems reasonable to believe that the South could have been made virtually indigestible for a Federal army which was not much larger and had far less mobility and firepower than the maximum American force in South Vietnam. Whether a resistance movement would have drawn clandestine support, from blockade running and through the trans-Mississippi area, is of course problematical, but here again other historical examples indicate that the small increment of outside help needed to keep a guerrilla war alive could have been found. Jefferson Davis had said in his inaugural address that no sacrifice would be too great to secure Southern independence, but Southern leaders decided instead to give up in 1865.

By quitting when they did, Southerners were able to believe that they had fought as long as they could, which was true by strictly conventional standards. Defeat was thus honorable. But they saved more than honor; they saved the basic elements— with the exception of slavery itself—of the Southern social, that is to say racial, order. The social order could not possibly have survived the guerrilla warfare which a continued resistance movement would have required. Too many blacks, a large part of the "people" on which guerrillas must depend, had already voted with their feet. By saving honor and preserving the social order, Southerners could claim that they had won a moral, if not a military, victory. And historians, from Buck to McKitrick, have explained how the Federal government and the people of the North, both deliberately and unwittingly, did not effectively refute the Southern claim to moral victory, but even sustained it, virtually conspiring with the South to prove that no one—no white man at least—had really lost the Civil War, and to demonstrate that both sides, as Americans, should take the brave deeds and great men of the war as their own.[25] The national cult of Robert E. Lee is only the most obvious case in point. The conspiracy survived until it died amidst the mawkish sentimentality of the Civil War Centennial, appropriately killed by the Civil Rights Movement. Before the conspiracy died, however, it had successfully drawn most of the psychological sting of defeat, although Southerners have often found it useful to play the role of a defeated and oppressed people, in part because so many Northerners have been such a sympathetic audience. For our purpose in describing the quality of the American military experience, we can simply note that the Civil War did surprisingly little to change basic American patterns of thought and action.

At this point, before entering the twentieth century, we should pause to reconsider the approach we have been taking to the American military past. There can hardly be any question that, whenever Americans before the end of the nineteenth century thought about questions of war or military force, their perception of those questions was strongly affected by certain peculiar attitudes and beliefs that, through the conditioning effect of long historical experience, had become almost reflexive. A dichotomous idea of national security, an unthinking optimism about the natural American aptitude for warfare, and an ambivalent attitude toward those Americans who specialized in the use of force, all have had consequences in the twentieth century, and it is easy enough to speculate about what those consequences have been. But it is difficult to

continue the discussion beyond 1900 in quite the way that we
have carried it on so far. Before 1900, military history is a
rather amorphous and often peripheral aspect of American society. Only sporadically, even in the colonial period, were military problems of central, explicit concern, while military institutions hardly existed apart from the inherent military strength
of the whole society. But by 1900 this situation was changing.
The problem of military security, in one form or another,
began—very slowly at first—to move toward the center of politics; and military institutions—again almost imperceptibly—
began to play an expanded social role. All public issues came to
be touched by the growing consciousness of military problems,
until at last a conservative President, a former general, could
warn the nation of the peril of a garrison state. Accordingly, as
it becomes more difficult to isolate military experience, our
analysis must become more complex.

On the very general level on which we have been operating
so far, we can say that, regarded in military terms, American
involvement in both World Wars certainly further reinforced
historically implanted attitudes and beliefs. Delayed entry in
both wars, followed by fairly uninterrupted progress toward
victory, made it possible in each case for Americans to overlook
the extent to which France, Britain, and Russia had worn down
German strength, and instead to believe that the United States
had really won the war. Even at the tactical level, American
self-confidence was confirmed. General John Pershing's naïve
demand for a return to open-field tactics could be realized only
under the special conditions of 1918, while the success of the
Normandy landings in 1944 seemed to prove that the British
had been unduly timid in their long argument with Americans
about the feasibility of a cross-Channel attack.[26] In other respects, the historic American outlook helps to explain what
otherwise might be hard to understand. Only a fundamental
self-confidence in the ability to fight, combined with a Mani-
chaean idea of security, made it natural to wait so long, to be so

peace-loving, before intervening in these World Wars, and then to intervene so massively on every front. Although Woodrow Wilson had earlier—and accurately—proclaimed peace without victory as the only satisfactory outcome for the United States, he responded to an essentially limited attack—submarine warfare—in a way that made a stalemate peace impossible, and thus guaranteed overwhelming Allied victory.[27] Franklin D. Roosevelt and his advisers had agreed in 1940 that Germany was the principal threat to American security, but virtually nothing was done to avert war with Japan, nor, once it had begun, was its prosecution kept strictly subordinate to European strategy.[28] Even the remarkable position of American military leaders in both wars, with strong political support but with little effective political guidance, reflects the ambivalent position of the military profession in American society.

By looking at twentieth-century American military experience in this way, we have simply extended an approach that seeks to define a broad consensus on military questions, an image of war which helps to explain the military behavior of the society as a whole. It does not emphasize technical military theories, which are international and not merely American in scope, and which actively interest only a small fraction of the society. We do know that American military leaders, from George Washington to William Sherman, were more responsive than is generally realized to European modes of military thought.[29] Yet we are able to subordinate such technical military ideas to broader and cruder forms of thought because, prior to about 1890, technical military thinking never played more than a secondary role. But by the end of the nineteenth century, when the rate of change in the technology of warfare had, in a few decades, become perhaps as great as it is today, military theory assumed an importance, even in American society, that requires us to treat it as a primary and independent variable.

If we focus on these technical ideas in the period since 1890, particularly on those that have become fully articulated and clearly differentiated systems of military thought (which may be called doctrines), we encounter an interesting fact: Of about a half-dozen doctrines which have informed Western military behavior in the twentieth century, three of them reached their most complete development in the United States.[30]

The doctrines, to describe them in their own technical terms, are those of Sea Power, Strategic Air Attack, and Limited War or, as it came to be known, Flexible Response. The doctrine of sea power as it was developed by Alfred T. Mahan stated that by offensive action a concentrated battle fleet could effectively deny the use of the sea to inferior naval forces and could pierce the coastal defense of any hostile power. The doctrine of strategic air attack, not an American invention but adopted and enthusiastically implemented by the United States, asserted that the hard military shell around the soft center of a modern industrial society could be outflanked from the air, with the result that the capacity of such a society to wage war could be quickly and completely destroyed. The doctrine of flexible response, a product of the great debate over military policy in the 1950's and a military reality only in the last decade, states that violence in any form can most effectively be dealt with by equivalent violence.

These technical doctrines have guided both thought and action on much broader issues involving war because they have had a responsive audience outside the narrow circle of military technicians. Theodore Roosevelt, Brooks Adams, and many other American intellectuals found Mahan's ideas exciting and persuasive.[31] Strategic air doctrine was worked out at Maxwell Field, but it was also actively promoted in the popular press, and its wide appeal was reflected, for example, in the columns of the *New Republic*, in the isolationist attack on Roosevelt by Charles Lindbergh, and in Roosevelt's own first decisions on strategy in 1938 and 1940.[32] Flexible response is a product less of the Pentagon than of American universities, and it could never have been realized without first capturing the imagination of the Kennedy Administration.[33]

Equally important is the fact that each doctrine emerged from a crisis within the military profession. More than military professionals in other societies, American career officers have always felt a special need to justify their very existence. But there were truly critical periods for the Navy in the 1880's, for the new Air Corps in the 1920's, and for the Army in the decade after 1945.[34] In these times of professional crisis, when it seemed as if a particular military service might almost wither away in the absence of any clear need for what it could do best, the doctrines of sea power, strategic air attack, and flexible response each carried considerable justificatory power on behalf of the service so threatened. Under the circumstances peculiar both to American society and to the particular crisis, it is not surprising that each doctrine was adopted and promoted with a zeal that blinded its proponents to alternative possibilities and to its inherent shortcomings.

Each doctrine can also be associated with an epoch of American foreign policy: sea power with imperialism and active intervention, especially in the Caribbean but also in the Far East; strategic air attack with isolationism not only in the interwar period but also in the sector of postwar strategy that depended solely on the threat to retaliate massively; and flexible response with global containment of Communist-supported revolution. The connections between technical doctrine and broad patterns of foreign policy are not all immediately obvious, and, especially in the case of the relationship between air power doctrine and isolationism, it is necessary to go beyond the apparent contradictions in order to see the underlying positive connections. But, in every case, military doctrine and foreign policy have been mutually and dynamically reinforcing.

This brings us to the last point about these doctrines: Do they reveal, when considered sequentially, some kind of fundamental shift during the twentieth century, or since 1945, in

the characteristic American outlook on war, some new lessons
from new experience? A positive answer might seem obviously
in order, because in substance each doctrine differs markedly
from the others, and each was developed in bitter opposition to
what had preceded it. Sea power doctrine was a critique of
traditional defensive notions of American security in the same
way that strategic air doctrine exploited the revealed weaknesses of sea power, and "limited-war" thinking grew out of the
logical and practical deficiencies of thermonuclear retaliation.
Moreover, all seem to break with a more distant past in their
emphasis on offensive military action, and the flexible-response
doctrine explicitly repudiates what were taken to be traditional
American ideas about the all-or-nothing use of force.

Even when all of the above is conceded, the elements of continuity are still most impressive: New ideas were absorbed and
reshaped by old, deeply imbedded modes of thinking about
war. Certainly the curious historical position of the military
profession in American society helps to account for the passionate, often obsessive, espousal of these doctrines by segments of the military elite. But the doctrines have also had
great political and even social resonance. They have not only
underpinned foreign policy; at times they have themselves
created foreign policy, as in 1964–65, when the existence of
military force and a doctrine for its employment seemed to
move into a vacuum of informed and constructive political
thinking. This resonance is fully explained only when we see
how each doctrine has rested upon, and drawn upon for emotional sustenance, the characteristic attitudes and beliefs that
were implanted, transmitted, and reinforced by almost four
centuries of American military experience. Each doctrine in-
corporates within it something like what we have called an absolute or dichotomous conception of security. The United
States is secure, or it is not; it is threatened, or it is not. None of
the doctrines, even flexible response, really allows for differences in the degree or quality of the threat. Both sea and air

doctrine argue that effective military action must be total, and that anything less is worse than useless. The doctrine of flexible response, while stating that force should be carefully proportioned to the military strength of the threatening force, implies that *all* unfriendly force endangers American security and so deserves forceful confrontation; it explicitly rejects the inherently passive posture of merely threatening to retaliate. All three doctrines also incorporate an extremely optimistic view of the skill with which American society can use force; in all three, there is a promise that, if the doctrine is followed, military success will be surgically swift and effective.

What has happened in the twentieth century is that, amidst rapid military and social change and unprecedented kinds of military experience, American society has been able to find—unconsciously, of course—the intellectual and psychological means to preserve much of an older response to military problems, and to preserve within that response much of its primitive force.

Throughout this essay, historical data have been ordered to fit the presumption that a society learns about war in much the same way that a rat learns to find food in a laboratory maze, or a child learns to cope with strange animals. As noted in the beginning, there are difficulties with such an approach. One, clearly, is evidential. Has anything been demonstrated beyond reasonable doubt? The answer is No. Once the theory is invoked, the data fall into place and the patterns become visible, but the relationship of act-thought-act remains unproved in any specific case, and is not easily reduced to a hypothetical statement which the historian can test by his usual methods. A second, theoretical difficulty follows closely on the first: May not military activity within American or any society be explained by other than prior military experience? The answer, surely, is Yes. Domestic political crisis, economic interest, child-rearing practices, the behavior of the enemy—any or all might indeed be part of complete explanation in a given case. The weakness here lies with the theory, which isolates the learner from the total context of his life. A third difficulty, mentioned earlier, is in the peril of equating an entire society with a biological individual; we have not been applying theory in any strict sense, but have simply been using a theoretical analogy.

Even faced with these unresolved difficulties, we can conclude that, in the future, those who seek to explain American governmental or popular behavior on issues involving war and the military must ask more seriously than they have before to what extent they are dealing with learned responses which operate beneath the level of full consciousness. The general national perception of the ethics and uses of war, and of the status and character of the military, is not the only important factor to be considered in understanding behavior in a particular war or positions taken on a question of military policy; but this perception is clearly a major factor, especially in American society with its unique pattern of military experience. Yet this perception is consistently ignored, partly because the time-frame of military studies is usually too short to take most sequential relationships into account, partly because the very notion of learned perception and response has seemed unusably vague.

Beyond its relevance to American society, the hypothesis that national military behavior is in a real sense learned behavior should have value for the study of any modern nation, or perhaps of any society. Certainly the constantly reinforcing pattern of American military experience has been extraordinary, just as the relationship between popular sentiment and governmental action has been exceptionally close throughout American history. Yet less democratic societies, with more varied military experiences, must also have learned to perceive military situations and to respond to them in ways that differentiate one society from another. Merely to ascribe significantly different patterns or styles of military behavior to differences in objective conditions—to size, wealth, geography, vulnerability, etc.—is to beg the difficult question of why nations often wage war in "strange" ways. We ask why governments collapse under military pressure, or capitulate, or run inordinate, even suicidal risks; why societies are militarily aggressive or apathetic, resist or yield under assault; why one, and not another, of several equally "rational" choices is selected. Definitive answers are probably beyond our power, but surely an approximation of truth must take into account the deep, primitive understanding of what war means in the life history of the tribe.

A last word is prompted by the admission that we have been using not a theory but an analogy. This admission gives us the freedom to look for other theoretical analogies in considering the present and future implications of our picture of the American military past. The nation appears to have reached a stage where its military learning is no longer appropriate, and so we wonder about the process of un-learning. Learning theory treats the so-called "extinction" of learning, but the theoretical discussion does not fit either the data or our impressions as well as before; extinction of learning appears in the literature as a relatively tame and straight-forward process compared to what we know about the convulsions of American society during the last five years. Our own historical analysis suggests that something more profound than "rat-finds-cheese" occurred in the course of several centuries of national military experience. The facts alone—that no other nation, not even Wilhelmine Germany, has had its official origin (Revolutionary War) and constitutional preservation (Civil War) so clearly linked to warfare, or has acquired such overwhelming military power after seeming so vulnerable—indicate that Freud and Erikson speak more directly to our current situation than do Pavlov and his successors.

If warfare is as tightly bound up with American national identity as the body of this essay argues, then we will need theories of personality, and not merely of learning, to help us understand the present and even anticipate the future. What

we find is a suggestion that our current condition is patholog-
ical, and that a considerable disruption of national personality
is inevitable. The first symptoms appeared during the Korean
War. Even if military failure can be acknowledged, the crisis
will be displaced onto other objects, and the costs to the organism will still be very high. Already there are signs that the military profession, and not just an occasional General Edwin
Walker or Curtis Lemay, is losing touch with its ambivalent but
satisfying role, a role which was largely self-policed. For the
first time, American soldiers may be as despised as they have
liked to claim to be when they were not. Disappointment and
disgust with failures, as much as moral and political disapproval
of wrong policies, have provided the emotional fuel for antiwar
action. Even the outrage of the young indicates how far they
were taught to expect a smoother, cleaner American military
performance, and how little prepared they were to face the
prospect of military failure; their expectations and standards
for judging international behavior are as inordinately high as
those of a John Foster Dulles or a Lyndon B. Johnson. For the
first time, very large numbers of ordinary Americans as well as
their leaders are deeply ashamed of their national identity, but
see no effective remedy. Many of them no doubt have mo-
ments when they think that they and the nation will ride it out,
that the Ten Years' War is only a bad dream which will soon be
over and forgotten, that the social and psychic damage can be
limited, and that other issues, other dangers are really more
urgent. Perhaps so; all gloomy prediction is mere speculation.
Nothing, however, in the historical record gives much support
to their modest optimism. On the contrary, the American military past, if I have interpreted it correctly, warns us that the effects of confessed failure are likely to be protracted, unpredictable, and severe.

Further Reflections

Rereading the last paragraph of the last essay in this book almost twenty years after it was written is to be reminded of the perils of prophecy. To pursue a bit further the Freudian metaphor used in that essay for the Vietnam experience, the fate of this painful episode in the American memory since 1976 has been a kind of national repression. Despite a memorial wall in Washington listing the names of more than fifty thousand Americans who died in the war, and despite a flow of films, memoirs, and televised versions claiming verisimilitude if not strict accuracy, the dominant images of the war in national memory have been gross, apparently compulsive distortions. Raised on *Rambo,* a legend more false than Davy Crockett, a generation of American students who enrolled in the popular college courses on the Vietnam War were surprised to learn that American leaders, however mistaken, had actually tried in some rational manner to analyze their problem and to formulate possible solutions, that not every aspect of the war was an unmitigated atrocity perpetrated by the United States, and that the American military was not in virtual mutiny and disintegration from the day of its arrival in Vietnam. Perhaps these students will retrieve and preserve a healthy, honest national memory of Vietnam. But most American appear to have done little more than try to forget this humiliating national failure.

The American military, while neither nursing its alienation nor plotting revenge, as I feared it might in 1976, has been a leader in national forgetfulness. All evidence indicates that the Vietnam War has never become a subject of serious study for the American military profession. Returning happily to the strategic and operational challenge of the Central European battlefield, the Army decided that there was more to be learned from refighting the Lorraine campaign of 1944 than from any further scrutiny of Ap Bac, Ia Drang, or Khe Sanh. After a brief flurry of military interest in euphemistically renamed "low intensity conflicts" in Third World locales, American military leadership has fixated on the NATO mission, which at this writing seems to be crumbling rapidly. The chief lesson of the Vietnam War for the Pentagon has been "never again," at least never without massive support from the American people. Not a bad lesson, perhaps, but not a substitute for careful research and frank discussion.

This contemporary military lesson of Vietnam directs attention back to where it belongs, on the American Revolution. It was widespread public support, though never undivided or unqualified, that made American independence feasible. British reluctance to accept the reality of that support, and to grasp its crucial importance, undermined every effort to suppress the American rebellion. American popular support for the struggle, manifested in thousands of voluntary acts by individuals and communities over an eight-year period, is what made the wartime experience so formative of American national consciousness after 1783. People innocent of political theory, mystified by arguments for and against bicameral legislatures, readily comprehended the brief, appealing message of the Declaration of Independence and its direct relevance to their own lives. Likewise, their memory of the years of danger, uncertainty, and more or less willing personal sacrifice gave special value—a different kind of reality—to what, after all, were only a few written words. All but the last chapter of this book are varying attempts to recapture this reality, to reconstruct some of the war-shaped process for America, 1750–1800, of what the Vietnam era once called "nation building."

As with Vietnam, the American Revolution has been heavily mythologized. The spectacular success of the United States after 1783, despite a few close calls, made it difficult to recall the moment of origin in anything like its actual historical complexity, full of the contingent and problematic. The Bicentennial of the American Revolution, planned amid a building national crisis and celebrated with little genuine zest, never promised to do more than reinforce old myths. But in fact the Bicentennial compelled us to do something, encouraged rethinking, my own included, and its net effect was to push our resistant memories a little closer to the historical truth. Here too the sobering experience of Vietnam, with all its ramifications, may have helped the process.

Sophisticated historians are as chary of talking about the truth as they are of asking, "What if . . . ?" And it would be outrageous for me, standing as I am on the shoulders of several generations of diligent and honest American historians, a few of them giants, to claim that the twelve essays in this book have some corner on historical truth. On the contrary, several of them play deliberately in that dangerously subjective zone where past meets present, and all of them may too naïvely reflect the special *Angst* of the 1960's and 1970's to give readers confidence in their interpretations, their judgments, and even their use of evidence. Yet I do not apologize for them or for my own angle of vision, and I will go so far as to claim that the personal element in each, the passion that moved me to do them in the first place, has been more valuable than otherwise. That passion was not primarily a desire to solve the riddle of American behavior in the present day, to be relevant, or to make my professional colleagues see the value of military history, although each of these thoughts has crossed my mind during the last thirty years. The driving passion was simply to come as close as I could to reconstructing a segment of the past, in the old discredited phrase, as it actually was—not merely the visible, official past that readily finds its way into the archives, but the look, feel, and sound of the past as real people experienced it, and also the deeply buried past, the invisible forces propelling those people in directions they seldom knew they were going. In other words—confessing all— to absorb as much of the truth as I could, and then to tell it, as best I knew how.

Notes

PREFACE TO THE REVISED EDITION

1. The term comes from J. H. Hexter, "The Historian and His Day," in *Reappraisals in History*, edited by Hexter (New York, 1963), 1–13.
2. *The Revolution Remembered: Eyewitness Accounts of the War for Independence* (Chicago, 1980).
3. *The Minutemen and Their World* (New York, 1976).
4. *A Revolutionary People at War: The Continental Army and American Character, 1775–1783* (Chapel Hill, 1979).
5. Buel, *Dear Liberty: Connecticut's Mobilization for the Revolutionary War* (Middletown, Conn., 1980), and Carp, *To Starve the Army at Pleasure: Continental Army Administration and American Political Culture, 1775–1783* (Chapel Hill, 1984). A full, critical survey of this new work in early American military history is Don Higginbotham, "The Early American Way of War," *William and Mary Quarterly,* 3rd series, XLIV (1987), 230–73.
6. *The First of Men: The Life of George Washington* (Knoxville, Tenn., 1988).

CHAPTER ONE

1. Among the many historians and philosophers of history who have discussed this point, the most stimulating and instructive are the early statements by Carl L. Becker, "Everyman His Own Historian," *American Historical Review,* XXXVII (1932), 221–32; the extreme statement that "relevance" not only *does* but *ought* to dictate by Edward Hallett Carr, *What Is History?* (New York, 1963); and the

iconoclastic second thoughts of J. H. Hexter, particularly "The Historian's Day," in his *Reappraisals in History* (New York, 1963), and "The Historian and His Society: A Sociological Inquiry—Perhaps," in his *Doing History* (Bloomington, Ind., 1971).

2. An excellent brief survey of historical writing on the Revolution is by Wesley Frank Craven, "The Revolutionary Era," in *The Reconstruction of American History,* edited by John Higham (New York, 1963); longer and more recent is the introduction by Jack Greene to his *Reinterpretation of the American Revolution* (New York, 1967); one view of the younger generation is expressed by Jesse Lemisch, "The American Revolution Seen from the Bottom Up," in *Towards a New Past: Dissenting Essays in American History,* edited by Barton J. Bernstein (New York, 1968).

3. Don Higginbotham, "American Historians and the Military History of the American Revolution," *American Historical Review*, LXX (1964), 18–34.

4. Wesley Frank Craven, *Why Military History?* (U.S. Air Force Academy, 1959).

5. Piers Mackesy, *The War for America, 1775–1783* (Cambridge, Mass., 1964).

6. John Shy, *Toward Lexington: The Role of the British Army in the Coming of the American Revolution* (Princeton, 1965).

7. Ira D. Gruber, *The Howe Brothers and the American Revolution* (New York, 1972). On the new appreciation of Clausewitz, see, for example, Bernard Brodie, *Strategy in the Missile Age* (Princeton, 1959).

8. Don Higginbotham, *Daniel Morgan: Revolutionary Rifleman* (Chapel Hill, 1961).

9. Don Higginbotham, *The War of American Independence* (New York, 1971).

10. The best picture of the "little war" of constant skirmishing, raid, and ambush is in the journal of Carl Leopold von Baurmeister, *Revolution in America,* translated and edited by Bernhard A. Uhlendorf (New Brunswick, N.J., 1957).

11. On British military and naval leadership, see George A. Billias, ed., *George Washington's Opponents* (New York, 1969).

12. Gruber, *Howe Brothers,* 112–26.

13. In addition to the works already mentioned, William B. Willcox, *Portrait of a General: Sir Henry Clinton in the War of Independence* (New York, 1964), and Franklin and Mary Wickwire, *Cornwallis: The American Adventure* (Boston, 1970), are important.

14. Mackesy, *War for America*. R. Arthur Bowler, *Logistics and the Failure of the British Army in America, 1775–1783* (Princeton, 1975), probes the question of corruption and British strategy more fully than any previous study.

15. Herbert Butterfield, *George III, Lord North, and the People, 1779–80* (London, 1949).

16. Evidence that the timing of the Declaration of Independence was in part intended to block negotiations with the British is in Weldon A. Brown, *Empire or Independence: A Study in the Failure of Reconciliation, 1774–1783* (Baton Rouge, 1941), 90–107. See also George Washington to John Augustine Washington, Philadelphia, May 31, 1776, *The Writings of George Washington*, edited by John C. Fitzpatrick, vol. V (Washington, D.C., 1932), 91–92.

17. A copy of the letter from Duportail to the Minister of War, the Comte de Saint-Germain, dated at the Whitemarsh camp, November 12, 1777, is in the papers of Sir Henry Clinton in the William L. Clements Library, Ann Arbor, Michigan. A summary of the letter is in the papers of the Earl of Shelburne, then in political opposition, also in the Clements Library. A published translation by Arthur P. Watts, based on another copy in the British Public Record Office, is in *Pennsylvania History*, I (1934), 101–6. The summary in the Shelburne papers indicates that the letter was intercepted in the English Channel, which Duportail himself guessed (see Elizabeth S. Kite, *Brigadier-General Louis Lebègue Duportail* [Baltimore, 1933], 59). Duportail was Minister of War early in the French Revolution, later fled to the United States, and died in 1802 on his way to join Napoleon.

18. In fact, pension files exaggerate the amount of longer service because the pension law of 1818 required a minimum of nine months service with Continental forces, and the law of 1832 required a minimum of six months with the militia. The large number who served even less than these minimum periods is apparent only in antiquarian local studies, like that by Howard K. Sanderson, *Lynn [Mass.] in the Revolution*, 2 vols. (Boston, 1909).

19. See, for example, the entries from 1779 onward in *Extracts from the Diary of Christopher Marshall*, edited by William J. Duane (Albany, 1877).

20. The best estimate of numbers of Loyalists is Paul H. Smith, "The American Loyalists: Notes on their Organization and Numerical Strength," *William and Mary Quarterly*, 3rd series, XXV (1968), 259–77.

21. Undated letter quoted in Ernst Kipping, *The Hessian View of America, 1776–1783*, translated by B. A. Uhlendorf (Monmouth Beach, N.J., 1971), 34–35.

22. To John Laurens, [Ramapo, N.J.], June 30, 1780, *The Papers of Alexander Hamilton,* edited by Harold C. Syrett and Jacob E. Cooke, vol. II (New York, 1961), 347–48.

23. To Edmund Randolph, Baltimore, Feb. 15, 1783, *The Papers of Thomas Jefferson,* edited by Julian P. Boyd, vol. VI (Princeton, 1952), 248. The prediction about "going down hill" appears in his *Notes On the State of Virginia,* edited by William Peden (New York, 1972), 161. The *Notes* were written in 1781.

24. *Jefferson Papers,* V, 455, 513, 566, 583–84, 593, 622, et passim.

25. Hannah Arendt, *On Revolution* (New York, 1963), stresses the absence of a "social question" in the American Revolution.

26. Lt. Benjamin Gilbert to his father, West Point, [late June 1783], *Winding Down: The Revolutionary War Letters of Lieutenant Benjamin Gilbert of Massachusetts, 1780–1783* (Ann Arbor, 1989), 108. On the Newburgh officer's "coup," there is Richard H. Kohn, "The Inside History of the Newburgh Conspiracy: America and the Coup d'Etat," *William and Mary Quarterly,* 3rd series, XXVII (1970), 187–220; Paul David Nelson, "Horatio Gates at Newburgh, 1783: A Misunderstood Role," with a rebuttal by Richard H. Kohn, *ibid.,* XXIX (1972), 143–58; and C. Edward Skeen, "The Newburgh Conspiracy Reconsidered," with a rebuttal by Richard H. Kohn, *ibid.,* XXXI (1974), 273–98.

27. This definition of war is in Maj. George S. Patton, Jr.'s unpublished thesis of 1932 in the Army War College archives, acc. no. 387-52, p. 46. The full passage is, "The guiding principle of [military] organization should be the endeavor to devise means of killing without getting killed."

CHAPTER TWO

1. Even the best military historians have done this, at least by implication. See Walter Millis, *Arms and Men* (New York, 1956), chap. I, especially the first sentence; or Louis Morton, "The Origins of American Military Policy, *Military Affairs,* XXII (1958), 75–82. Daniel Boorstin, author of the most provocative essay yet written on the subject, says: "Allowing for some variations, there was an impressive uniformity in the way colonists organized (or failed to organize) their defense." *The Americans: The Colonial Experience* (New York, 1958), 356, in the part entitled "A Nation of Minute Men." The

most important of the polemicists on the militia question were Emory Upton, John A. Logan, and John McAuley Palmer.

2. It is emphasized that what follows are hypotheses suggested by research done in another connection, and are intended to stimulate further inquiry. Professor Clyde R. Ferguson of Kansas State University discussed these hypotheses, when they were presented as a paper, knowledgeably and perceptively. While not accepting some of his views, I have profited by his criticism, as I have by that of Professor Wesley Frank Craven.

3. William Waller Hening, ed., *The Statutes at Large: Being a Collection of All the Laws of Virginia*...(Richmond, 1810–23), I, 174.

4. *Acts and Resolves, Public and Private, of the Province of Massachusetts Bay* (Boston, 1869–1922), V, 445–54.

5. Philip A. Bruce, *Institutional History of Virginia in the Seventeenth Century* (New York, 1910), II, 5–6. Bruce says slaves were excused, but Hening, ed., *Statutes at Large*, I, 226, says "negroes."

6. Wesley Frank Craven, "Indian Policy in Early Virginia," *William and Mary Quarterly*, 3rd series, I (1944), 73–76.

7. See the manifestly impracticable laws in Hening, ed., *Statutes at Large*, I, 140–41, 292–93.

8. Bruce, *Institutional History*, II, 101–20.

9. Hening, ed., *Statutes at Large*, II, 326–36, 341–50. See the discussion in Wilcomb E. Washburn, *The Governor and the Rebel: A History of Bacon's Rebellion in Virginia* (Chapel Hill, 1957), 35–63.

10. Douglas Leach, *Flintlock and Tomahawk: New England in King Philip's War* (New York, 1958), emphasizes that New Englanders disliked the draft, but also makes it clear that many of them were drafted. See especially pp. 45–46, 103–4, 123, and 185–87.

11. E. B. O'Callaghan and B. Fernow, eds., *Documents Relative to the Colonial History of the State of New-York* (Albany, 1853–87), I, 153–54, 389, 392, 397, 427–28, 438; II, 112.

12. Jasper Danckaerts, who saw New York militia muster in 1680, wrote: "I have never seen anything worse." Bartlett Burleigh James and J. Franklin Jameson, eds., *Journal of Jasper Danckaerts, 1679–1680* (New York, 1913), 239. Shortly thereafter he was favorably impressed by the Boston militia; *ibid.*, 271. For New York's continuing troubles with militia, see O'Callaghan and Fernow, eds., *Doc. Rel. Col. Hist. N.-Y.*, III, 373, 478; IV, 185, 870–79, 968; V, 60, 253.

13. Spotswood to the Lords Commissioners of Trade, Sept. 14, 1713, in R. A. Brock, ed., *The Official Letters of Alexander Spotswood*...(Richmond, 1882–85), II, 37. In a long report to the Board of Trade in 1716

(*ibid.,* 194-212), Spotswood proposed the abandonment of the militia system in Virginia in favor of a force that would comprise only one-third of the available military manpower, but would be paid by a tax on the other two-thirds who would be excused from service. Spotswood's proposal has a certain similarity to the modern American Reserve and National Guard. He was certain that most Virginians would be happy to pay a small tax to avoid traveling 20 or 30 miles to muster, but foresaw opposition from "Persons of Estates," who "would not come off so easily as they do now." As Spotswood saw it, under the militia system, in practice "no Man of an Estate is under any Obligation to Muster, and even the Servants or Overseers of the Rich are likewise exempted; the whole Burthen Iyes upon the poorest sort of people."

14. Governor Joseph Dudley to the Board of Trade, Apr. 8, 1712, in Cecil Headlam, ed., *Calendar of State Papers, Colonial Series, America and West Indies, July, 1711-June, 1712* (London, 1925), 257-58.

15. The Council and Assembly of South Carolina to the Council of Trade and Plantations, Jan. 29, 1719/20, *ibid., January, 1719 to February, 1720* (London, 1933), 319.

16. Lieutenant Governor William Bull to the Board of Trade, May 25, 1738, Egremont Papers, Public Record Office 30 (Gifts and Deposits), Piece 47, XIV, 55-56, Public Record Office, London.

17. Contents of the First Charter of South Carolina, 1663. Thomas Cooper and D. J. McCord, eds., *Statutes at Large of South Carolina* (Columbia, 1836-41), I, 29; "Journal of the...Yemassee War," *Year Book—1894, City of Charleston, So. Ca.* (Charleston, n.d.), 323 et passim.

18. In a memorial to the King, Apr. 9, 1734, the Governor, Council, and Assembly argued that the presence of three Negroes for every white man made provincial self-defense impossible. *Cal. State Papers, Col., Amer. and W. Indies, 1734-1735* (London, 1953), 173-75.

19. For Negroes, see Benjamin Quarles, "The Colonial Militia and Negro Manpower," *Mississippi Valley Historical Review*, XLV (1959), 643-52. For servants, see Richard B. Morris, *Government and Labor in Early America* (New York, 1946), 279-90, which shows that a considerable number of servants fought in the eighteenth century, despite the protests of their masters; and Abbot E. Smith, *Colonists in Bondage: White Servitude and Convict Labor in America, 1607-1776* (Chapel Hill, 1947), 279, which shows that servants were not usually mustered into the militia during the eighteenth century. There is scattered evidence for the existence of migratory free white men not enrolled

in the militia: Nathaniel B. Shurtleff, ed., *Records of the Governor and Company of the Massachusetts Bay in New England* (Boston, 1853–54), V, 242; *Colonial Laws of New York from the year 1664 to the Revolution* (Albany, 1894–96), I, 454; Governor Dudley to the Council of Trade and Plantations, Nov. 15, 1710, in Headlam, ed., *Cal. State Papers, Col. Amer. and W. Indies, 1710–June, 1711* (London, 1924), 268, where Governor Dudley reported that all his "loose people" had gone in the expedition to Nova Scotia; Smith, *Colonists in Bondage*, 281–82, which discusses the impressment of vagrants; Colonel George Washington to Governor Dinwiddie, Mar. 9, 1754, in R. A. Brock, ed., *The Official Records of Governor Robert Dinwiddie...* (Richmond, 1883–84), I, 92, where George Washington complains that his soldiers in 1754 are "loose, Idle Persons that are quite destitute of House and Home." For Indians, either as allies or as individual recruits, examples abound. Perhaps the overall tendency was exemplified by the New York Assembly in 1711; when asked to provide 600 men for the expedition against Canada, it voted 350 "Christian" volunteers, 150 Long Island Indians, and 100 Palatine Germans, who were not only outside the militia system but recently had been disarmed for their unruly behavior. In addition, 100 more Palatines were sent by the Assembly as recruits to the four British regular companies statoined in the province.

20. Richard L. Morton, *Colonial Virginia* (Chapel Hill, 1960), II, 526–27, 535. The laws quoted are in Hening, ed., *Statutes at Large*, VI, 438; *ibid.*, VII, 70.

21. L. H. Butterfield et al., eds., *The Adams Papers: Diary and Autobiography of John Adams* (Cambridge, Mass., 1961), I, 110 et passim.

22. In a private letter to the Earl of Loudoun, Feb. 25, 1758, Major General James Abercromby urged that the provincial troops be improved "by drafting them out of the militia, in place of whom they send out at an extravagant premium the rif-raf of the continent." Loudoun Papers, No. 5668, Henry E. Huntington Library, San Marino, California.

23. Stanley M. Pargellis, *Lord Loudoun in North America* (New Haven, 1933), 108–9.

24. J. C. Webster, ed., *The Journal of Jeffery Amherst* (Toronto, 1931), 331. Pargellis, *Loudoun*, III, gives the lower figure of 670 based on the report enclosed in Amherst to Samuel Martin, Nov. 1, 1762, Amherst Papers, War Office 34, LXXIV, fol. 176, Public Record Office. But a comparison of this report with the list in Amherst's *Journal* shows

an increase in the number of recruits supplied by Massachusetts, Rhode Island, Connecticut, and New York, suggesting that the former document is an incomplete report.

25. In 1761 Governor Thomas Fitch of Connecticut went so far as to propose the enlistment of French prisoners of war, then in his colony, in the provincial forces. Jeffery Amherst to Thomas Fitch, Apr. 15, 1761, Connecticut Historical Society, *Collections,* XVIII (Hartford, 1920), 109-10.

26. *Acts and Resolves,* IV, 193.

27. James Otis, *The Rights of the British Colonies Asserted and Proved...* (Boston, 1764), 58. Lieutenant Colonel Ralph Burton was the officer disgusted by the American camp; to Lord Loudoun, Aug. 5, 1756, Loudoun Papers, No. 1424, as quoted in Pargellis, *Loudoun,* 95.

28. Gage to Dartmouth, June 25, 1775, in Clarence E. Carter, ed., *The Correspondence of General Thomas Gage* (New Haven, 1931-33), I, 407. Though the argument advanced in this essay is meant to apply only to the colonial period, the author being willing to admit that the Revolution brought rapid and extensive changes, there remains at least a trace of persistent difference between Virginia and Massachusetts after 1775. In 1777, Jefferson opposed a draft from the Virginia militia: "It ever was the most unpopular and impracticable thing that could be attempted. Our people even under the monarchial government had learnt to consider it as the last of all oppressions." Adams, in reply, agreed that it was "only to be adopted in great Extremities." But he added: "Draughts in the Massachusetts, as they have been there managed, have not been very unpopular, for the Persons draughted are commonly the wealthiest, who become obliged to give large Premiums, to their poorer Neighbours, to take their Places." Jefferson to Adams, May 16, 1777, and Adams to Jefferson, May 26, 1777, in Lester J. Cappon, ed., *The Adams-Jefferson Letters: The Complete Correspondence between Thomas Jefferson and Abigail and John Adams* (Chapel Hill, 1959), I, 4-5. More recently, Fred Anderson, *A People's Army: Massachusetts Soldiers and Society in the Seven Years' War* (Chapel Hill, 1984), has argued that Massachusetts soldiers in this last colonial war were not marginal members of society but made up a representative cross section. The soft spot in his argument is that systematic evidence of soldiers' social background exists only for the year 1756; there is nothing comparable for the subsequent six annual recruiting drives. In other long wars, including the Revolutionary War, the later years are when more marginal members of society are induced to join the army. This is not to say

that Anderson is wrong, but simply that his case is not proved by the evidence extant.

CHAPTER THREE

1. Their host was Joseph Cradock, who wrote of the evening in his *Literary and Miscellaneous Memoirs* (4 vols.; London, 1826), II, 178–80.

2. *Ibid.*, I, 253, 277–78; also J. G. Sulzers, *Tagebüch…1775 und 1776* (Leipzig, 1780), 122. Ellis's book is *A Voyage to Hudson's Bay…in the Years 1746 and 1747* (London, 1748). For his other offspring, see his will in Land Registry Office, London, willbook "Pitt," f. 777.

3. There are two biographies, one by an English descendant, Charles A. W. Pownall (London, 1908), which is predictably biased and unscholarly, though interesting and informative; the other by John A. Schutz (Glendale, Calif., 1951), which is scholarly but disappointing. A better account of Pownall's parliamentary career is in Sir Lewis Namier and John Brooke, *The House of Commons, 1754–1790* (London, 1964), III, 316–18. To "make a figure" is of course Chesterfield's admonition to his son, since made famous by Namier as a key to British political behavior in the mid-eighteenth century.

4. [Phillip Thicknesse], *The Modern Characters from Shakespeare* (London, 1778), 68: quotation from *As You Like It* (Act II, scene VII) on "G----r P--n--l." By contrast, Thicknesse had only compliments for his friend Ellis; see John Nichols, *Literary Anecdotes* (London, 1812–15), IX, 533.

5. Cradock, *Memoirs,* II, 179.

6. The specific office tendered to him by Hillsborough is my conjecture, but there is no doubt about the offer itself; Henry Ellis to William Knox, Dec. 30, 1767, Knox papers, 1/25, William L. Clements Library, Ann Arbor, Michigan. The summary of this letter in *Historical Manuscripts Commission, Various Collections,* VI (Dublin, 1909), 95, is misleading. The other points concerning Ellis's career are discussed below.

7. William W. Abbot, *The Royal Governors of Georgia* (Chapel Hill, 1959), 57–83, contains an excellent account of his governorship.

8. *A Voyage to Hudson's Bay*, xvii–xviii, 93–94, and 212 ff.

9. On his thinking as governor, see especially his memorial to the Board of Trade, Oct. 5, 1756, which was sent to the Treasury because it requested funds for presents to the Indians; in Treasury papers 1/367, Public Record Office, London. His work for Egremont is documented in the Egremont papers (Public Record Office, London, 30/47), vol. 14, ff. 65–66, and vol. 22, ff. 37–41, 67–92, and 105–

10. Some of these items are signed by Ellis; others are in his hand; the remainder in one way or another reflect the influence of his position and thinking. William Knox, John Pownall (the brother of Thomas), Maurice Morgann, and certainly Halifax himself were others who contributed actively to the formulation of an American policy in this critical period, although it is difficult to be precise in the allocation of credit within a welter of anonymous memoranda. Knox, who served under Ellis in Georgia and whose ideas matched those of his patron, was most likely the author of a series of "Hints" on American policy, done either for Ellis or directly for Egremont. The formulation of policy for the West is discussed most fully in Jack M. Sosin, *Whitehall and the Wilderness* (Lincoln, Nebr., 1961), 37–65, while military policy is treated in my *Toward Lexington* (Princeton, 1965), 52–58. Neither book quite finds and fits together all the pieces of this very interesting puzzle. In particular, a comparison of handwriting now leads me to believe that it was Ellis himself who drew up the "Plan of Forts and Garrisons" (or "Plan of Forts and Establishments" as it is in the early draft in the Egremont papers, PRO 30/47/22, ff. 84–87) which Egremont sent to the Board of Trade for its guidance. The belief that Ellis drafted the Proclamation of 1763 is expressed in Francis Maseres to Fowler Walker, Quebec, Nov. 19, 1767, *The Maseres Letters,* edited by W. Stewart Wallace (Toronto, 1919), 62–63. Evidence of Ellis's ideas and influence is also found in *The Papers of Sir William Johnson,* ed. Alexander C. Flick, et al., 14 vols. (New York, 1921–65), III, 294, and X, 209; in Governor Lyttleton of Jamaica to William Knox, Spanish Town, Dec. 30, 1762, Knox papers, I/ii, Clements Library; and especially in Knox's memoir of the Earl of Shelburne in *Historical Manuscripts Commission, Various Collections,* VI, 282–83.

10. Dec. 8, 1773, Knox papers, II/5, Clements Library. In other letters, he frequently admitted to laziness.

11. In a letter to Knox, Oct. 17, 1772, Knox Papers, I/57, Clements Library, he speaks of a friendly visit to "Beckett," Barrington's country house.

12. Ellis to Knox, Marseilles, Mar. 23, 1774, *Historical Manuscripts Commission, Various Collections,* VI, iii.

13. Caroline Robbins, *The Eighteenth Century Commonwealthman* (Cambridge, Mass., 1959), 312.

14. Schutz, *Pownall,* ii; and *The Papers of Benjamin Franklin,* ed. Leonard W. Labaree and Whitfield J. Bell (New Haven and London, 1962), V, 339–40n., where the date of the first edition of *Administration of the*

Colonies is mistakenly given as 1765 instead of 1764. See also Labaree, *Royal Government in America* (New Haven, 1930), 43, for an earlier expression of the same opinion.

15. To William Tudor, Quincy, Feb. 4, 1817, *The Works of John Adams,* edited by Charles F. Adams (Boston, 1856), X, 243.

16. There is a bibliography of his writings in Schutz, *Pownall.*

17. *Administration,* 1764 ed., 1. Compare the sympathetic if sarcastic response which these words evoked in James Otis, *Rights of the British Colonies Asserted and Proved* (Boston, 1764), 40–41.

18. I have transposed the order of these quotations, but their sense is unaltered.

19. In the extensive analysis of the book by Schutz there is no hint that Pownall proposed, or at the very least condoned, taxation of the colonies (p. 189). Schutz's treatment of *Administration of the Colonies* is in a few other respects misleading. For example: p. 192, to the effect that neither Indian affairs nor the military establishment were discussed in the first or later editions; p. 207, which implies that the first two editions did not discuss taxation at all; p. 209, where it is suggested that the "considerable person" mentioned by Pownall in the fourth edition was the Earl of Chatham, when the fifth edition (p. 29n.) states that it was the Duke of York; p. 188, where Schutz says that Pownall accepted the idea of "balanced government" as the guarantor of liberty, when in fact his mind was notably free of that particular cliché of eighteenth-century political thought. On this last point, Harrington's influence helps to understand Pownall's position; see J. G. A. Pocock, "Machiavelli, Harrington, and English Political Ideologies in the Eighteenth Century," *William and Mary Quarterly,* 3rd series, XXII (1965), 549–83. To my knowledge Edmund S. and Helen M. Morgan are the only historians to state clearly what Pownall actually said about taxation: *The Stamp Act Crisis* (Chapel Hill, 1953), 74. A recent treatment is G. H. Guttridge, "Thomas Pownall's *The Administration of the Colonies:* The Six Editions," *William and Mary Quarterly,* 3rd series, XXVI (1969), 31–46, although there were in fact only five editions.

20. Pownall to Pitt, Jan. 24, 1765, Chatham papers, Public Record Office, London, 30/8/53, ff. 170–71, in which Pownall expressed uncertainty about revealing his identity as the author of *Administration,* whose first edition was anonymous. Later he claimed that the second and third editions (1765, 1766) were not "dedicated" to Grenville, but only "addressed" to him; yet the running head in the second edition reads "DEDICATION."

21. Pownall to Halifax (?), July 23, 1754, edited by Beverley McAnear, *Mississippi Valley Historical Review,* XXXIX (1953), 745.

22. See note 9 for my own belief that Ellis himself drew up the "Plan of Forts and Garrisons" of early 1763, the final version of which proposed a regional division of the supreme military command.

23. The idea of Parliamentary representation for the colonies is of course not original; it was proposed by, among others, Governors William Shirley and Francis Bernard of Massachusetts, James Otis, Benjamin Franklin, and William Knox. Richard Koebner, *Empire* (Cambridge, England, 1961), 175–77, implies that Pownall first presented these ideas in the third edition (1768). More serious is Koebner's distortion of Pownall's point of view; for Pownall, the shift in the center of power was a danger to be averted while there was still time, not an inevitable development, as Koebner would have it.

24. Dowdeswell to Rockingham, Jan. 16, 1766, Rockingham papers, R1–558, Wentworth-Woodhouse Muniments, Sheffield City Library.

25. Pownall to Samuel Cooper, May 9, 1769, in Frederick Griffin, *Junius Discovered* (Boston, 1854), 229.

26. *William and Mary Quarterly,* 3rd series, XXII (1965). 549–83.

27. See James Harrington, "A System of Politics," in *The Oceana...and His Other Works* (London, 1737), ed. John Toland, 496. See also Koebner, *Empire,* 59–67, and especially the notes, on Harrington's categories and their etymology.

28. The best account of his political career at this point is in Sir Lewis Namier and John Brooke, *House of Commons, 1754–1790,* III. 316–18.

29. I refer here to the work of R. A. Humphreys, Charles R. Ritcheson, John Brooke, Jack M. Sosin, and John Norris, though the conclusion is my own.

30. These page references are to the annotated copy of the 1768 edition in the British Museum, accession number C.60.i.9.

31. Koebner uses these marginal comments to reach even harsher conclusions about Burke; *Empire,* 184–92.

32. For example, there are such suggestions in two recent, important, and erudite works written from totally opposed points of view: Bernhard Knollenberg, *Origin of the American Revolution, 1759–1766* (New York, 1960), 13–24; and Lawrence H. Gipson, *The British Empire Before the American Revolution* (New York, 1965), XI, 70–82.

33. For example, see Koebner, *Empire,* 125.

34. Edmund S. Morgan, "The American Revolution: Revisions in Need of Revising," *William and Mary Quarterly,* 3rd series, XIV

(1957), 3–15. Even Professor Morgan indulges in "if-history"; see p. 12.

35. On this, see Koebner, *Empire,* 85ff.

36. Sir Lewis Namier and John Brooke, *Charles Townshend* (London, 1964), 27–28, 37–45, 76–77, 138–42, and esp. 179.

37. Here I must register strong disagreement with Koebner, *Empire,* esp. pp. 117–18, where the incoherence of imperial thought is stressed, and p. 125, where it is said that there was no systematic conception of empire in 1763. The opposite was more nearly true, and Koebner's own analysis of Pownall, Franklin, and Francis Bernard will, if read carefully, support that opinion. This is a remarkable book, from which I have learned a great deal, but Koebner was perhaps excessively literal in his treatment of these ideas, and moreover seems to have been led by his aim of depriving the idea of "empire" of any emotional content to seek diversity rather than coherence in the thought of this epoch.

CHAPTER FOUR

1. Quoted in John C. Long, *Lord Jeffery Amherst, a Soldier of the King* (New York, 1933), 41. The information on Gage's family and early life comes from John R. Alden, *General Gage in America* (Baton Rouge, 1948), a sound study that is the only full biography of Gage.

2. Massachusetts Historical Society, *Collections,* 4th series, IV (Boston, 1858), 369–70, in reply to the queries of historian George Chalmers.

3. Oct. 17, 1754, quoted in Robert Wright, *The Life of Major-General James Wolfe* (London, 1864), 293.

4. And it was not for lack of contemporary criticism of the conduct of the campaign in general, because invective flew after the battle. The principal sources are Winthrop Sargent, ed., *The History of an Expedition Against Fort DuQuesne in 1755* (Memoirs of the Historical Society of Pennsylvania, vol. V; Philadelphia, 1855); Stanley M. Pargellis, ed., *Military Affairs in North America, 1748–1765: Selected Documents from the Cumberland Papers in Windsor Castle* (New York, 1936), 77–132, hereafter *Military Affairs;* and Charles Hamilton, ed., *Braddock's Defeat* (Norman, Okla., 1959). A case of modern, uninformed criticism is in the editorial note by Hamilton, pp. xvi–xvii, which is not supported by any contemporary account. The most interesting analysis is by Pargellis, "Braddock's Defeat," *American Historical Review,* XLI (1936), 253–69, though I cannot agree with all of his opinions, and the fullest account is in Lee McCardell, *Ill-Starred General: Braddock of the Coldstream Guards* (Pittsburgh, 1958).

5. July 25, 1755, Pargellis, *Military Affairs,* 117.

6. Gage to the Earl of Albemarle, July 24, 1755, in Thomas Keppel, *The Life of Augustus, Viscount Keppel* (London, 1842), I, 213–18.

7. Gage to Major Craven, June 19, 1759 (copy), LO 6114, Loudoun Papers, Henry L. Huntington Library and Art Gallery, San Marino, California, hereafter Huntington Library.

8. To the Duke of Cumberland, Oct. 2, 1756, Pargellis, *Military Affairs,* 235.

9. J. Clarence Webster, ed., *The Journal of Jeffery Amherst* (Toronto, 1931), 171.

10. Huck to Loudoun, Dec. 3, 1759, LO 6153, Loudoun Papers, Huntington Library. Huck may have been grinding some ax in this letter for Loudoun's benefit, but I doubt it.

11. The fullest account of these battles is in Lawrence H. Gipson, *The Great War for the Empire: The Victorious Years, 1758–1760 (The British Empire Before the American Revolution,* vol. X; New York, 1949).

12. The introduction to Stanley M. Pargellis, *Lord Loudoun in North America* (New Haven, 1933), is an excellent discussion of defense policy before 1775.

13. A good discussion of the rationale for an American garrison is in Bernhard Knollenberg, *Origin of the American Revolution: 1759–1766* (New York, 1960), 27–28, 87–98, though he is wrong in his contention that the Indian problem had little to do with the decision.

14. Secretary of State Halifax to Amherst (received by Gage), Oct. 11, 1763, Clarence E. Carter, ed., *The Correspondence of General Thomas Gage. . .1763–1775* (New Haven, 1931–33), II, 2–3, hereafter *Gage Correspondence.*

15. Halifax to Gage, "Private," Jan. 14, 1764, *ibid.,* 10.

16. Gage to Barrington, "Private," June 28, 1768, *Gage Correspondence,* II, 479–80; Gage to Hillsborough, Sept. 26, 1768, *ibid.,* I, 197.

17. John Pownall to the Earl of Dartmouth, Sept. 22, 1773, Dartmouth Papers, I (2), no. 882, William Salt Library, Stafford, England, hereafter Salt Library.

18. Alden, *Gage,* 149; and John Armstrong to George Washington, Dec. 24, 1773, Stanislaus M. Hamilton, ed., *Letters to Washington and Accompanying Papers* (Boston and New York, 1898–1902), IV, 290–91.

19. Abercromby to Loudoun, Dec. 2, 1773, LO 6447, Loudoun Papers, Huntington Library; Harvey to Governor Johnstone of Minorca, Sept. 21, 1773, War Office Papers 3/23, pp. 126–27, Public Record Office, London. I have repunctuated and expanded abbreviations in these sentences for clarity.

20. James Grant to [James Wemyss], June 14, 1773, Wedderburn Papers, I, p. 38. William L. Clements Library, Ann Arbor, Michigan, hereafter Clements Library.

21. Captain J. Marsh to Brigadier Haldimand, Jan. 22, 1768, British Museum Additional Manuscripts 21728, London.

22. King to North, Feb. 4, 1774. Sir John W. Fortescue, ed., *The Correspondence of King George the Third* (London, 1927–28), III. no. 1379, hereafter *Correspondence of George III*.

23. Massachusetts Historical Society *Collections*, 4th series, IV (Boston, 1858), 371, in reply to the queries of historian George Chalmers.

24. "Private Diary of Gen. Haldimand," Douglas Brymner, *Report on Canadian Archives, 1889* (Ottawa, 1890), 129.

25. Cabinet minutes, April 7, 1774, Dartmouth Papers, II, 883, Salt Library.

26. John Andrews to William Barrell, May 18, 1774, Massachusetts Historical Society, *Proceedings*, VIII (Boston, 1866), 328.

27. Warren to Josiah Quincy, Jr., Nov. 21, 1774, Josiah Quincy, *Memoir of the Life of Josiah Quincy, Junior* (Boston, 1875), 178–79.

28. Gage to Dartmouth, Sept. 2, 1774, *Gage Correspondence*, I, 371. I have rearranged the order of the sentences slightly.

29. Gage to Dartmouth, Sept. 25, 1774, two letters, one of them private, *ibid.*, 275–77. His specific proposals were made in a private letter to Thomas Hutchinson, which he asked Dartmouth to peruse.

30. Dartmouth to Gage, "Private," Aug. 23, 1774, *ibid.*, II, 171–72. Gage received the letter Oct. 28.

31. William Knox to John Pownall, Sept. 13, 1774, Knox Papers, II, no. 17, Clements Library; Knox to Dartmouth, Nov. 15, 1774, and Pownall to Dartmouth, Dec. [16], 1774, Dartmouth Papers, II, nos. 994 and 1022, Salt Library.

32. Hutchinson to Gage, Nov. 19, 1774, Gage Papers, Clements Library.

33. Barker's diary is printed in the *Atlantic Monthly*, XXXIX (1877), 389–401, 544–54.

34. Peter O. Hutchinson, ed., *The Diary and Letters of . . . Thomas Hutchinson* (Boston, 1883–86), I, 232.

35. John Andrews to William Barrell, Mar. 18, 1775, Massachusetts Historical Society, *Proceedings*, VIII (Boston, 1866), 401.

36. Horace Walpole, *Journal of the Reign of George the Third*, ed. John Doran (London, 1859), 445; King to North, *Correspondence of George III*, III, no. 1556.

37. Quoted in Allen French, "General Haldimand in Boston," Massachusetts Historical Society, *Proceedings*, LXVI (Boston, 1942), 91.

38. Major Philip Skene to Lord North, Jan. 23, 1775, Dartmouth Papers, II, no. 1116, Salt Library.

39. Dartmouth to Gage, "Secret," Jan. 27, 1775, *Gage Correspondence*, II, 179-83. The circumstances surrounding this letter are discussed in John R. Alden, "Why the March to Concord?" *American Historical Review*, XLIX (1944), 446-54. Barrington's private letter, Feb. 3, 1775, is in the Gage Papers, Clements Library.

40. "Intelligence" received Apr. 3, 1775, Gage Papers, Clements Library.

41. Burgoyne to Lord George Germain, Aug. 20, 1775, Germain Papers, Clements Library.

42. Gage to Barrington, "Private," June 26, 1775, *Gage Correspondence*, II, 686-87. I do not agree with Alden, *Gage*, p. 254, that Gage understood the importance of New York *before* the battle of Bunker Hill.

43. Burgoyne to Lord George Germain, Aug. 10, 1775, Germain Papers, Clements Library; Wemyss quoted in Allen French, *The Day of Lexington and Concord* (Boston, 1925), 61.

44. I am indebted to Professor Howard H. Peckham, former director of the Clements Library, where he lived many years with Gage, for the suggestion that Gage's crucial role was political.

CHAPTER FIVE

1. Peter Paret, "The History of War," *Daedalus*, C (1971), 376-96, discusses the way in which military history has been cut off from the study of history in general.

2. Benjamin Rush, Nov. 13, 1775, in *Lee Papers*, Collections of the New York Historical Society, 4 vols. (New York, 1871-74), I, 216.

3. The adjutant general of Hessian troops described Rawdon's Volunteers of Ireland as one of the finest regiments in the army. Bernard A. Uhlendorf, ed., *Revolution in America* (New Brunswick, N.J., 1957), 264. Rawdon's original letter to Major Rugeley, Camden, July 1, 1780, and his subsequent explanation to Cornwallis, Dec. 5, 1780, British Public Record Office, London, Colonial Office 5/101, 283-84, 413. Robert L. Meriwether, *The Expansion of South Carolina, 1729-1765* (Kingsport, Tenn., 1940), 136-46, describes the character of the Waxhaws settlement, while more information on the origins of some of the settlers is in Robert W. Ramsey, *Carolina Cradle* (Chapel Hill, 1964).

4. The best overall account of colonial American society in the eigh-

teenth century is James Henretta, *The Evolution of American Society, 1700–1815* (Lexington, Mass., 1973).

5. The classic account of the phenomenon is Benjamin Franklin, "Observations Concerning the Increase of Mankind" (1751), in *The Papers of Benjamin Franklin*, edited by Leonard W. Labaree and William B. Willcox, 15 vols. to date (New Haven, 1959–), IV, 255ff. A modern analysis is J. Potter, "The Growth of Population in America, 1700–1860," in *Population in History*, ed. D. V. Glass and D. E. C. Eversley (London, 1965).

6. James G. Leyburn, *The Scotch-Irish: A Social History* (Chapel Hill, 1962), 172.

7. Potter, "Growth of Population."

8. See Leyburn, *The Scotch-Irish*, on the Scotch-Irish. A recent estimate for German immigration is in Howard B. Furer, *The Germans in America, 1607–1970* (Dobbs Ferry, N.Y., 1973), 4. James T. Lemon, *The Best Poor Man's Country* (Baltimore, 1972), discusses both Scotch-Irish and Germans in eighteenth-century Pennsylvania, where most of the impact of immigration was felt. Philip D. Curtin, *The Atlantic Slave Trade: A Census* (Madison, Wisc., 1969), 140, is the best estimate of black immigration; and Winthrop D. Jordan, *White Over Black* (Chapel Hill, 1968), 116 ff., discusses the general fear of slave insurrection after about 1740.

9. The best picture of this elite is still Leonard W. Labaree, *Conservatism in Early America* (New York, 1948); but see also James K. Martin, *Men in Rebellion* (New Brunswick, N.J., 1973). The operation of "deference" is discussed in J. R. Pole, "Historians and the Problem of Early American Democracy," *American Historical Review*, LXVII (1961), 626–46.

10. The major instances of violent outbreaks included the Green Mountain Boys, waging civil war over land grants between the Connecticut and Champlain valleys well before the Revolution; land riots in New Jersey and New York; something like open warfare between Pennsylvania authorities and Connecticut settlers in the upper Susquehanna Valley; the so-called Paxton Boys in the middle Susquehanna, massacring Indians and threatening Philadelphia itself; Regulators in both North and South Carolina, using vigilante violence, with a pitched battle needed to stamp them out in the former colony; and, while the seaboard debated the Boston crisis in 1774–75, fighting between Pennsylvania and Virginians for control of the Pittsburgh area.

11. Bernhard Knollenberg, *George Washington: The Virginia Period, 1732–1775* (Durham, N.C., 1964), 44–50.

12. For two New England towns and their early response to the war, see Howard K. Sanderson, *Lynn in the Revolution,* 2 vols. (Boston, 1909), and Jonathan Smith, *Peterborough, New Hampshire, in the American Revolution* (Peterborough, N.H., 1913).

13. *Historical Statistics of the United States, Colonial Times to 1957* (Washington, D.C. 1960), 756; Allen French, *The First Year of the American Revolution* (Boston, 1934), 52; and Charles H. Lesser, ed., *The Sinews of Independence: Monthly Strength Reports of the Continental Army* (Chicago, 1976), 2–3, for July.

14. Russell F. Weigley discusses Washington's "orthodoxy" in *The American Way of War* (New York, 1973), 13–17, and his views on citizen soldiers in *Towards an American Army* (New York, 1962), 1–9. Paul David Nelson of Berea College is currently engaged in a study of American military leaders' attitudes toward the militia during the Revolutionary period.

15. Quoted in Allen French, "General Haldimand in Boston," *Massachusetts Historical Society Proceedings,* LXVI (1942), 91.

16. Richard H. Kohn, *Eagle and Sword* (New York, 1975), explores the connection between Federalism and the army after the war.

17. Charles A. Lofgren, "Compulsory Military Service under the Constitution: The Original Understanding," *William and Mary Quarterly,* 3rd series, XXXIII (1976), 76–79, is an informed sketch of actual practice during the war.

18. The point is illustrated and developed in chapter 7 of this volume.

19. The best account of wartime finance is E. James Ferguson, *The Power of the Purse* (Chapel Hill, 1961), and the most thorough treatment of military supply and its problems is by Erna Risch, *Supplying Washington's Army* (Washington, D.C., 1981). The basic prosperity of America failed to sustain the war effort because that prosperity had three components: surplus production, marketing mechanisms, and a distribution system. The war simply overtaxed the distribution system and, eventually, the marketing mechanisms. The distribution system had developed in the colonial period as a pattern of fairly short, low-volume overland hauls to navigable water, which was by far the most efficient means of transportation. The war effectively closed the routes of water transportation, and required long-distance, high-volume overland shipments, frequently *across* the river valleys; i.e., in "unnatural" directions for which there was little or

no colonial precedent. The marketing mechanisms had developed in the colonial period on the basis of paper money and credit, both dependent on mutual confidence; runaway wartime inflation naturally broke down these marketing mechanisms. Surplus production no doubt diminished during the war, but did not disappear; the problem lay in marketing and distributing the surplus. J. A. Edwards of University College Swansea (Wales) helped me to clarify my thinking on this point, and I am indebted to him.

20. This analysis of British strategy and its problems is derived from chapter 10, of this volume. My understanding of the subject depends heavily on the work of Piers Mackesy, William B. Willcox, Paul H. Smith, and Ira D. Gruber.

21. The view of the Loyalists as essentially "minority" groups belongs to William H. Nelson, *The American Tory* (Boston, 1961), 85–92. Robert McCluer Calhoon, *The Loyalists in Revolutionary America, 1760–1781* (New York, 1973), is the fullest, most recent survey; on p. 562 Calhoon indicates that Nelson's concept has stood up well to the test of further research.

22. Not often do contemporary records or local historians describe the line between Whigs and Tories in ethnic or religious terms; there were good reasons not to do so during the war, and there have been well-known inhibitions against doing so ever since. But close study of the areas committed to one side or the other supports the view that ethnic and religious differences were important determinants of Revolutionary behavior. For example, German settlements in the Carolina back-country appear to have provided much of the manpower for Loyalist militia units in that region, although the Scottish role is better known; while other Tories in arms were often described as "regulators," referring to the prewar vigilante insurrections. But on German Loyalism, see Edward McCrady, *The History of South Carolina in the Revolution 1775–1780* (New York, 1901), 33 ff., and Robert O. Demond, *The Loyalists in North Carolina during the Revolution* (Durham, N.C., 1940), 54–55. And for an Anglican view of the Waxhaws settlement before the war, there is the Reverend Charles Woodmason (Jan. 25, 1767): "a finer body of land is no where to be seen—But it is occupied by a sett of the most lowest vilest crew breathing—Scotch Irish Presbyterians from the North of Ireland" (Richard J. Hooker, ed., *The Carolina Backcountry on the Eve of the Revolution* [Chapel Hill, 1953], 14).

23. This transition in political attitudes between 1776 and 1787 is fully

and beautifully described by Gordon S. Wood, *The Creation of the American Republic, 1776-1787* (Chapel Hill, 1969), but Wood does not relate the transition specifically to the experience of war; I do.

CHAPTER SIX

1. John R. Alden, *General Charles Lee, Traitor or Patriot?* (Baton Rouge, 1951).

2. There are three hints, all of which are susceptible to other interpretations. One is in a letter to his sister, Dec. 23, 1763, *Lee Papers, New-York Historical Society Collections, 1871-74,* I, 48; hereafter referred to as *Lee Papers.* Another is in a letter about Lee when he was staying at Lucca, during his return from the second journey to Poland; it is quoted in a note by Alden, p. 317, n. 15. The third is the attempt by his first biographer, Edward Langworthy, to prove that Lee liked women, rumors to the contrary notwithstanding; in *Lee Papers,* IV, 163-64.

3. The description is borrowed from Eric Hoffer, *The True Believer* (New York, 1951).

4. Douglas Southall Freeman, *George Washington* (New York, 1948-57), especially vols. IV and V.

5. Lee to Sidney Lee, Mar. 28, 1772, *Lee Papers,* I, 110.

6. See Lee to Washington, May 9, 1776, *ibid.,* II, 12, for an indication that Lee was on Braddock's march with Washington.

7. Lee to George Colman (the elder), May 8, 1769, *Lee Papers,* I, 81-82.

8. He mentioned a proposed visit to Silesia to see a Prussian military review in a letter from Warsaw to the Earl of Charlemont, June 1, 1765, *ibid.,* 41. His view of the French and Indian War is best expressed in his influential pamphlet, *Strictures on...A "Friendly Address to All Reasonable Americans... "* (Philadelphia, 1774), *Lee Papers,* I, 162.

9. The three commanders were Loudoun, Abercromby, and Amherst. For the encounter with the king, see Horace Walpole, *Last Journals* (London, 1910), I, 404-5.

10. Lee to Sidney Lee, Mar. 28, 1772, *Lee Papers,* I, 111.

11. In particular, see the letters of John Adams in Edmund Burnett, ed., *Letters of Members of the Continental Congress* (Washington, D.C.,1921-36), I, 136-37; hereafter, Burnett, *Letters.*

12. James Warren to Sam Adams, July 9, 1775, in William V. Wells, *The Life and Public Services of Samuel Adams* (Boston, 1866), II, 316.

13. Lee to Sullivan, July 24, 1775, *Lee Papers,* I, 199. Historians usually credit Washington or Sullivan with the movement forward to Ploughed Hill, but contemporary accounts describe it as Lee's ac-

tion. See the *Virginia Gazette,* Oct. 21, 1775, and the *Magazine of American History,* VIII (1882), 125.

14. George W. Greene, *The Life of Nathanael Greene* (New York, 1867), I, 131; Thompson to his brother, Sept. 10, 1775, in William T. Read, *The Life and Correspondence of George Read* (Philadelphia, 1870), 112.

15. John Adams to Lee, Feb. 19, 1776, *Lee Papers,* I, 312.

16. For a sympathetic eye-witness account of Lee's effect in Newport, see Franklin B. Dexter, ed., *The Literary Diary of Ezra Stiles* (New York, 1901), I, 646–47.

17. Letters expressing his attitude during these months are in *Lee Papers,* I, 233ff. Curtis Nettels, *George Washington and American Independence* (Boston, 1951), describes the problems of this period and puts Lee's activity in proper perspective.

18. For the politics of this resolution, see Burnett, *Letters,* I, 329, 339, 354, 389, 405, and 408.

19. To John Augustine Washington, Mar. 31, 1776, in John C. Fitzpatrick, ed., *The Writings of George Washington* (Washington, D.C., 1931–44), IV, 450–51. All quotations from Washington's letters are from the Fitzpatrick edition unless otherwise noted. This work is referred to hereafter as Washington, *Writings.* Lee's question was asked in a letter to Robert Morris, Jan. 23, 1776, *Lee Papers,* I, 255.

20. Lee to Washington, Feb. 19, 1776, *ibid.,* 309.

21. See Eric Robson, "The Expedition to the Southern Colonies, 1775–1776," *English Historical Review,* LXVI (1951), 535–60, for the British side.

22. Lee to Washington, July 1, 1776, *Lee Papers,* II, 100–103.

23. Lee to Moultrie, July 7, 1776, *ibid.,* 126.

24. John Drayton, *Memoirs of the American Revolution* (Charleston, 1821), II, 313 and 280ff.

25. William Moultrie, *Memoirs of the American Revolution* (New York, 1802), I, 141.

26. Lee to Gates, Oct. 14, 1776, *Lee Papers,* II, 261–62.

27. Tilghman to Duer, Oct. 17, 1776, quoted in Henry P. Johnston, *The Campaign of 1776 Around New York and Brooklyn* (New York, 1878), 271. See also note on p. 270.

28. The incident is recounted by Major General William Heath, who was not sympathetic to Lee in general, in Rufus R. Wilson, ed., *Heath's Memoirs of the American War* (New York, 1904), 87–88; hereafter Heath, *Memoirs.*

29. Washington to Lund Washington, Aug. 20, and to Richard Henry Lee, Aug. 29, 1775, Washington, *Writings,* III, 433 and 450.

30. Lee to Burke, Dec. 16, 1774, *Lee Papers,* I, 147.

31. Lee to Rush, Nov. 13, 1775, *ibid.,* 216.

32. Lee to Rush, Oct. 10, 1775, *ibid.,* 212.

33. *Ibid.,* 332, and 417–18.

34. *Ibid.,* II, 283.

35. Washington to Reed, Aug. 22, 1779, Washington, *Writings,* XVI, 152.

36. Rush to John Adams, Sept. 21, 1805, in Lyman H. Butterfield, ed., *Letters of Benjamin Rush* (Princeton, 1951), II, 906; hereinafter, *Letters of Rush.*

37. Reed to Lee, Nov. 21, 1776, *Lee Papers,* II, 293–94.

38. Howe to Germain, Nov. 30, 1776, in Peter Force, ed., *American Archives,* 4th series (Washington, D.C., 1837–53), V, 926.

39. Washington to Lee, Nov. 21, 1776, *Lee Papers,* II, 296.

40. His words about "treason" were used in another connection to James Bowdoin, Nov. 22, 1776, *ibid.,* 303, but they do indicate his state of mind. He wrote of reconquering New Jersey to Heath, Dec. 9, 1776, *ibid.,* 340.

41. See Freeman, *George Washington* IV, 232–90.

42. Lee to Rush, Nov. 20, 1776, and to Bowdoin, Nov. 30, 1776, *Lee Papers,* II, 298 and 324.

43. Heath, *Memoirs,* 107.

44. The sequence of letters, and the indications that some letters are missing, are found in *Lee Papers,* II, 326–44, and Washington, *Writings,* IV, 318–42. For further evidence that Washington was neither quite as desperate in early December nor as certain about what Lee should do as tradition suggests, see the letters in Greene, *Life of Nathanael Greene,* I, 280–85.

45. Lee to Washington, Dec. 11, 1776, *Lee Papers,* II, 345.

46. Lee to Gates, Dec. 12/13, 1776, *ibid.,* 348.

47. The document is printed in *Lee Papers,* II, 361–66. It is discussed by George H. Moore, *The Treason of Charles Lee* (New York, 1860); in *Lee Papers,* IV, 335–427; and by Alden, 174–79.

48. "A Plan for the Formation of the American Army...[April, 1778]," *Lee Papers,* II, 383–89.

49. Alexander Hamilton to Elias Boudinot, July 26, 1778, in Harold C. Syrett and Jacob E. Cooke, eds., *The Papers of Alexander Hamilton* (New York, 1961–), I, 528–29; hereafter, *Hamilton Papers.*

50. The following account of the Monmouth campaign is based on the revealing record of Lee's court-martial, except where noted (*Lee Papers,* III, 1–208), and on several visits to the ground itself.

51. Nathanael Greene best expressed the optimistic view of the American strategic dilemma to George Washington, June 24, 1778, quoted in Theodore Thayer, *Nathanael Greene, Strategist of the American Revolution* (New York, 1960), 244. Greene wrote: "People expect something from us. . . . I think we can make a partial attack without suffering them to bring us to a general action."

52. Hamilton to Boudinot, July 5, 1778, *Hamilton Papers*, I, 510.

53. Most published sketch maps of the battle of Monmouth that I know of are misleading and inaccurate. One of the best, oddly, is in Jared Sparks, ed., *The Writings of George Washington* (Boston, 1834–37), V, 430. William S. Stryker, *The Battle of Monmouth*, edited by William S. Myers (Princeton, 1927), makes no attempt to plot the battle graphically. The most important contemporary map is reproduced in Louis Gottschalk, *Lafayette Joins the American Army* (Chicago, 1937), 222.

54. William B. Willcox, ed., *The American Rebellion; Sir Henry Clinton's Narrative of His Campaigns, 1775–1782* (New Haven, 1954), 91–98. Clinton, who did not like Lee, thought Lee had been unjustly treated.

55. The letters are in *Lee Papers*, II, 435–38.

56. Morris to Washington, Oct. 26, 1778, Burnett, *Letters*, III, 465; Laurens to Hamilton, Dec. 5, 1778, *Hamilton Papers*, I, 593; Rush to William Gordon, Dec. 10, 1778, *Letters of Rush*, I, 220; Alden, *General Charles Lee*, 253–54.

57. The epithet was used by Major John Eustace, Lee's aide; Eustace to Lee, Nov. 28, 1779, *Lee Papers*, III, 394.

58. Lee to Sidney Lee, Dec. 11, 1781, *ibid.*, 464–65.

59. Benjamin Rush, *Autobiography*, edited by George W. Corner (Princeton, 1948), 155–56.

60. Alexander Graydon, *Memoirs of a Life* (Edinburgh, 1822), 337–39.

61. Lee had expressed keen interest in light infantry to Sidney Lee, Mar. 1, 1761, *Lee Papers*, I, 29. For the rapidly growing European interest in light infantry tactics and partisan warfare at this time, see Max Jähns, *Geschichte der Kriegswissenschaften* (Munich and Leipzig, 1889–91), III, 2710–20.

62. For a brilliant account of the military revolution that accompanied the political revolutions of the late eighteenth century, see Robert R. Palmer, "Frederick the Great, Guibert, Bülow: From Dynastic to National War," in Edward M. Earle, ed., *Makers of Modern Strategy* (Princeton, 1941), 49–74.

63. Marcus Cunliffe, *George Washington: Man and Monument* (Boston, 1958), in the third chapter of his book was the first to develop the idea of Washington as a military conservative.

CHAPTER SEVEN

1. Clinton Rossiter wrapped the argument of a large book around the first opinion from Adams: *Seedtime of the Republic* (New York, 1953). For a discussion of Adams's second opinion, see William H. Nelson, *The American Tory* (Oxford, 1961), 92. Robert R. Palmer, *Age of the Democratic Revolution* (Princeton, 1959–65), I, 200, has followed John R. Alden, *The American Revolution* (New York, 1954), 87, in saying that Adams made no such estimate; but, in fact, he did: Charles F. Adams, ed., *The Works of John Adams* (Boston, 1856), X, 63 and 87.

2. Peter Oliver, *Origin and Progress of the American Rebellion,* edited by Douglass Adair and John A. Schutz (San Marino, Calif., 1961); the interview is on pp. 129–30.

3. Scott can be identified through Francis B. Heitman, comp., *Historical Register of Officers of the Continental Army,* 2nd ed. (Washington, D.C., 1914), 485–86; Heitman has actually confused two William Scotts, who were cousins, but there is no doubt that the officer wounded and captured at Bunker Hill was a William Scott.

4. Scott's Peterborough origins were traced through the huge compilation, *Massachusetts Soldiers and Sailors of the Revolutionary War* (Boston, 1896–1908), XIII, 929–30. Once Scott had been located in space, Jonathan Smith, *Peterborough, New Hampshire, in the American Revolution* (Peterborough, 1913), was vastly informative, especially 10–11 and 326–33.

5. The discussion of Peterborough rests on analysis of the exhaustive biographical data in Smith, *Peterborough,* 165–394.

6. Analyses similar to that for Peterborough have been done for Lynn, drawing on the biographical data in Howard K. Sanderson, *Lynn in the Revolution,* 2 vols. (Boston, 1909), an exhaustive compilation similar to that done by Smith for Peterborough; for Berks County, drawing on Morton L. Montgomery, *History of Berks County, Pennsylvania, in the Revolution, from 1774 to 1783* (Reading, Pa., 1894), less useful than Smith or Sanderson, but supplemented by tax data in *Pennsylvania Archives,* 3rd series, XVIII, and the military rolls in *ibid.,* 5th series, particularly vols. I–V; for the Maryland recruits, by Edward C. Papenfuse and Gregory A. Stiverson, "General Smallwood's Recruits: The Peacetime Career of the Revolutionary War Private," *William and Mary Quarterly,* 3rd series, XXX (1973), 117–32; for the 2nd, 4th, 9th, and 13th Massachusetts Regiments, by John Sellers, "The Origins and Careers of the New England Soldier: Non-Commissioned Officers and Privates of the Massachusetts Continental Line" (unpublished paper, 1972); and for the Virginia

pension applicants, drawing on John F. Dorman, comp., *Virginia Revolutionary Pension Applications,* 16 vols. (Washington, D.C., 1958–), in progress, and another paper by John Sellers, "The Common Soldier in the American Revolution" (1974), based on a sample of 658 Virginia pension applicants. See chap. II, n. 27.

7. James T. Lemon and Gary B. Nash, "The Distribution of Wealth in Eighteenth-Century America: A Century of Changes in Chester County, Pennsylvania, 1693-1802," *Journal of Social History,* II (1968), 1–24, is the best survey of this trend; see also Charles S. Grant, *Democracy in the Connecticut Frontier Town of Kent* (New York, 1961), 83-103, 171-72, and 214.

8. Peter Force, comp., *American Archives,* 4th series, I, 406-7, 434, 531-34.

9. Edmund C. Burnett, ed., *Letters of Members of the Continental Congress* (Washington, D.C., 1921-36), I, 18-19, 34, and 36.

10. Force, *American Archives,* 4th series, III, 696, for example, on Dutchess County, New York.

11. Paul H. Smith, "The American Loyalists: Notes on Their Organization and Numerical Strength," *William and Mary Quarterly,* 3rd series, XXV (1968), 259-77.

12. Nelson, *American Tory,* chap. V, esp. p. 91.

CHAPTER EIGHT

1. Paul H. Smith, "The American Loyalists: Notes on Their Organization and Numerical Strength," *William and Mary Quarterly,* 3rd series, XXV (1968), 259-77.

2. Paul H. Smith, *Loyalists and Redcoats: A Study in British Revolutionary Policy* (Chapel Hill, 1964); William B. Willcox, *Portrait of a General: Sir Henry Clinton in the War of Independence* (New York, 1964); Piers Mackesy, *The War for America, 1775-1783* (London and Cambridge, Mass., 1964).

3. Hannah Arendt, *On Revolution* (New York, 1963), 111ff., 215, et passim.

4. R. R. Palmer, *The Age of the Democratic Revolution* (Princeton, 1959-65), I, 188-90; Gordon S. Wood, "A Note on Mobs in the American Revolution," *William and Mary Quarterly,* 3rd series, XXIII (1966), 635-42.

5. Oscar Zeichner, "The Rehabilitation of Loyalists in Connecticut," *New England Quarterly,* XI (1938), 308-30. Zeichner's statement that there is no general study of Loyalists after the war is still true.

6. Richard Cobb, *The Police and the People: French Popular Protest, 1789-1820* (Oxford, 1970).

7. A fuller discussion of this shift in British strategy is in chaper 10.

8. Alexander C. Flick, *Loyalism in New York during the American Revolution* (New York, 1901), 88.

9. Adrian C. Leiby, *The Revolutionary War in the Hackensack Valley* (New Brunswick, 1962), 36–37.

10. Carlisle to Lady Carlisle, July 21, 1778, *Historical Manuscripts Commission,* 14th Report: *Carlisle MSS.,* V, 356–57.

11. Memorandum, Aug. 1, 1778, Clinton Papers, William L. Clements Library, Ann Arbor, Michigan.

12. Memorandum, Jan. 24, 1778, Clinton Papers.

13. Conversation quoted in Rawdon to Clinton, Feb. 12, 1779, Clinton Papers.

14. [Elijah Hunter], Apr. 2, 1779, Clinton Papers. Hunter is identified as a double agent by Carl Van Doren, *Secret History of the American Revolution* (New York, 1941), 237 and 300–301. On Holmes: Robert Bolton, *A History of the County of Westchester* (New York, 1848), I, 27–28.

15. New York, Feb. 1, 1779, *Carlisle MSS.,* V, 415–16.

16. Abraham C. Cuyler to Thomas Ward, June 7, 1780, Clinton Papers. Italics mine.

17. The whole story is in the Clinton Papers: Samuel Hayden to John André, June 27, 1780; Cortlandt Skinner to André, July 4; André to Stephen Payne Adye, July 11; minutes of a board of inquiry, July 18; André to Beverley Robinson, July 19.

CHAPTER NINE

1. Jan. 6, 1778, from the Jungkenn papers in the William L. Clements Library, University of Michigan, Ann Arbor, Michigan, and translated in Ernst Kipping, *The Hessian View of America* (Monmouth Beach, N.J., 1971), 34.

2. "Journal from London (Most Secret)," July 26, 1778, in British Museum Additional Manuscripts (hereafter cited as BM Add. MSS.) 46491, 42, British Museum, London, and William Eden to Alexander Wedderburn, New York, Sept. 6, 1778, *ibid.,* 48–49.

3. Lord George Germain to General Sir Henry Clinton, "Most Secret," Mar. 8, 1778, Historical Manuscripts Commission (hereafter cited as HMC) *Stopford-Sackville,* II, 96.

4. Ira Gruber, "Britain's Southern Strategy," in *The Revolutionary War in the South,* edited by W. Robert Higgins (Durham, N.C., 1979), 205–38.

5. Excellent on the role of Loyalism in British strategy is Paul H. Smith, *Loyalists and Redcoats: A Study in British Revolutionary Policy* (Chapel Hill, 1964).

6. One well-informed observer's view of what was being attempted is in "Advices from [Andrew] Elliot," New York, Dec. 12, 1778, HMC *Carlisle,* 392–93.

7. Germain to Clinton, Mar. 8, 1778, HMC *Stopford-Sackville,* II, 94–99. Clinton received this letter on May 9, at the same time he received the letter of March 21, which modified the earlier directive and is discussed below.

8. Howe to Germain, Philadelphia, Jan. 16, 1778, Colonial Office (hereafter cited as CO) 5/95, 127–28, Public Record Office, London.

9. Germain to Clinton, "Most Secret" Mar. 21, 1778, CO 5/95, 179–83, 194–97.

10. Germain to Clinton, Aug. 5, 1778, CO 5/96, 49–52.

11. Clinton to Germain, New York, July 27, 1778, CO 5/96, 123–26, extracted and summarized in HMC *Stopford-Sackville,* II, 116–17.

12. For example, Colonel Israel Angell of the Second Rhode Island Continentals entered in his diary on Aug. 23, 1778, that the French fleet "left us in a most Rascally manner and what will be the Event God only knows" (Edward Field, ed., *Diary of Col. Israel Angell* [Providence, R.I., 1899], 4).

13. Clinton to Germain, Sept. 15, 1778, CO 5/96, 217–19.

14. Germain to Eden, Oct. 15, 1778, BM Add. MSS. 46491, 54–55, is an example of his tendency to make everything "vital." Germain to Clinton, "Secret and Confidential," Jan. 23, 1779, CO 5/97, 25–33, illustrates the effect of this tendency on his orders to Clinton.

15. Clinton to Germain, New York, Oct. 5, 1778, CO 5/96, 347–49, and April 4, 1779, CO 5/97, 467–70. The latter is also in HMC *Stopford-Sackville,* 124–25.

16. Prevost's letters to Clinton of Feb. 14, Mar. 1, and June 11, 1779, were enclosed in Clinton to Germain, July 26, 1779, CO 5/98, 316, 323–24, and 355–56.

17. May 20, 1779, enclosed in Clinton to Germain, June 18, 1779, CO 5/98, 12.

18. May 23, 1779, in *ibid.,* 23–24.

19. "Private," May 22, 1779, CO 5/97, 679–83.

20. Germain to Clinton, "Secret," Sept. 27, 1779, CO 5/98, 169–87 (also in HMC *Stopford-Sackville,* II, 143–45), as well as a separate, "Most Secret" letter of the same date, suggesting that a chance to plunder the Spanish colonies would attract deserters from the Continental army; and Clinton to Germain, Sept. 26 and Oct. 9, 1779, CO 5/98.

21. Dec. 4, 1779, CO 5/98, 709–18.

22. See, for example, Clinton's instructions to Major Patrick Ferguson, as inspector of militia, May 22, 1780, extracted in William B. Will-

cox, ed., *The American Rebellion: Sir Henry Clinton's Narrative* . . . (New Haven, 1954), 441.

23. Clinton to Germain, May 14, 1780, CO 5/99, 517–19.

24. Simpson to Clinton, May 15, 1780, enclosed in Clinton to Germain, May 16, 1780, CO 5/99, 533ff.

25. Arbuthnot to Germain, Dec. 16, 1779, and May 2 [actually after 11], 1780, HMC *Stopford-Sackville,* II, 149, 161–62.

26. Tarleton to Clinton, Camp on Bronx, July 2, 1779 (enclosed in Clinton to Germain, July 25, 1779, CO 5/98); Ferguson to Clinton, Aug. 1, 1778, Clinton Papers, Clements Library; Carlisle to Lady Carlisle, New York, July 2, 1779, HMC *Carlisle,* 356; Hutchinson to the Earl of Hardwicke, London, May 31, 1779, BM Add. MSS. 35247 f. 186; Rodney to Germain, St. Lucia, Dec. 22, 1780, HMC *Stopford-Sackville,* II, 192; and Tryon to Clinton, New York, July 20, 1779 (enclosed in Clinton to Germain, July 25, 1779, CO 5/98).

27. Dec. 15, 1779, CO 5/99, 55–56.

28. Franklin Wickwire and Mary Wickwire, *Cornwallis: The American Adventure* (Boston, 1970), 182–83, discuss the effect of the proclamation. I do not share their opinion that a campaign of terror surely would have won the war in the South.

29. Clinton to Germain, June 4, 1780, CO 5/99, 589, also in HMC *Stopford-Sackville,* II, 167.

30. Aug. 25, 1780, CO 5/100, 173–80.

31. Cornwallis to Clinton, July 14, 1780, enclosed in Clinton to Germain, Aug. 25, 1780, CO 5/100, 221–26, also in B. F. Stevens, ed., *The Campaign in Virginia 1781,* 2 vols. (London, 1888), I, 235–41.

32. Cornwallis to Clinton, Aug. 6, 29, 1780, CO 5/100, 233–34, 515–19; Lord Rawdon to Major General Alexander Leslie, Oct. 24, 1780, *ibid.,* 685; Rawdon to Clinton, Oct. 29, 1780, CO 5/101, 85–90; (also in HMC *Stopford-Sackville,* II, 185–86, but misdated Oct. 28, 1778); Captain James Stuart to his brother Charles, Camden, S.C., Jan. 7, 1781, *Journal of the Society for Army Historical Research,* XX (1955), 135; and Bull to Germain, Charleston, Feb. 16, 1781, HMC *Stopford-Sackville,* II, 202.

33. William B. Willcox describes the Cornwallis revealed in his letter to Clinton of Apr. 23, 1781 as "a man beyond the point of clear thinking. None of his reasons make sense." See "The British Road to Yorktown," *American Historical Review,* LII, (1946), 12–13.

34. See, for example, Germain to Clinton, Jan. 3, Mar. 7, Apr. 4, and May 2, 1781, CO 5/101, 1–8, 311–15, 337–44, 623–31.

CHAPTER TEN

1. Don Higginbotham. "American Historians and the Military History of the American Revolution," *American Historical Review*, LXX (1964), 18–34, surveys the military historical writing about the Revolution and describes the recent revival of interest in the subject. But it is remarkable how little even this revival has impinged on study of the Revolution as a whole. Higginbotham's *The War of American Independence* (New York, 1971), more than any previous general account, seeks to relate the military and nonmilitary segments of the war; basic research in this direction, however, has hardly begun.

2. J. Franklin Jameson, *The American Revolution Considered as a Social Movement* (Princeton, 1926).

3. Frederick B. Tolles, "The American Revolution Considered as a Social Movement: A Re-evaluation," *American Historical Review*, LX (1954), 1–12, reprinted in the paperback edition of Jameson (Princeton, 1967), surveys the critical attack on Jameson's argument. Two unjustly neglected books that seek to relate the direct pressure of warfare to major political developments are Bernhard Knollenberg, *Washington and the Revolution* (New York, 1940), and Curtis Nettels, *George Washington and American Independence* (New York, 1951). While both Bernard Bailyn, *The Ideological Origins of the American Revolution* (Cambridge, Mass., 1967), and Gordon S. Wood, *The Creation of the American Republic, 1776–1787* (Chapel Hill, 1969), stress the intellectual and even psychological changes wrought by revolution, the former stresses prewar Whig-Tory conflict, while the latter rarely (e.g., 324) sees wartime events as agents of intellectual change. Jackson T. Main, *The Social Structure of Revolutionary America* (Princeton, 1965), finds, on the whole, relatively little perceptible change in socioeconomic structure and so is not disposed to consider the possible effects of the war.

4. Richard Hofstadter, *The Progressive Historians: Turner, Beard, Parrington* (New York, 1968).

5. On military history, see Peter Paret, "The History of War," *Daedalus*, C (1971), 376–96. On the principles of war, see Bernard Brodie, "Strategy as a Science," *World Politics*, I (1949), 467–88.

6. For another, differently directed discussion of the relevance of the twentieth century to the eighteenth, see Thomas C. Barrow, "The American Revolution as a Colonial War for Independence," *William and Mary Quarterly*, 3rd series, XXV (1968), 452–64. Of the reverse relationship—the relevance of the American Revolution to

twentieth-century revolution—there is no question here, although Richard B. Morris and Clinton Rossiter, among others, have written books on the subject.

7. Allan Nevins, *The American States During and After the American Revolution, 1775-1789* (New York, 1924), 574; E. James Ferguson, *The Power of the Purse: A History of American Public Finance, 1776-1790* (Chapel Hill, 1961), 63, 69. The *specie value* of unredeemed certificates issued by the Quartermaster and Commissary departments was $3,723,000 at the end of the war; the *paper value* of all certificates was over $100,000,000.

8. Charles S. Grant, *Democracy in the Connecticut Frontier Town of Kent* (New York, 1961), 96-103; James T. Lemon and Gary B. Nash. "The Distribution of Wealth in Eighteenth-Century America: A Century of Change in Chester County, Pennsylvania, 1693-1802," *Journal of Social History,* II (1968), 1-24; Allan Kulikoff, "The Progress of Inequality in Revolutionary Boston," *William and Mary Quarterly,* 3rd series, XXVIII (1971), 375-412. All of these authors found an increase in the relative number of "poor" during the war, but none attempted to connect this change to the war itself.

The question is made more difficult by the lack of systematic thought about the "impact" of war on society. The most recent bibliography, Kurt Lang, *Military Institutions and the Sociology of War* (Beverly Hills and London, 1972), has sixty-four entries under "Costs and Consequences of War," but only five of them published later than 1960, when revolutionary war began—again—to be a matter of concern. Worth reading is Arthur Marwick, "The Impact of the First World War on British Society," *Journal of Contemporary History,* III (1968), 51-63.

9. Since this essay was first published, Howard H. Peckham has compiled a chronological list of military and naval actions, *The Toll of Independence* (Chicago, 1974), and thereby revised our estimate of rebel casualties upward to more than 25,000 deaths in service (p. 130).

10. There is a large but generally polemical and low-grade literature on "revolutionary war." Chalmers Johnson, "Civilian Loyalties and Guerrilla Conflict," *World Politics,* XIV (1962), 646-61, and Peter Paret, *French Revolutionary Warfare from Indochina to Algeria* (Princeton, 1964), are good introductions.

11. Robert C. Pugh, "The Revolutionary Militia in the Southern Campaigns, 1780-1781," *William and Mary Quarterly,* 3rd series, XIV (1957), 154-75, makes a sensible case for the military importance of the mili-

tia without the sentimentalism that impairs other similar efforts. Russell F. Weigley, *Towards an American Army* (New York and London, 1962), 1–9, sketches Washington's view, while Peter Paret, "Colonial Experience and European Military Reform at the End of the Eighteenth Century," *Bulletin of the Institute of Historical Research*, XXXVII (1964), 47–59, clarifies both the tactical and international contexts of the militia question.

12. A fuller development of this argument is in the essay on Lee, chapter 6.

13. The outstanding recent works on the British side of the war are Piers Mackesy, *The War for America, 1775–1783* (London, 1964); William B. Willcox, *Portrait of a General: Sir Henry Clinton in the War of Independence* (New York, 1964); and Paul H. Smith, *Loyalists and Redcoats: A Study in British Revolutionary Policy* (Chapel Hill, 1964). My understanding of the British war effort derives heavily from these three books, although at numerous points their evidence and arguments have been checked by my own research. Mackesy and Willcox also helped to revise the original version of this essay, which they both read, by giving me some incisive criticism, for which I here thank them and absolve them of all responsibility. Several other works are especially valuable: Ira Gruber, *The Howe Brothers and the American Revolution* (New York, 1972); Robert D. Bass, *The Green Dragoon: The Lives of Banastre Tarleton and Mary Robinson* (New York, 1957); George Athan Billias, ed., *George Washington's Opponents: British Generals and Admirals in the American Revolution* (New York, 1969); and Franklin and Mary Wickwire, *Cornwallis: The American Adventure* (Boston, 1970). Troyer Steele Anderson, *The Command of the Howe Brothers During the American Revolution* (New York, 1936), a carefully reasoned study based on limited evidence, is still very much worth consulting.

14. The final crisis, and the thinking that shaped it on the British side, can be traced in Bernard Donoughue, *British Politics and the American Revolution: The Path to War 1773–1775* (London, 1964); Benjamin W. Labaree, *The Boston Tea Party* (New York, 1964); and John Shy, *Toward Lexington: The Role of the British Army in the Coming of the American Revolution* (Princeton, 1965), chap. 9.

15. How Boston kept itself from being effectively isolated can be followed in Richard D. Brown, *Revolutionary Politics in Massachusetts: The Boston Committee of Correspondence and the Towns, 1772–1774* (Cambridge, Mass., 1970).

16. Gage to Secretary at War Barrington, "Private," June 26, 1775,

Clarence E. Carter, ed., *The Correspondence of General Thomas Gage . . . 1763–1775* (New Haven, 1931–33), II, 686–87.

17. Burgoyne to Germain, Aug. 20, 1775, Germain Papers, William L. Clements Library, Ann Arbor, Michigan. The psychological effects of Bunker Hill, of course, were the opposite of those expected by Burgoyne. One British officer, who had a line to general headquarters, wrote: "Our confidence in our own troops is much lessened since the 17th of June . . . We have a great want of discipline both amongst officers and men." Lord Rawdon to his uncle, the Earl of Huntingdon, Charlestown, Mass., Aug. 3, 1775, *Report on the Manuscripts of the Late Reginald Rawdon Hastings . . .*, Historical Manuscripts Commission, *Twentieth Report* (London, 1934), III, 159, hereafter cited as *MSS of Hastings,* III.

18. Mackesy, *War for America,* 35, 42; Willcox, *Clinton,* 55, 58; Smith, *Loyalists,* 41. The question of strategic intentions and expectations, especially in the case of General Howe, is murky. Although he said that he expected to destroy Washington's army in battle, there is some reason to believe that he hoped to win a decisive victory in the chess-like manner idealized by Maurice de Saxe (see Jon M. White, *Marshal of France* [London, 1962], 272–73), by maneuvering Washington out of richer, more populous areas and into a tactically hopeless position, where the only rational choice would be for the rebel army to break up and flee, all without major bloodshed. This kind of strategic thinking, so characteristic of the ancien régime, would later move Clausewitz to scorn (*On War,* trans. O. J. Matthijs Jolles [Washington, D.C., 1950], 210); but even Clausewitz elsewhere admitted that battles unfought, like the unpaid bills of commercial credit, functioned as the nexus of strategy (*ibid.,* 27, 123). The point here is that Howe, by threatening to fight only under favorable circumstances, no doubt hoped to minimize fighting. The tension, obvious to Clausewitz and to ourselves, between the conquest of territory and the destruction of enemy armed force, was less felt in the eighteenth century, when the very objects of war tended to be territorial and the costs of major battle, even to the victor, seemed extraordinarily high.

19. Leonard Lundin, *Cockpit of the Revolution: The War for Independence in New Jersey* (Princeton, 1940), 157ff.

20. E. H. Tatum, ed., *The American Journal of Ambrose Serle, Secretary to Lord Howe, 1776–1778* (San Marino, Calif., 1940), 155; "Journals of Lieut.-Col. Stephen Kemble," *The Kemble Papers,* New York Historical Society, *Collections,* XVI (New York, 1884), I, 160.

21. W. A. Whitehead et al., eds., *Archives of the State of New Jersey, 1631–1800*, 2nd series (Trenton 1901), I, 276ff, contains numerous accounts of minor skirmishes and affrays, reported in newspapers on both sides. Col. Charles Stuart to his father, the Earl of Bute, Feb. 4, 1777, E. Stuart-Wortley, ed., *A Prime Minister and His Son* (London, 1925), 99, is an especially clear statement of the problem. Some British officers, like the young Lord Rawdon, had expected positive results from the brutal conduct of the army in New Jersey. While still at New York he had written: "I think we should (whenever we get further into the country) give free liberty to the soldiers to ravage it at will, that these infatuated creatures may feel what a calamity war is." To the Earl of Hastings, Sept. 25, 1776, *MSS of Hastings*, III, 185.

22. The loss of British control in New Jersey is illustrated in a letter written by James Murray, a British officer, to his sister, from Perth Amboy, Feb. 25, 1777: "As the rascals are skulking about the whole country, it is impossible to move with any degree of safety without a pretty large escort, and even then you are exposed to a dirty kind of *tiraillerie*. . . . Would you believe that it was looked upon as a rash attempt to go [to New Brunswick] by land accompanied by two Light Dragoons, tho' there are not above 5 or 6 miles of the road, and these next to the shore, but what are occupied by our troops?" Eric Robson, ed., *Letters from America, 1773–1780* (Manchester, 1951), 38–42.

23. Adrian Leiby, *The Hackensack Valley in the American Revolutionary War* (New Brunswick, 1962), 20.

24. Mackesy, *War for America*, 103–24; Smith, *Loyalists*, 44–59. Although the basic strategic concept remained that of "proving the superiority of the British troops over the army of the rebels" in order to produce a collapse of American morale and a more or less automatic political settlement (Germain to Gen. Howe, Oct. 18, 1776, Germain Papers, Clements Library), there is evidence of growing British interest in the attitudes of the local population. See, for example, Burgoyne to Clinton, Quebec, Nov. 7, 1776, Clinton Papers, Clements Library; Gen. Howe to Germain, Dec. 20, 1776 (extract), and Howe to Clinton, Apr. 5, 1777, Germain Papers.

25. On the popular response to the British march from Elkton, Maryland to Philadelphia, see B. A. Uhlendorf, ed., *Revolution in America: Confidential Letters and Journals, 1776–1784, of Adjutant General Major Baurmeister of the Hessian Forces* (New Brunswick, 1957), 95–113, and Alexander Graydon, *Memoirs of His Own Time* (Philadelphia, 1846), 285, 306. In Uhlendorf, ed., *Revolution in America*, 134–39, 148, 157,

162, 169, Baurmeister gives a graphic account of guerrilla warfare around Philadelphia during the following winter and spring.

26. Mackesy, *War for America,* 121–44. Historians continue to explain the failure of the campaign almost solely in terms of the famous "forgotten despatch," though, as Mackesy, 117–18, demonstrates, long-available evidence does not confirm the emphasis given to this incident, in which General Howe allegedly was not told that General Burgoyne might be needing some help around Albany. The reasons for the failure of the campaign are far more complicated and in a sense more damning of the British high command, but the story and its point are apparently too good to give up. Additional evidence is in the letter of Adj. Gen. Edward Harvey to Lt. Gov. James Murray of Minorca, May 16, 1777; Harvey in London clearly understood what Howe and Burgoyne planned to do: "I think that we may place H[owe] in possession of Philadelphia and a great part of Pennsylvania in the month of June. If the Canada Army can get, in tolerable time to Albany, much may be done, but much certainly depends on that measure." W. O. 3/23/214–215, Public Record Office.

27. The special constraints on strategy imposed by eighteenth-century tactics and organization are discussed and revealed in Stanley M. Pargellis, "Braddock's Defeat," *American Historical Review,* XLI (1936), 253–69, and *Lord Loudoun in North America* (New Haven, 1933), and in C. P. Stacey, *Quebec, 1759* (New York, 1959). The Wickwires, *Cornwallis,* 90, refuse to accept at face value the testimony of Cornwallis when he said, concerning Howe's failure to destroy Washington's army at Long Island in August 1776, "that I never did hear it suggested by anyone that those lines could have been carried by assault." But other eye-witness accounts, written during the events of the campaign of 1776, bear out Cornwallis's words. The young Lord Rawdon wrote to his uncle, from New York, Sept. 25, 1776, "that everything is at stake and that one daring attempt, if unsuccessful would ruin our affairs in this part of the world, and the difficulty of getting troops, is so great that we ought not to hazard our men without the evident prospect of accomplishing our purpose." *MSS of Hastings,* III, 186. The more experienced Frederick Mackenzie, during the pursuit of Washington later in the fall, noted in his diary on Nov. 3, 1776, only the question of whether the British army would extend its winter quarters into New Jersey, not whether Washington would be pursued to destruction. *The Diary of Frederick Mackenzie . . .* (Cambridge, Mass., 1930), 95. Military historians have

tended to judge Howe and other eighteenth-century military leaders by Napoleonic standards, which are simply not appropriate to the historical situation. See note 18, above.

28. Mackesy, *War for America,* 156–58, 252–56; Willcox, *Clinton,* 260ff.

29. Smith, *Loyalists,* 79–99; Mackesy, *War for American,* 252ff.

30. The king to Lord North, June 11, 1779, John W. Fortescue, ed., *The Correspondence of King George the Third* . . . (London, 1927–28), III, 351. Almost five years earlier, Lord Barrington, secretary at war until 1778 and a fairly consistent hard-liner on American policy, had used North's logic and reached the same conclusion: "Our disputes with North America have not at present the foundation of Interest, for the contest will cost us more than we can ever gain by our success." Even if the Americans were defeated, Barrington thought that they would have to be held down by armies, "which would be ruinous and endless." To Dartmouth, Dec. 24, 1774, Barrington Letterbook 1766–1775, East Suffolk Record Office, Ipswich, England, HA 174 acc. 1026, 283–89. Thomas Hutchinson, however, former governor of Massachusetts and a man of penetrating intelligence, used cost-benefit analysis in a letter to Lord Hardwicke, Aug. 31, 1778, to reach the opposite position; without some great military victory, Hutchinson argued, Britain would lose not only the thirteen colonies but the West Indies and the Newfoundland fisheries as well, and he stated that whatever the cost of defeating the colonies it would be far less than the harm done by such a loss. Additional Manuscripts 35427, fol. 141, British Museum.

31. Mackesy, *War for America,* 267–68; Smith, *Loyalists,* 100–105, 126–42.

32. Quoted from the Clinton Papers, Clements Library, in Wickwire. *Cornwallis,* 427, n. 55. On the success of British irregular tactics, see *ibid.*, 132–33, 164–65, and Bass, *Tarleton.*

33. "Colonel Robert Gray's Observations on the War in Carolina," *South Carolina Historical and Genealogical Magazine,* XI (1910), 153. This is a remarkable document, conveying a vivid sense of the chaotic situation in those areas of South Carolina not occupied in strength by British forces. On the failure of British pacification even before the appearance of Greene's army, see Lord Rawdon to Maj. Leslie, Oct. 24, 1780, *Report on the Manuscripts of Mrs. Stopford-Sackville* . . . , Hist. MSS Comm., *Fifteenth Report* (London, 1910), II, 185, hereafter cited as *MSS of Stopford-Sackville,* II.

34. Wickwire, *Cornwallis,* 169–95. But see also Willcox, *Clinton,* 352–53, and Macksey, *War for America,* 343–45.

35. Macksey, *War for America,* 404–36, 473–77, 487–94. On p. 512, the

author suggests that the British might reasonably have continued the war after Yorktown. He makes a strong case, but it rests on his belief that American rebels by 1781 were too war-weary to survive the withdrawal of French and Spanish support. I do not agree; American complaints are not to be taken at face value, although— as the first essay in this book argues—they must be taken seriously.

36. Among the senior commanders, General Clinton, for all his faults, had the clearest and earliest grasp of what was happening. In planning for the campaign in the South, he wrote to Secretary of State Germain, Apr. 4, 1779, cautioning against a premature capture of Charleston: "It might induce a number of persons to declare for us whom we might afterwards be obliged to abandon, and thus might destroy a party on whom we may depend if circumstances will permit a more solid attempt in proper season." *MSS of Stopford-Sackville*, II, 125. See also the observation of Frederick Mackenzie, Aug. 5, 1781, *Diary of Mackenzie*, 581–82.

A decade after the war, Charles Stedman, in discussing the reversal of popular attitudes in New Jersey in 1776–77, gave a succinct version of how the British lost their ability to control public opinion. Before the battle of Trenton, Stedman wrote, many New Jerseyans were "well affected" and ready to fight for the king. "But when the people found that the promised protection was not afforded them; that their property was seized, and most wantonly destroyed; that, in many instances, their families were insulted, stripped of their beds—nay, even of their very wearing apparel; they then determined to try the other side.... And it is but justice to say that the Americans never took anything from their friends, but in cases of necessity; in which cases they uniformly gave receipts ... always living, as long as they could, upon their enemies; and never suffering their troops to plunder their friends with impunity. But at the same time it is to be noticed, that the American troops were suffered to plunder the Loyalists, and to exercise with impunity every act of barbarity on that unfortunate class of people; frequently inflicting on them even scourges and stripes." Stedman, *The History of the Origin, Progress, and Termination of the American War* (London, 1794), I 242–43.

Some argued, both at the time and subsequently, that a more wholehearted resort to fire and sword would have terrorized the Americans into submission. For example: Thomas Hutchinson to Lord Hardwicke, May 31, 1779, Add. MSS 35427, fol. 186, Brit.

Museum. But young Col. Charles Stuart, who had served in America for several years and could hardly be suspected of pro-rebel sympathies, rejected a strategy of terror on other than humanitarian grounds. He not only questioned the physical capacity of the British army and navy to carry on "a war of ravage and destruction" but argued that there was no reason to believe that "acts of severity will cause these people to submit." Everywhere the British army had gone, Stuart wrote to his father on Sept. 16, 1778, "every species of barbarity has been executed," doing nothing more than to plant "an irrecoverable hatred." Stuart-Wortley, ed., *Prime Minister and His Son,* 132. For a fuller exploration of the question of terrorism, see chapter 8, above.

37. Barrow, "American Revolution as a Colonial War for Independence," *William and Mary Quarterly,* 3rd series, XXV (1968), 459, also thinks that neutral or moderate elements were "often a majority."

38. Uhlendorf, ed., *Revolution in America,* contains the most revealing account of British and Allied day-to-day awareness of rebel militia.

39. Baron Ludwig von Closen, a member of the French expeditionary force, noted in his journal on Apr. 12, 1781: "The Americans lose 600 men in a day, and 8 days later 1200 others rejoin the army; whereas, to replace 10 men in the English army is quite an undertaking." Evelyn M. Acomb, ed. and trans., *The Revolutionary Journal of Baron Ludwig von Closen, 1780–1783* (Chapel Hill, 1958), 75. In Uhlendorf, ed., *Revolution in America* esp. 353–54, Baurmeister describes the rebel militia at its best, near the end of the war. See also the "Journal of John Charles Philip von Krafft, of the Regiment von Bose, 1776–1784," New York Historical Society, *Collections,* XV (New York, 1883), 43–142.

40. Charles J. Hoadly, ed., *The Public Records of the State of Connecticut* (Hartford, 1894), I, 91ff.

41. *Ibid.,* 259–60. An interesting study of the Maryland militia, its sociology and political role, during the early years of the war, is an unpublished paper by David Skaggs. "Flaming Patriots and Inflaming Demagogues." It confirmed my own belief that mobilization often meant politicization. Richard Buel of Wesleyan University is undertaking a general comparative study of this process in the American Revolution.

42. H. E. Egerton, ed., *The Royal Commission on the Losses and Services of American Loyalists, 1783 to 1785* (Oxford, 1915), 49; also 10, 32, 35, 41, 43–44, 48.

43. V. H. Paltsits, ed., *Minutes of the Commissioners for Detecting and Defeating Conspiracies in the State of New York: Albany County Sessions, 1778–1781* (Albany, 1909), I, 369.

44. *Ibid.*, II, 735.

45. Minutes of the Council of Safety, *Pennsylvania Archives*, 1st series, XI, 38, 54–55; 94; Edmund Pendleton to William Woodford, May 24, 1779, David J. Mays, ed., *Letters and Papers of Edmund Pendleton* (Charlottesville, 1967), I, 285–86.

46. The Penobscot episode can be followed in the reports to Clinton in Hist. MSS Comm., *Report on American Manuscripts in the Royal Institution of Great Britain* (London, 1904–9), I, 458–60; II, 14–18, 45, 52, 66, 83, 144, 258. Some interesting observations are in Uhlendorf, ed., *Revolution in America*, 313, to the effect that McLean "is probably the first Briton who understands the art of winning the confidence of the inhabitants. He has organized militia twenty miles inland." See also 342.

47. Certain strongly held opinions appear with greater frequency in the British record near the end of the war: that the Americans were war-weary; that the Americans were virtually unanimous in opposition to royal government; that British leniency was losing the war; that British brutality was losing the war; and that British inconsistency toward the Americans was losing the war.

48. On virtue, see Wood, *Creation of the American Republic*, 65–70.

49. For the exchange between Hamilton and Burke, see Harold C. Syrett and Jacob E. Cooke, eds., *The Papers of Alexander Hamilton* (New York, 1961–), VI, 333–37, 357–58.

CHAPTER ELEVEN

1. *The Collected Works of Abraham Lincoln*, Roy P. Basler et al., eds., 9 vols. (New Brunswick, N.J., 1953), I, 108–15.

2. Gage to Lord Dartmouth, Sept. 25, 1774 (two letters), *The Correspondence of General Thomas Gage*, Clarence E. Carter, ed., 2 vols. (New Haven, 1931–33), I, 275–77.

3. Barrington to Lord Dartmouth, Nov. 12, 1774, Barrington Letterbook, Ipswich Record Office; General Harvey to General John Irwin, June 30, 1775, W.O. 3/5, 36–37, British Public Record Office.

4. *Observations on Civil Liberty and the Justice and Policy of the War with America* (London, 1776). On Price and the reception given his pamphlet, see the *Dictionary of National Biography*, XLVI, 335.

5. The best estimate I know of the numbers who served actively in the

Revolutionary War on the American side is in an unpublished paper by Theodore J. Crackel. Crackel projected backward from the number and age-profile of pensioners in the National Archives, using a modified mortality table. His estimate of 185,000 serving six months or more may be too low, because his working assumptions are uniformly conservative ones.

6. The best estimate of Loyalist numbers is Paul H. Smith, "The American Loyalists; Notes on their Organization and Numerical Strength," *William and Mary Quarterly,* 3rd series, XXV (1968), 259–77. For blacks, see *Historical Statistics of the United States, Colonial Times to 1957* (Washington, D.C., 1960), 756, and Benjamin Quarles, *The Negro in the American Revolution* (Chapel Hill, 1961), ix.

7. Howard H. Peckham, ed., *The Toll of Independence: Engagements and Battle Casualties of the American Revolution* (Chicago, 1974), 130.

8. The population of Israel was estimated at 3,164,000 by the May 1972 census. The *Annual Register* for 1973, p. 202, lists casualties in the Yom Kippur War as 2,512 dead, 508 missing.

9. The various pension laws are compiled in Robert Mayo and Ferdinand Moulton, *Army and Navy Pension Laws and Bounty Land Laws* (Washington, D.C., 1852). An account of the number of veterans who were pensioned under these laws is in William H. Glasson, *Federal Military Pensions in the United States* (New York, 1918), 23–96.

10. On war casualties, the literature is large, but unsatisfactory. The brief discussion in Quincy Wright, *A Study of War . . . ,* 2 vols. (Chicago, 1942), I, 224ff; is still a useful guide to the standard works. An even briefer note in Mark M. Boatner, comp., *Encyclopedia of the American Revolution* (New York, 1966), 187, 189, states that three or four were wounded for every man killed; but if we are concerned with *serious* wounds then a ratio of one-to-one seems reasonably conservative. The assertion in the text about death by disease is a guess, but a very conservative one based on study of other pre-twentieth-century wars; some historians assert that disease killed more, but they tend to include non-service deaths. Ernst Kipping, *The Hessian View of America, 1776–1783* (Monmouth Beach, N.J., 1971), 39, indicates that 4,626 "Hessians" died in the whole war while 357 were killed but this proportion, if applied to American losses (ca. 8,000 known killed) would put total deaths well over 100,000—an obvious impossibility.

11. The estimate of "Loyalist" emigrés is lower than that given in Wallace Brown, *The Good Americans: The Loyalists in the American Revolution*

(New York, 1969), but Brown recently (November 1974) said at a conference in London on Loyalism that a lower figure of 66,000 was probably correct.

12. Quarles, *Negro in the American Revolution,* 119, 172–81; Robin W. Winks, *The Blacks in Canada: A History* (New Haven and Montreal, 1971), 29–95, 99, 143, 237. Wallace Brown, at the conference noted above, estimated that 15,000 blacks emigrated.

13. The best case study of the impact of the Revolutionary War on Indians is Anthony F. C. Wallace, *Death and Rebirth of the Seneca Nation* (New York, 1969); a general account is Jack M. Sosin, *The Revolutionary Frontier, 1763–1783* (New York, 1967).

14. Francis B. Heitman, in compiling the *Historical Register of Officers of the Continental Army,* 2nd ed. (Washington, 1914), found about 14,000 officers, although he made no effort to search systematically for militia officers.

15. Chapter 2 in this volume; Charles A. Lofgren, "Compulsory Military Service under the Constitution: The Original Understanding," *William and Mary Quarterly,* 3rd series, XXXII (1976), 61–88.

16. Jerry A. O'Callaghan, "The War Veteran and the Public Lands," *Agricultural History,* XXVIII (1954), 163–68.

17. E. James Ferguson, *The Power of the Purse: A History of American Public Finance, 1776–1790* (Chapel Hill, 1961), 3–47.

18. Louis C. Hatch, *The Administration of the American Revolutionary Army* (New York, 1904); Victor L. Johnson, *The Administration of the American Commissariat During the Revolutionary War* (Philadelphia, 1941). Since this essay was written, valuable new work has appeared: by Wayne Carp, *To Starve the Army at Pleasure: Continental Army Administration and American Political Culture, 1775–1783* (Chapel Hill, 1984); by Erna Risch, *Supplying Washington's Army* (Washington, D.C., 1981); and by Wayne K. Bodle and Jacqueline Thibaut, eds., *Valley Forge Historical Research Report,* 3 vols. (Valley Forge, Pa., 1980).

19. For example, Washington's General Orders of Dec. 29, 1779, at Morristown, in which he said that American soldiers were behaving more like "a band of robbers than disciplined troops called forth in a defence of the rights of the Community." *The Writings of George Washington,* John C. Fitzpatrick, ed., 39 vols. (Washington D.C., 1931–44), XVII, 331.

20. The best account is still in Allan Nevins, *The American States During and After the Revolution, 1775–1789* (New York, 1924).

21. David Ramsay, *The History of the American Revolution,* 2 vols. (London, 1793 edition), II, 136.

22. Glasson, *Federal Military Pensions,* and the unpublished work by Crackel mentioned in note 5.

23. *A Census of Pensioners for Revolutionary or Military Services* (Washington, D.C., 1841). The total listed in the Sixth Census (1840), p. 475, is 20,797, but some of those were veterans of the War of 1812, and the listed age of a few indicate that they were children of veterans. The name of John Lockridge, and the surnames of Maxcy and Crowder, appear in Lincoln's early correspondence, though no connection has been positively established. Sangamon County had a population of about 14,000 in 1838.

24. See Kenneth Lockridge, "Land, Population, and the Evolution of New England Society 1630–1790," *Past and Present,* XXXIX (1968), 62–80; Jackson Turner Main, *The Social Structure of Revolutionary America* (Princeton, 1965); and James A. Henretta, *The Evolution of American Society, 1700–1815* (Lexington, Mass., 1973).

25. *The Age of the Democratic Revolution: A Political History of Europe and America, 1760–1800,* 2 vols. (Princeton, 1959–65), I, 188–90.

26. This view of the effect of the Revolution on slavery is suggested by Gerald W. Mullin, *Flight and Rebellion: Slave Resistance in Eighteenth-Century Virginia* (New York, 1972), 124ff. Winthrop Jordan, *White Over Black: American Attitudes Toward the Negro, 1550–1812* (Chapel Hill, 1968), might disagree (cf. 367–68), but I find much in his book to support the idea advanced herein. In conversation, Duncan J. MacLeod, author of *Slavery, Race and the American Revolution* (Cambridge, 1974), has strongly challenged this causal conjecture mainly on the ground that "tightening" is not evident until the 1790's when factors other than the Revolution are clearly operative.

27. This is the conclusion reached by Theodore J. Crackel in his unpublished study of Revolutionary War veterans from New Jersey. John R. Sellers, "The Common Soldier in the American Revolution," in *The Military History of the American Revolution,* edited by Stanley J. Underdal (Washington D.C.), 151–68, reaches similar conclusions.

28. Jackson T. Main, "Government by the People: The American Revolution and the Democratization of the Legislatures," *William and Mary Quarterly,* 3rd series, XXIII (1966), 391–474: Henry J. Young, "The Spirit of 1775," *John and Mary's Journal,* I (1975), 53–55.

29. Charles S. Grant, *Democracy in the Connecticut Frontier Town of Kent* (New York, 1961), 96–103; James A. Henretta, "Economic Development and Social Structure in Colonial Boston," *William and Mary Quarterly,* 3rd series, XXII (1965), 75–92: James T. Lemon, *The Best*

Poor Man's Country: A Geographical Study of Early Southeastern Pennsylvania (Baltimore, 1972), 11, 69, 88.

30. Allan Kulikoff, "The Progress of Inequality in Revolutionary Boston," *William and Mary Quarterly*, 3rd series, XXVIII (1971), 375–412, clearly thinks the Revolution made the distribution of wealth *less* democratic, but Main, *Social Structure*, the only general study so far, is uncertain about the net effect.

31. *History of the American Revolution* (1793 ed.), II, 136–37.

32. *Ibid.*

33. Leonard W. Labaree, *Conservatism in Early American History* (New York, 1948), and James K. Martin, *Men in Rebellion: Higher Governmental Leaders and the Coming of the American Revolution* (New Brunswick, N.J., 1973), describe the colonial elite, while J. R. Pole sets forth the concept of a "deferential" society in "Historians and the Problem of Early American Democracy," *American Historical Review* LXVII (1962), 626–46.

34. To Richard Henry Lee in 1775 (Aug. 29), Washington wrote of "an unaccountable kind of stupidity" which "prevails but too generally" among the Massachusetts officers, who made it "one of the principal objects of their attention . . . to curry favour with the men" (*Writings*, III, 450–51). To Brigadier General Charles Scott in 1778 (Oct. 8) he wrote of "the unpardonable inattention of Officers, and their scandalous sacrifice of every other consideration to the indulgences of good Quarters" (*Writings*, XIII, 47). Examples could easily be multiplied.

35. This idea, that more or less incompetent military service during the Revolutionary War weakened the position of the early American elite, emerged from discussion in a seminar for college teachers during the summer of 1975 at Ann Arbor, and I hereby acknowledge my debt to that lively group.

36. "Fame" as an influential factor in American Revolutionary behavior is best set forth by the late Douglass Adair, *Fame and the Founding Fathers: Essays by Douglass Adair*, edited by Trevor Colbourn (Williamsburg and New York, 1974), 3–26.

CHAPTER TWELVE

1. Perhaps the most articulate proponent of accidentalist explanation has been Arthur Schlesinger, Jr., *The Bitter Heritage: Vietnam and American Democracy, 1941–1966* (New York, 1966).

2. Fred J. Cook's *The Warfare State* (New York, 1962) is a sensational

account of the military-industrial complex, but William A. Williams's *The Tragedy of American Diplomacy* (Cleveland, 1959) is one of the earliest and best structural interpretations.

3. C. Wright Mills, *The Causes of World War III* (New York, 1956), chaps. 8–9.

4. One succinct cultural interpretation is Sir Denis Brogan's "The Illusion of American Omnipotence," first published in 1952, and reprinted in his *American Aspects* (London, 1964), 9–21. Most versions of cultural explanation, however, take the form of casual statement rather than extended discourse.

5. The best discussion of the problem of national character is Alex Inkeles and Daniel J. Levinson, "National Character," in Gardiner Lindzey and Elliott Aronson, eds., *The Handbook of Social Psychology*, 2nd ed. (Reading, Mass., 1969), IV, 418–506.

6. On learning in general, Ernest R. Hilgard and Gordon H. Bower, *Theories of Learning*, 3rd ed., (New York, 1966); Albert Bandura and Richard H. Walters, *Social Learning and Personality Development* (New York, 1963). On the last two hypotheses mentioned, Jerome S. Bruner, Jacqueline J. Goodnow, and George A. Austin, *A Study of Thinking* (New York, 1956), 68–69, and chap. IV, esp. 85–87.

7. One need only examine the tables of contents of a number of books on current military affairs, as well as course syllabi dealing with the subject. A distinguished exception is Bernard Brodie, *Strategy in the Missile Age* (Princeton, 1959), but even its four-chapter introduction on the historical development of strategic-bombing doctrine stands apart from the main body of the book.

8. C. Vann Woodward, "The Age of Reinterpretation," *American Historical Review*, LXVI (1960), 1–19. Woodward applies the term "age of free security" to *all* American history before World War II; I like the label, but have modified his use of it.

9. William Goetzmann, *When the Eagle Screamed; The Romantic Horizon in American Diplomacy, 1800–1860* (New York, 1966), 105 et passim.

10. Howard Mumford Jones, *O Strange New World* (New York, 1964), is an outstanding exception.

11. M. Eugene Sirmans, *Colonial South Carolina: A Political History, 1663–1763* (Chapel Hill, 1966), and Gary B. Nash, *Quakers and Politics: Pennsylvania, 1681–1726* (Princeton, 1968), convey the rawness and insecurity of even the later seventeenth century.

12. David B. Quinn, *The Elizabethans and the Irish* (New York, 1966) and *Raleigh and the British Empire* (London, 1947).

13. Perry Miller, *Errand into the Wilderness* (Cambridge, Mass., 1956), best explores the hopes and disillusionment of converting Indians to Christianity.

14. For an account of the way in which European warfare had become limited by the eighteenth century, see Walter Dorn, *Competition for Empire* (New York, 1940).

15. Klaus Knorr, *On the Uses of Military Power* (Princeton, 1966), 83. Kenneth Waltz, *Man, the State and War* (New York, 1959), and Alastair Buchan, *War in Modern Society* (London, 1966), have also informed me here and elsewhere on the functions of military force.

16. A narrative account of early American warfare is Howard H. Peckham, *The Colonial Wars, 1689–1762* (Chicago, 1962).

17. A detailed study of these problems around 1750 is in Lawrence H. Gipson, *The British Empire before the American Revolution* (New York, 1936–42), vols. I–V.

18. For example, "Canada Survey'd," *Calendar of State Papers, Colonial Series, America and West Indies, June, 1708–1709* (London, 1922). no. 60.

19. Benjamin Franklin, *The Interest of Great Britain Considered* (London, 1760). It is in an anonymous letter to the press that he uses the word "extirpation."

20. The origins of this ambivalent attitude are discussed in John Shy, *Toward Lexington: The Role of the British Army in the Coming of the American Revolution* (Princeton, 1965); the fullest exploration is Marcus Cunliffe, *Soldiers and Civilians: The Martial Spirit in America, 1775–1865* (Boston, 1968).

21. Thomas A. Bailey's account of these crises is particularly good: *A Diplomatic History of the American People*, 7th ed. (New York, 1958); but Pierre Renouvin, *Histoire des relations internationales* (Paris, 1954–55), V–VI, puts them in general perspective.

22. See Russell F. Weigley, *History of the United States Army* (New York, 1967).

23. Two of the most revealing documents on nineteenth-century American attitudes toward the prospect of war are *Letter of Mr. [Robert J.] Walker, of Mississippi, Relative to the Reannexation of Texas* (Philadelphia, 1844), and the speech of Senator Redfield Proctor of Vermont on March 17, 1898, in the *Congressional Record*, XXXI, part 3, 2916–19. Both Walker and Proctor were intelligent men, sincerely interested in the cause of peace, who were able to persuade themselves and others that war was inevitable and just.

24. C. Vann Woodward, *The Burden of Southern History*, rev. ed., (Baton Rouge, 1968), 187–91; Robert Penn Warren, *The Legacy of the Civil War* (New York, 1961), 14–15.

25. Paul H. Buck, *Road to Reunion, 1865–1900* (Boston, 1938); Eric L. McKitrick, *Andrew Johnson and Reconstruction* (Chicago, 1960). The most penetrating account of the intellectual and psychological aspects of the Civil War is Edmund Wilson, *Patriotic Gore* (New York, 1962).

26. James G. Harbord, *The American Army in France, 1917–1919* (Boston, 1936), 169, 407–8; Kent R. Greenfield, ed., *Command Decisions* (New York, 1959), chaps. 6, 8, 13.

27. Edward H. Buehrig, *Woodrow Wilson and the Balance of Power* (Bloomington, 1955); Arthur S. Link, *Wilson the Diplomatist* (Baltimore, 1956).

28. See Louis Morton, "Japan's Decision for War," in Greenfield, *Command Decisions,* chap. 3. My view that the Americans did not adhere to their "Germany-first" agreement is controversial; another view is expressed in Samuel Eliot Morison, *Strategy and Compromise* (Boston, 1958). My case must rest mainly on the very complex question of the allocation of sea-lift, which can be followed in Richard M. Leighton and Robert W. Coakley, *Global Logistics and Strategy, 1940–1945,* 2 vols. (Washington, 1955 and 1968).

29. Russell F. Weigley, *Towards an American Army* (New York, 1962); T. Harry Williams, "Military Leadership, North and South," in David Donald, ed., *Why the North Won the Civil War* (Baton Rouge, 1960).

30. In addition to the three doctrines discussed below, the others may be described as the doctrines of the Short Total War (exemplified in pre-1914 war planning, which stressed the offensive power of mass armies and the fragility of modern industrial society), Blitzkrieg (which in both its German and Japanese forms stressed lightning thrusts for limited ends, to be followed by consolidation and defense of *faits accomplis*), and *Guerre révolutionnaire* (usually involving guerrilla warfare but always combining political and military action, directed at the masses, for either revolutionary or counter-revolutionary ends). Others that might be considered, although they never achieved the same state of definition or acceptance, were doctrines of Material Attrition (Western Front in World War I, and German and American use of submarine blockade) and Psychological Attrition (Sir Basil Liddell Hart's concept of the Indirect Approach). Still others, like American amphibious doctrine, never reached the level of uniting political and military aspects of warfare.

31. Walter Lafeber, *The New Empire: An Interpretation of American Expansion, 1860–1898* (Ithaca, 1963).

32. Michael Sherry, *The Rise of American Air Power* (New Haven, 1987).

33. Robert McNamara was, of course, the key figure, but the key books were produced in the 1950's by William Kaufmann, Robert Osgood, Henry Kissinger, Bernard Brodie, Maxwell Taylor, and Thomas Schelling. Kaufmann's eulogistic account of McNamara may be said to close the circle: *The McNamara Strategy* (New York, 1964).

34. Alfred T. Mahan, *From Sail to Steam* (New York, 1907), 267ff. Harold and Margaret Sprout, *The Rise of American Naval Power, 1776–1918* (Princeton, 1939), 165–201; Alfred F. Hurley, *Billy Mitchell: Crusader for Air Power* (New York, 1964); Walter Millis et al., *Arms and the State* (New York, 1959), part III.

Index

Abbott, William W., 307

Abercromby, Gen. James, 87, 101, 106-7, 305

Adair, Douglass, 340

Adams, Brooks, 288

Adams, John, 39, 47, 138-39, 141, 165, 171, 221, 306; opinion of Pownall, 52

Adams, Samuel, 47, 140, 160, 174

Albany, N.Y., 35, 87, 137, 240

Albermarle, Earl of, 84

Alden, John R., 311, 314, 318, 322

Alexander, John, 172

Allds, Benjamin, 172

Almon, John, 53

American character, 267-69

American colonial society, affluence in, 24-25, 122-24; appearance of anarchy in, 124; elitism in, 123-24; ethnic diversity in, 123, 130-31; military origins of first settlements, 274-75; nutrition in, 122; personal freedom in, 124; population growth in, 122, 124; "provincialism" in, 124-25; widespread voting in, 123

American colonies: characteristics of society in 1760, 122-25; Parliamentary representation of, 64-67, 70

American diplomacy, character of, 281

American elite: threatened by British policies, 125-26; transformation of, 261-62

American invincibility, sense of, 279-80

American military commanders, abilities of, 22

American public opinion, Revolutionary-era, 20-21, 126-28, 232-33, 235-44

American Revolution: American victory or British defeat?, 215; British causes of, 45-80, 93-94, 107; British strategies, 193-212, 222-34; as a civil war, 183; estimates of casualties, 249, 337; estimates of financial cost, 217; estimates of numbers of participants, 217, 248-49, 337; estimates of numbers of refugees, 250; ethnic divisions perpetuated by, 226, 317; and French Revolution compared, 183; historiography of, 12-15, 215; local studies of, 322-23; political effect of presence of British army, 236; popular imge of, 166; popular mythology of, 26; as "social process of political education," 235-44; viciousness of, 22-23; wartime atrocities, 281 (*see also* Atrocities, wartime); weakness of American war effort, 22-24; why British lost, 17-20

American Revolution, effects of, 3, 217-63; counterrrevolutionaries eliminated,

345

Ann Arbor Paperbacks